Teaching and Social Behavior

Teaching and Social Behavior

Toward an
Organizational Theory of Instruction

Phillip C. Schlechty

The University of North Carolina

ALLYN AND BACON, INC.
boston london sydney toronto

Library of Congress Cataloging in Publication Data

Schlechty, Phillip C   (date)
    Teaching and social behavior.

    Bibliography: p.
    Includes index.
    1. Educational sociology. I. Title.
LC189.S33   370.19'3   75-45138
ISBN 0-205-05494-3

Contents

Preface

This book is written for those who are seriously interested in schools as well as for those who are merely curious about them. My effort has been to describe and analyze the nature of schools and school-related behavior from the perspective of a sociologist—a sociologist interested in the study of human behavior in complex social organizations. At a descriptive level the reader will find much he or she too could have written, especially if the reader happens to be a teacher or school administrator. However, this book goes beyond simple description and storytelling. In addition to providing an accurate report on the nature of social life in schools, it provides some insight into those structural characteristics of schools that seem to account for some of the behavior one observes in classrooms.

As a part of the discussion in this book I hope to help the teacher and the school administrator gain a clearer understanding of some of the more perplexing realities they confront as they go about their jobs. For example, most teachers jealously guard their classroom doors from invasion by other adults, and when other adults do appear behind a teacher's closed classroom door, the situation is typically tense and fraught with the potential for conflict. Why is this so? Why is it that teachers, unlike most other professionals, find it necessary to do most of their work outside of the view of other adults, and especially other professionals? Even more curious, perhaps, is the tendency of faculties and students, especially in times of interpersonal tension, to take on characteristics more associated with hostile camps than with enlightened intellectual communities. The consequences are often strange indeed. For example, when a student and a teacher have a disagreement, the building principal may feel constrained to support the teacher—even if the principal believes that the teacher is wrong—to avoid loss of status with the teaching staff. What is it about schools that creates such conditions? In attempting to discover the organizational sources of teacher and student behavior and in attempting to give some consistent meaning to observations about life in schools, I have found sociological theory especially useful. In building my interpretations of the social realities of schools, I have drawn on conflict theory, social action theory, symbolic interactionism, and functionalism.

My search is for a logical and consistent set of explanations about the relationships between teachers, students, and school organizations. The basic question to which this book is addressed is "How do school organizations affect the behavior of teachers and students in classrooms?" Every chapter, page, paragraph, and sentence of this book is written as an effort to provide some part of an answer to that question.

Chapter 1 may be read as both an introductory and a concluding chapter. As an introductory chapter it leaves much unsaid. Some readers may wish that the chapter had been omitted completely; others may wish it had been considerably expanded. As a concluding chapter it does not say enough, for by the end of the book I would hope the reader would agree with me that there are understandable reasons for our ignorance about schools, and that chief among those reasons is our propensity to ask the wrong questions.

Chapters 2 and 3 (and to a lesser degree chapter 4) have been written to orient the reader, particularly the nonsociologist, to some basic distinctions between social and psychological explanations. Another purpose of these chapters is to encourage the reader, especially the educational researcher and the theoretician, to consider the possibility of basing inquiries into school life on social theory as well as on psychological theory.

In chapters 5 through 7 I have attempted to describe and analyze some of the differences between and among schools that seem most likely to directly influence the behavior of teachers and students. These chapters are especially important since they provide the framework for most of the discussion in chapters 8 through 12. The reader is especially advised that the appendix of this book was written to illustrate the ideas underlying the typology of schools presented in chapter 5. It is probably wise, therefore, to read the appendix along with chapter 5. The appendix is an integral part of this book. Read in connection with chapter 5, it assists the reader in working through the more intricate aspects of a discussion that refers to thirty-six distinct types of schools.

Chapters 8 through 12 have been written to illustrate the practical and theoretical significance of looking at schools from the perspective of social theory. I have attempted to center my illustrations on issues of concern to both teachers and researchers. For example, chapter 8 provides a discussion of classroom management issues and chapter 12 addresses the persistent issue of the relationship between teacher personality and school performance.

In summary, it is my hope that the reader will find this book useful, whether for the purpose of making sense out of one's own life in school, or for the purpose of making theoretical sense out of school life. For the practicing teacher and administrator I hope this book provides useful insights, but I also hope they will not confuse description with prescription. Although I present typologies of teachers and schools, too little is known about schools to recommend one of these types over all others.

For the educational researcher and theoretician I hope this book provides some fruitful hypotheses. It is well to be critical of this book as "little more than informed speculation," but it is also well to remember that informed speculations are very close to researchable ideas. I am personally convinced that the perspective suggested in this book is pregnant with research prospects, and that such research promises to be more fruitful than has been the case with most educational research. Little of the research done in education makes a real difference in the day-to-day operation of schools. The perspective presented here can move us closer to that much-desired but seldom-achieved union between theory and practice.

Many individuals have contributed, directly and indirectly, to the publication of this book. I would especially like to acknowledge my debt to the numerous graduate students who have served as sounding boards for my ideas and critics of my views, and who have provided encouragement when it was needed. Among these students are Norman Ellis, Sylvia Polgar, Betheda Justice, James Blackburn, Hugh Huff, Glenn Freedman, Eric Rice, Joyce Jaffee, and Helen Atwood.

Many of the ideas developed in this book were first suggested to me by Professor Robert E. Jewett, who has also served as an advisor and friend. Professor Ronald G. Corwin has also contributed immensely to my thinking. Indeed, it was as a student in a seminar that he directed that I was first taken by the idea of applying organizational theory to the routine concerns of classroom teachers.

I am also deeply obliged to Dean Norton L. Beach of the University of North Carolina School of Education for using his office to provide time for me to complete this book, and to my colleagues in the school who unselfishly took up my duties so that I could give my full attention to this task. I am especially indebted to one of my colleagues, Professor Richard Phillips, who carefully read most of this manuscript and gave much thoughtful advice.

In the latter stages of preparing the manuscript I met three individuals without whom I would never have mastered the many details of producing a book. Ms. Susan Fields spent many dull and tedious hours checking and verifying footnotes and other bibliographical materials. Mr. Steve Mathews has demonstrated again and again what it is to be a competent editor.

I am especially happy with the excellent and sympathetic treatment my manuscript received from Ms. Sheryl Avruch, who is a production editor with few peers.

It is always a doubtful policy to dedicate a book, for to do so may be to inflate its importance beyond that which is deserved. I would, however, like to thank my wife, Shelia, for her tireless efforts as typist and helpful critic. I would like also to thank my daughters, Krista and Jenny, who provide me with very selfish reasons for caring about schools and teachers, and who also provide me with much firsthand information about the way the school looks from the student vantage point.

Teaching and Social Behavior

1

The State of the Art

Are organizational differences among and within schools related to differences in student learning? Questions of this kind have been raised only in recent years, and right now there is scant assurance that educational researchers will be able to answer this question affirmatively. Until the publication of *Equality of Educational Opportunity*,[1] few educational researchers had even expressed doubt about whether differences among schools were significant factors in explaining differences in student learning. Indeed, most of the reform movements in education during the fifties and sixties had been predicated upon the assumption that the "form" of school organization is significantly related to learning outcomes. Thus, Conant[2] advocated the comprehensive high school, the federal government spent abundant funds to "equalize" the financial support of schools, and local schools tried a variety of organizational innovations, such as team teaching, differentiated staffing, and the "open classroom." In every instance, however, such decisions and actions were based not on empirical evidence but solely on an *a priori* acceptance of the tenability of the assumption that differences in schools do make a difference in learning outcomes—in other words, upon an act of faith.

Evidence to support the proposition that schools make a difference is less than overwhelming. Some educational researchers would go so far as to suggest that "if enough individual background characteristics were controlled, any effects

1

of schools per se ultimately would disappear."[3]   Nonetheless, other researchers are convinced that school-related differences cause real differences in student learning.   Yet, those who believe in the efficacy of school organizations have difficulty in producing convincing evidence to support their position.   For example, both the tone of the discussion and the direction of the analyses presented by McDill and Rigsby[4] leave little doubt that the authors are sympathetic toward the idea that differences in schools do make significant differences in student learning.   But, after presenting data which demonstrate that certain contextual factors do make *some* differences in student achievement levels, the authors conclude that their study "demonstrates that school quality (regardless of how it is measured) can have only modest effects on the achievement of students."[5]

If school-related differences do indeed make little difference in student learning, then the implications for educational planners are staggering.   But right now we simply do not know.   Perhaps one reason why researchers have failed to demonstrate significant relationships between variations in schools and learning outcomes is that they have been hampered by a limited, and perhaps even faulty, conceptualization of educational research.   Should this turn out to be the case, it could be disastrous for educators to base critical policy decisions upon the data that have been generated by much recent research.[6]

Most research in the domain of school effectiveness has been based upon the assumption that school-related variables like size, financing, and instructional patterns should be treated as independent variables, and student learning as a dependent variable.   Upon initial inspection, this assumption seems viable; yet there is reason to believe that it is precisely this assumption that makes it so difficult for investigators to identify "the cause" of significant differences in student achievement between schools.

Most of those who have seriously addressed the questions related to school and teacher effects have been primarily concerned with questions of measurement.   Those who deal with measurement problems, perhaps unfortunately, are often more intrigued with issues related to instrumentation and statistical analysis than with theoretical and conceptual issues. Measurement and statistical analysis are not small matters, and anyone who would do research on schools and teaching would do well to give serious attention to the issues involved. But there is much more to measurement than sampling, validating, scoring, coding, and statistical analysis. One of the fundamental concerns in measurement is the problem of conceptualization. If the concepts or categories employed in the development of measurement devices and techniques are inappropriate to the questions asked, the measurement will be useless regardless of its technical sophistication and statistical nicety. It is at the level of conceptualization and theory that educational research has been lacking. On this subject Dreeben writes:

> There is an ironical association between our familiarity with schools and our ignorance about them. It is fair to say that no adequate description or formulation of their structural characteristics currently exists, perhaps because the schooling process so obviously involves psychological change that the most reasonable way to study it—or so it would seem—is to look for those psychological changes that appear related to the main business of the school, which is instruction.[7]

Before the effects of teachers and schools can be discussed with any precision, it will be necessary to develop a systematic conceptualization of the structural properties of schools. Without such a conceptualization one cannot reasonably speculate on, let alone measure, how the structural characteristics of schools affect students or student-related outcomes. Because this task has not been managed, knowledge of the relationship between the social organization of schools and the behavior of teachers and students has advanced very little since Willard Waller's[8] classic formulation of the issue. And this is true in spite of the fact that since Waller, a number of tightly controlled and technically sophisticated studies have been undertaken to shed light on the subject.[9] The work of Willard Waller remains a prototype of the kind of work that is needed if inquiry into the nature of schooling is to advance. Modern researchers may criticize Waller's methodology, his lack of "hard data," and his reliance on fictionalized accounts of school life, but few will suggest that his insights are insignificant. Waller also provides a convincing defense for his procedures when he writes:

> But if one is to show the school as it really is, it is not enough to be unprejudiced. It is necessary to achieve some sort of literary realism. . . . To be realistic, I believe, is simply to be concrete. To be concrete is to present materials in such a way that characters do not lose the qualities of persons, nor situations their intrinsic human reality. Realistic sociology must be concrete. In my own case, this preference for concreteness has led to a relative distrust of statistical method, which has seemed, for my purposes, of little utility. Possibly the understanding of human life will be as much advanced by the direct study of social phenomena as by the study of numerical symbols abstracted from those phenomena.[10]

The immediate concern is the need to know what differences among and within schools produce differences in the behavior of students. Only after this question has been answered will it be possible to deal effectively with the question, "Within a given social context, what kinds of student behavior are likely to 'produce' the most significant student learning?" Until educators can secure a reasonably clear notion about how the social organization of schools affects the behavior system of classrooms, there is little point in discussing the differences between schools nor in assessing what effect these differences have on the learning of individual students. At present there exists no systematic formulation of those organizational variables that may be relevant to understanding behavioral differences in schools. Furthermore, there have been few significant attempts to link, either theoretically or empirically, the organizational characteristics of schools and the classroom behavior of students. What is needed, then, is a theoretical framework that makes it possible to build a conceptual linkage between the structural characteristics of schools and the behavior patterns within classrooms. It is the purpose of this book to contribute to the development of such a theory and research methodology.

A STATEMENT OF PURPOSE

This book represents a beginning effort in the development of what will be called an organizational theory of instruction. Proceeding from the assumption that schools are complex social organizations, the following types of questions are asked: How is it that the organizational properties of schools are translated into the behavioral properties of classrooms? Are the patterns of influence in classrooms somehow related to the structural properties of schools? To what extent is it possible, and useful, to separate the structural characteristics of schools and classrooms from the personal characteristics of the participants in the life of schools? To what degree is the classroom behavior of teachers and students a product of idiosyncratic factors like intelligence, attitudes, and personality structures and to what degree is school behavior more directly attributable to the role requirements incumbent upon those who occupy the positions of teacher and student? Is it possible to formulate a theory of instruction that gives primacy to the structural characteristics of schools and classrooms and considers the individual characteristics of students and teachers as tangential? If such a theory is constructed, what can it be expected to explain that cannot be explained by existing psychological theories of learning and schooling?

No single statement should purport to provide a definitive answer to even one of these questions, to say nothing of the entire range. Given the present state of empirical research and theoretical knowledge concerning the schooling process, the best that can be hoped for is to point toward areas in which answers might lie. Such a treatment will necessarily be uneven, for more is known about some of these subjects than about others. Much more is known, for example, about the classroom role of teachers than is known about the role of teachers in other dimensions of school life (e.g., the teacher as faculty member, liaison with parents, member of a profession) and practically nothing is known about the roles of students. Indeed, the assumption that "student" is a unitary position in the school, and that the position carries equal expectations for all who occupy it, is in itself evidence that current understanding of the complexity of school organizations is quite simplistic.

It is not necessary to start from scratch when beginning to develop theoretical explanations of the relationship between teachers, students, and schools. Waller's work stands as a benchmark. One would do exceedingly well to add even a little to what is explicit or implicit in his work. Other researchers like Gordon,[11] Corwin,[12] and Coleman[13] have given careful consideration to some aspects of school social structures, and are useful guides in the development of an organizational theory of instruction. There are, however, serious deficiencies in the literature on schools as organizations. In summarizing the research on school organizations, Bidwell writes:

> To understand what schools are like as organizations—what their characteristic structures, processes, and functional problems are —we now must rely on empirical work, much of which either was not explicitly directed toward these questions or was narrowly focused on some subsystem, process, or activity within the school, without being informed by a more general conception of the school as an organization.[14]

Much of the empirical evidence presented in these research efforts is, nonetheless, instructive. It is especially useful when one is attempting to weave a relational web between classroom behavior and school organization. Of particular relevance to the task at hand are the works of Jackson,[15] Adams and Biddle,[16] and Good and Brophy.[17] Some of these studies are implicitly based on social science theory although the researchers often fail to recognize this fact or fail to make it clear and explicit.[18]

In working toward an organizational theory of instruction, it is necessary to have in mind some guidelines relating to the process of theory building. In this regard, Timasheff's formulation seems an appropriate point of reference:

> Theory cannot be derived from observations and generalization merely by the means of rigorous induction. The construction of theory is a creative achievement. . . . There is always a jump beyond the evidence, a hunch, corresponding to the creative effort. But every theory thus obtained then must be subjected to *verification*. It is considered verified, in a preliminary way, if no known fact or generalization seems to contradict it. If there is a contradiction, the tentative theory must be rejected or at least modified.[19]

The hunch that has guided the construction of the formulation presented in this book is that a key to understanding school effects lies in the understanding of how power, influence, and authority are distributed throughout school systems. This hunch has its basis in the commonplace observation that one of the central concerns of schools and teachers is the motivation, direction, and control of students. Though critics may lament that this is so, how could it be otherwise? Schools are, after all, purposeful human organizations, and chief among their purposes is to induce students to behave in ways that are assumed to influence learning. That some teachers and some schools develop strategies of inducement that are malignant and counterproductive seems beyond dispute. But equally beyond controversy is the fact that schools are legitimately concerned with the direction, motivation, and control of student behavior.

More important than the legitimacy of teacher and school influence on student behavior is the centrality of power, influence, and compliance[20] in the human life of schools. The ways in which schools gain compliance from students has been the subject of much shrill criticism, but little thoughtful analysis. Clearly, schools differ in the kinds of power and influence strategies they use. For example, some schools routinely rely on corporal punishment, whereas other schools prohibit the practice. Some schools seem to rely heavily on student voluntarism to accomplish organizational ends, whereas other schools rely on coercion and, furthermore, what is true of differences between schools seems equally true between teachers. Some teachers are able to gain student compliance by simply "asking" for it; others cannot gain student compliance even when it is demanded.

The conventional way of expressing differences between and among schools is in terms of the communities they serve (e.g., lower class—middle class), the geographic location (e.g., urban—rural), or some other classification system that fastens on variables that are highly correlated with these conventional typologies, such as racial composition, school size, or financial resources. If, however, useful comparisons of the effects of schools and teachers are to be developed, the variables toward which one looks for causal mechanisms must have their locus in the social structure of the school or the classroom. For example, schools are composed of distinct organizational units such as departments, work groups, and classrooms. Other "informal" social units such as friendship cliques and interest groups also operate in schools. The ways in which these social and organizational units are related to each other, and the ways in which they differ in respect to their organizational characteristics (e.g., cohesiveness, scope of authority, behavioral expectations, and boundary permeability) are likely to be different from school to school. (At least such an assumption has considerable support in the literature on schools and, more particularly, in the literature related to the sociological study of complex social organizations.) These variations may be related to the classroom behavior of teachers and students. It seems useful, therefore, to develop a systematic means by which the structure of schools can be related to behavior in classrooms. A purpose of this book is to develop a means of categorizing schools according to the ways they vary in their organizational properties (which will be referred to as *mode of organization*) and then to examine the relationships between different modes of school organization and the behavioral networks found in the classroom in those schools.

The prevailing control networks in classrooms affect the behaviors of both teachers and students within those classrooms. It seems likely that these differences in classroom behavior systems are related to differences in student learning. In this regard, Bredemeier states that:

> however important it is to ascertain the familial sources of various salient student characteristics in the hope of optimizing them, it is at least equally important to accept those characteristics, once present, as given, and then to ascertain *what their implications* are for children's embracement of or distance of alienation from *various structurings* of the student role.[21]

Before one can discuss the implications of different student roles for students with different characteristics, means must be made available for specifying the structural characteristics of student roles, as well as for pinpointing the sources that create or legitimize those roles. Therefore, another component of this book is to develop a method for studying the behavior networks and normative structures of classrooms.

One of the more promising ways of dealing with these aspects of classroom behavior systems is to think of the classroom as a control network within the organizational context of the school. Central to this type of analysis would be the concepts of power, influence, compliance, and adaptation. Although most efforts in the analysis of classroom interaction patterns tend to be inductive and do not lend themselves easily to generalization, it seems reasonable to infer from recent work in classroom analysis (e.g., Adams and Biddle[22]) that classrooms do, indeed, possess distinct patterns of influence. Both teachers and students exercise power and influence in the classroom, and both teachers and students adapt to, or comply with, the influence efforts of other participants in the life of the classroom. Describing how this state of affairs arises and the effects it has is the major task of this book.

A POINT OF VIEW

The business of theory construction is a highly personalized undertaking. There is no simple formula to follow as one goes about the task. One must move from abstraction to fact, and back again. One must remember that when abstraction moves too far from fact there is the danger of distorting reality, but that there is no pristine virtue in always "sticking with the facts." There are times when important questions must have tentative answers before facts are readily available. One of the functions of theory, and one of the reasons for constructing theories, is that theories shed light on what varieties of facts might be needed, and what remains yet to be determined. In this regard, Mills's observation that "facts discipline reason; but reason is the advance guard in any field of learning"[23] seems quite appropriate. In the process of applying reason to the problems of interpreting school life, a writer does well, however, to keep in mind Waller's statement: "A sociological writer cannot, in the present state of our science, hope to get very far ahead of common sense, and he is usually fortunate if he does not fall behind it."[24]

NOTES

1. James S. Coleman, Ernest Q. Campbell, et al., *Equality of Educational Opportunity* (U.S. Department of Health, Education and Welfare, Office of Education, Washington, D.C.: U.S. Government Printing Office, 1966).

2. James B. Conant, *The American High School Today* (New York: McGraw-Hill Book Company, Inc., 1959).

3. A. W. Astin, "A Re-examination of College Productivity," *Journal of Educational Psychology*, 52 (1961), 173–178, as summarized by Sarane S. Boocock, *An Introduction to the Sociology of Learning* (Boston: Houghton Mifflin Company, 1972), p. 200.

4. Edward L. McDill and Leo C. Rigsby, *Structure and Process in Secondary Schools: The Academic Impact of Educational Climates* (Baltimore: Johns Hopkins University Press, 1973).

5. Ibid., p. 118.

6. See, for example, John Walton, "Anti-Scholastic Bias in the Study of Equality of Educational Opportunity," *Intellect*, 102 (October, 1973), 36–37.

7. Robert S. Dreeben, *On What Is Learned in School* (Reading, Mass.: Addison-Wesley Publishing Company, 1968), p. vii.

8. Willard Waller, *The Sociology of Teaching* (New York: John Wiley & Sons, Inc., 1932, reprinted 1967).

9. See, for example, McDill and Rigsby, *Structure and Process in Secondary Schools.*

10. Waller, *The Sociology of Teaching*, preface. Reprinted by permission of John Wiley & Sons, Inc.

11. C. Wayne Gordon, *The Social System of the High School: A Study in the Sociology of Adolescence* (Glencoe, Ill.: Free Press of Glencoe, 1957).

12. Ronald G. Corwin, *A Sociology of Education: Emerging Patterns of Class, Status, and Power in the Public Schools* (New York: Appleton-Century-Crofts, 1965).

13. James S. Coleman, *The Adolescent Society: The Social Life of the Teenager and Its Impact On Education* (New York: Free Press, 1961).

14. Charles E. Bidwell, "The School as a Formal Organization," in *Handbook of Organizations*, ed. James G. March (Chicago: Rand McNally & Company, 1965), p. 972.

15. Philip W. Jackson, *Life in Classrooms* (New York: Holt, Rinehart and Winston, Inc., 1968).

16. Raymond S. Adams and Bruce J. Biddle, *Realities of Teaching: Explorations with Video Tape* (New York: Holt, Rinehart and Winston, Inc., 1970).

17. Thomas L. Good and Jere E. Brophy, *Looking in Classrooms* (New York: Harper & Row Publishers, Inc., 1973).

18. More will be said on this subject later, but the fact that most who do applied research on teaching and schools are by training or inclination psychologists goes far to explain why there has yet to be a significant breakthrough in the creation of adequate theories relating classroom behavior and school organization.

19. Nicholas S. Timasheff, *Sociological Theory: Its Nature and Growth* (New York: Random House, 1967), p. 10.

20. Many of the fundamental structures that underlie the analysis that follows were initially suggested in Amitai Etzioni, *A Comparative Analysis of Complex Organizations: On Power, Involvement,*

and Their Correlates (New York: The Free Press of Glencoe, Inc., 1961). Particularly crucial is Etzioni's observation that such a formulation permits the theoretician to articulate social systems and personality systems in a fashion that makes theoretical sense. Central to the potential of this kind of theory as a basis for an organizational theory of instruction is the fact that such a formulation "combines a structural and motivational aspect: structural, since we are concerned with the kinds and distribution of power in organizations; motivational, since we are concerned with differential commitments of action to organizations." p. xv.

21. H. C. Bredemeier, "Schools and Student Growth," *The Urban Review*, 2 (1968), 24.

22. Adams and Biddle, *Realities of Teaching*.

23. C. Wright Mills, *The Sociological Imagination* (New York: Oxford University Press, 1959), Evergreen edition, 1961, p. 205.

24. Waller, *The Sociology of Teaching*, p. 3.

2

Some Issues of Perspective

Theories of teaching have their basis in the psychology of learning. The practice of teaching has its basis in the social realities of classrooms and schools. Willard Waller summed up the relationship between educational theory and practice this way:

> both the theory and practice of education have suffered in the past from an overattention to what ought to be and its correlative tendency to disregard what is. When theory is not based upon the existing practice, a great hiatus appears between theory and practice, and the consequence is that the progressiveness of theory does not affect the conservatism of practice. The student teacher learns the most advanced theory of education, and goes out from school with a firm determination to put it into practice. But he finds that this theory gives him little help in dealing with the concrete social situation that faces him. After a few attempts to translate theories into educational practice, he gives up and takes his guidance from conventional sources, from the advice of older teachers, the proverbs of the fraternity, and the commandments of principals.[1]

Jackson, among others, has recently provided evidence to support what many educators have long suspected; teachers find very little that is relevant or useful in existing theories of teaching and learning.[2] Jackson's basic explanation for the gap between educational theory and practice is that teachers are concerned with the immediacy of classroom behavior, while most theoreticians are concerned with long-term outcomes.[3] A similar conclusion is implicit in Waller's statement. Why, then, have educational theoreticians not thought systematically about the social realities of schools? Why have educators not developed theories of instruction that are more clearly based on the existing practices of teachers and schools? At least three conditions in American education suggest answers to these questions. First, there is a psychological bias that dominates American education. Second, there is a lack of clear distinction among the concepts of teaching, school, behavior, and learning, which is compounded by a tendency to see learning and its concomitants (e.g., attitudes and perceptions) as the essential dependent variables in educationally relevant research design. Third, a preference exists for individualistic interpretations of leadership phenomena—especially teacher leadership.

THE PSYCHOLOGICAL BIAS OF AMERICAN EDUCATORS

The role of psychology in developing insight into the problems faced by educators is not to be dismissed. The basic aim of the school is, after all, to bring about psychological change. One would be foolish to dismiss as irrelevant a discipline that takes as one of its central concerns the explanation of psychological change. When a particular mode of explanation comes to dominate a field, or when particular orientations become so deeply imbedded in thoughtways of scholars in the field that few submit these assumptions to critical analysis, one is justified in suggesting the possibility of bias. Psychological perspectives clearly dominate the thinking of educational researchers and theoreticians. This dominance seems sufficiently clear and widespread to warrant the use of the term bias.

Psychology and Teacher Training

In his *Talks to Teachers,* William James, certainly not a minor figure in educational psychology, said the following:

> Fortunately for you teachers, the elements of the mental machine can be clearly apprehended, and their workings easily grasped. And, as the most general elements and workings are just those parts of psychology which the teacher finds most directly useful, it follows that the amount of this science which is necessary to all teachers need not be very great. Those who find themselves loving the subject may go as far as they please, and become possibly none the worse teachers for the fact, even though in some of them one might apprehend a little loss of balance from the tendency observable in all of us to overemphasize certain special parts of a subject when we are studying it intensely and abstractly. But for the great majority of you a general view is enough, provided it be a true one; and such a general view, one may say, might almost be written on the palm of one's hand.[4]

It is unlikely that modern educational psychologists would agree with James. Many would suggest that James was wrong in the first place. Others might be willing to accept James's premise as appropriate to his time and place, but point to advances in the field as evidence that teachers nowadays must know more about psychology than can be written easily on the palm of one's hand. The course pattern of the typical teacher education program indicates just how much more. It is not at all unusual to require teachers in training to take at least one course in general-experimental psychology, one course, at least, in educational psychology, a course in child growth and development, and perhaps a course in child or adolescent psychology.[5] Course patterns and content vary from institution to institution, but rare indeed is the teacher training institution that does not place heavy emphasis on the "psychological foundations" of education, and courses formally designated as psychology are not the only ones that are psychologically oriented. Other courses, like teaching methods, guidance, tests and measurement, and even educational philosophy and educational sociology, may be so oriented that the issues considered could be as well taken up in courses on learning theory, psychometrics, and social psychology. From a humble beginning, in which a responsible psychologist might suggest that teachers could write all they need to know of psychology on the palm of their hands, educational psychology has come to a place of considerable prominence in the education of teachers. Whether this prominence is warranted by the circumstances is not of concern here. What is of importance is that no other academic discipline is so clearly present in the preparation of teachers as is the discipline of psychology.[6]

Psychological Basis of Research in Education

A second, perhaps more critical, dimension of the psychological bias of educators is to be found in the persistence of a research tradition that places an undue reliance on the study of the psychological determinants of behavior, with relative inattention to social scientific explanations of behavior. To the extent that educational research considers social variables at all, these variables are taken as factors that should be statistically controlled in order to isolate the "true" effects of idiosyncratic differences. Most educational researchers do control for variables like social class, race, and sex, for it is now commonly accepted that social variables do have an impact on personality development and perhaps even on cognitive development. But few educational researchers seem to understand that social variables may exist outside of the consciousness of individuals.[7] Many educational researchers seem to ignore the fact that the social structures of schools and teachers' roles in those structures serve to constrain the performance of the teacher. More central to the present argument, however, is the nature of the research that is now being done, both in regard to teacher effects and student learning. Until the early 1960's most research on teaching consisted of attempts to relate such characteristics as value orientation, open-mindedness, or attitude to student or administrator ratings of teachers.[8] Other studies have attempted to compare teachers as a group with other groups of individuals, apparently in the hope that there would be some indication of those characteristics which distinguished teachers from other occupational types. With some exceptions (e.g., Ryans's study of teacher characteristics[9]) most studies prior to 1960 did not even attempt to relate teacher characteristics to actual classroom behavior. Rather, they related teacher characteristics to what researchers assumed to be logical effects of teacher behavior: student ratings, administrator ratings, or student achievement.

The results of this line of research are summarized by Getzels and Jackson as follows:

> Despite the critical importance of the problem and a half-century of prodigious research effort, very little is known for certain about the nature and measurement of teacher personality, or about the relation between teacher personality and teaching effectiveness. The regrettable fact is that many of the studies so far have not produced significant results.[10]

The relative fruitlessness of this line of research has not, however, dissuaded researchers from continuing in the quest. As a survey of dissertation abstracts or professional journals will clearly indicate, many researchers cling to the assumption that differences in teacher effectiveness or performance must somehow be independently related to the personality structures of teachers. The advent of high-speed computers and sophisticated statistical techniques, particularly multivariate analysis, has given new hope to that stubborn band of researchers who insist that teacher personality is the basic determinant of teacher behavior and effectiveness. These researchers, and their number is substantial, argue that the lack of conclusive evidence to support their position results from the crude quality of measurement and analytic techniques. By more careful attention to the problems of reliability and validity, careful research design and reliance on factor analysis, multivariate analysis, and high-speed computers, they hope to demonstrate that their belief—perhaps bias would be a better term—has a basis in reality.

Another group of educational researchers, while not giving up on the idea that teacher characteristics are a chief determinant of student learning, have developed a new approach to the problem. Following the lead provided by researchers like Ryans,[11] they are attempting to relate the personality character- istics of teachers to teacher classroom behavior. Others attempt to relate patterns of teacher behavior to student learning. Al- though this represents a significant departure from earlier re- search, the procedures employed continue to reflect an inclination toward psychological interpretations of classrooms. Almost all of these studies take some psychologically based factor as either an independent or a dependent variable. For example, Fland- ers's[12] initial work employed teacher influence patterns as an independent variable, and student attitudes and achievement as a dependent variable. Ryans[13] viewed teacher behavior as a dependent variable, and the personal characteristics of teachers as independent. Few classroom analysts view teacher and stu- dent behavior as an outgrowth of a reciprocal social relationship,[14] and even fewer have conceived of the behavior system of the classroom as a dependent variable, with the independent variables being related to the organizational properties of the school itself.[15] Indeed, most behavior category systems used by classroom analysts assume that influence flows in a linear fashion from individual teacher to individual student. Very few of the existing behavior category systems reflect the reciprocity of influence in group interaction, although the terms interaction analysis and social interaction are used freely. Furthermore, many of the labels used in these category systems indicate that the researchers are more interested in the mental processes that may be occurring "in" individual minds than they are in the social dynamics of the classroom (e.g., the teacher accepts feelings, or the student presents a hypothesis). It would appear that there exists no system for categorizing classroom behavior that is consciously based on a systematic *social* theory of group interaction.[16] Most systems designed to generate social data about classrooms are based on concepts that are more appropriate to the understanding of psychological processes than to the understanding of social processes. Therefore, the data are often useless for purposes of social analysis. Since few of these systems are linked to a systematic theory of learning, many are of dubious value even for the purpose of studying individual psychological processes.

Concluding Remarks

In addition to patterns of training and research, evidence regarding a psychological bias among educators can be adduced from the statements of observers from both inside and outside the fields of professional education. At least one such observer, a sociologist, is both cognizant of the bias and convinced that it stands in the way of an adequate understanding of education. Wilson writes:

> We shall not have an adequate understanding of education until we renounce an exclusively psychological approach that obscures the significance of the social system, the adolescent subculture, the influence of peer groups, and the like. Psychology, and especially that brand called Educational Psychology (as though to distinguish it from other sorts of psychology that are mis- or un-educational!) focuses on the individual. From the psychological point of view, as the pedagogical cliché goes, the function of education is to develop to the utmost the potential of the individual. This posture is consonant with many of our pieties—I do not deride them but mean only to call attention to certain plausible consequences—about the dignity of the individual, respect for the individual, the character of a democracy in contrast to totalitarian states, the Good Shepherd who would leave the ninety and nine to seek the single lost sheep.[17]

Wilson's point of view probably has more appeal to sociologists than to professors of education, but there is evidence that educational researchers are becoming aware of the existence of a psychological bias. For example, one entire edition of the

Review of Educational Research,[18] a publication of the prestigious American Educational Research Association, was given over to the discussion of social factors in education. The editors' introduction gives some indication of how recently educational researchers have come to recognize the potential contribution of the social sciences to their enterprise.

> This issue of the *Review* has departed significantly from the usual procedures for selecting articles for publication in this journal. For the first time the selection was limited to one Division of AERA, in this instance, Division G, the Social Context of Education. . . . The purpose of bringing these papers together in this one issue was twofold—to give special recognition to this relatively new and rapidly growing division of the Association, and to encourage broader social science representation in the *Review* and other AERA journals.[19]

This introduction clearly suggests that the social sciences are a long way from being adequately represented in educational research journals, to say nothing of the thoughtways of educational researchers.

However, the aim should not be to supplant the bias toward psychology with a bias toward sociology or the social sciences, for distortions of the realities of school life would still result. Learning is a central factor of understanding schools, and no one is so well equipped as the psychologist to understand the processes by which learning occurs. But there is much more to school than learning. How students behave in school and how teachers behave is clearly related to the structure of the relationships that exist in schools. A psychological perspective can give guidance to understanding the relationship between student behavior in schools and school-related learning. But psychology is not in a position to explain the nature and significance of the social relationship between teachers and students in schools. As Boocock so rightly points out:

> Regardless of the structural defects in the student-teacher relationship, the notion persists that the teacher is important, and

most readers can recall a teacher who had a distinct impact on his life for better or worse. In view of the almost universal importance attached to the teacher role, it is surprising how little can be said about the kind of teacher and teaching which produces the best learning results. Research has been done on the social background and status of teachers . . . but very little is known about the relationships between what teachers *do* in the classroom and the subsequent behavior of their students.[20]

So long as the basic research thrust in education is toward relating behavior to learning and learning to behavior, very little will be known about the subject of the behavioral effects of teaching. What teachers do and how this relates to the subsequent behavior of students has to do with the structure of the social relationships, in schools and in classrooms, and it is in the understanding of such social relationships that sociology finds much of the grist for its mill. But as Wilson points out:

It is, apparently, hard to see that a group does not consist of a collection of people, that the sociologist is dealing with the structure of *relationships*, and their constituent roles, and the dimensions of analysis are quite different from those used in the study of personality systems. Even thoughtful people are likely to fall into the nominalist fallacy: only the concrete individual has reality. This is reinforced by the strong position psychology has enjoyed in our intellectual tradition. It has deflected our attention from relationships *between* self and other to those *within*; emotional, cognitive, and neurological.[21]

SCHOOLS, TEACHERS, AND LEARNING

Consistent with the psychological perspective that dominates educational thought is the view that teaching theories should be based on or deduced from theories of learning. For example, DeCecco writes, ". . . a theory of learning is much broader and more basic than a theory of teaching. In fact, theories of teach-

21

ing must be based on theories of learning."[22] The assumption
that learning theory is the appropriate basis for teaching theory
is so deeply embedded in the conventional wisdom of education
that the suggestion that there are reasonable alternatives to this
assumption is likely to raise considerable controversy.[23] In spite
of the fact that efforts to generate useful teaching theories from
learning theories have been generally fruitless, educators still
persist in the belief that efforts to deduce teaching theories from
learning theories are worthy of continued effort. The reason for
this persistence is clear.

> From a commonsense viewpoint, the linkage between teaching
> and learning is so intimate—or appears to be—that an under-
> standing of the one process would seem to imply an understand-
> ing of the other. If we knew all there was to know about learning
> we ought to know, or be able to deduce, all there is to know
> about teaching. At least, so it would seem. This expectation, in
> one form or another, has enjoyed widespread popularity among
> psychologists and educators alike. It has bolstered the hope that
> a scientific theory of learning will be developed which will have
> immediate and direct consequences for the improvement of the
> teacher's work.[24]

Even those scholars who are sympathetic to the idea that learning
theory may not be an appropriate basis for teaching theory find
it difficult to discard a psychological view of the world. Some,
like Jackson, argue that the demonstrated inability of learning
theory to generate teaching theories, combined with the low
level of current understanding of life in classrooms, suggests that
the best that can be hoped for in the immediate future is ". . . the
emergence of several critical perspectives from which to view
classroom events. Each perspective, it may be hoped, will provide the practitioner and the researcher with a unique strategy
of inquiry with which to examine educational affairs."[25]
   Others, like Amidon,[26] are more blatantly empirical in their
orientation and are pursuing a course of research that promises
to yield little more (or less) than a series of empirical generaliza-

tions[27] concerning correlations between quantitative measures of discrete types of teacher or student classroom behavior and student achievement. The hope of this latter group of researchers is that the empirical generalizations they produce will become the basis for an inductively derived theory of classroom behavior.[28]

It is possible to develop deductively derived theories of classroom behavior that are based on other than psychological premises. Cohen, for example, suggests that such theories are possible, and goes some way toward demonstrating that her case has merit.[29] But Cohen would limit her theories to problems of very narrow scope and limited range. She writes: ". . . a theory helpful in understanding and manipulating status systems in the classroom will probably not be the same theory which will prove helpful in changing the authority structure of the classroom."[30] There is, though, reason to hope that it will be possible to construct theories of instruction that are more broadly based than Cohen seems to think possible. Perhaps something akin to what Robert Merton has called theories of the middle range:

> Middle-range theory is principally used in sociology to guide empirical inquiry. It is intermediate to general theories of social systems which are too remote from particular classes of social behavior, organization and change to account for what is observed and to those detailed orderly descriptions of particulars that are not generalized at all. Middle-range theory involves abstractions, of course, but they are close enough to observed data to be incorporated in propositions that permit empirical testing. Middle-range theories deal with delimited aspects of social phenomena, as is indicated by their labels. One speaks of a theory of reference groups, of social mobility, or role-conflict and of the formation of social norms just as one speaks of a theory of prices, a germ theory of disease, or a kinetic theory of gases.[31]

Before middle-range theories of instruction can be developed, however, it will be necessary for educators to put their conceptual house into a different order than now exists. It will be particularly crucial that the central concepts employed in research be ordered in such a way that one can easily distinguish between social processes and psychological effects. Though psychological effects may be the long-run goal of teaching, the immediate problem of teaching theory is to explain the social processes of classrooms and schools. As Jackson puts it:

> The problem turns, it would seem, on the distinction between the teacher's *primary* concern and his *ultimate* concern, on the thoughts and practices dominating his immediate actions with students, as contrasted with his hopes and expectations concerning the long-term achievement of individuals within his class. Teachers, particularly in the lower grades, seem to be more activity-oriented than learning-oriented. That is, they commonly decide on a set of activities which they believe will have a desirable outcome and then focus their energies on achieving and maintaining student involvement in those activities. Learning is important, to be sure, but when the teacher is actually interacting with his students it is at the periphery of his attention, rather than at the focus of his vision.
>
> In the interactive setting the teacher commonly encourages his students to do what he thinks will be good for them without giving too much thought to the precise outcome of his instructional effort. At first glance this lack of precision might appear to be a pedagogical shortcoming, and indeed it is criticized as such by proponents of so-called behavioral objectives, . . . but an analysis of some of the qualities of classroom life already examined in this volume does much to dispel such hasty criticism. Considering only the numerical facts, so to speak—the number of hours spent in school, the number of students in each room, and the number of subjects in the curriculum—the teacher's imprecision in establishing goals becomes understandable, if not forgiveable.[32]

Since conceptualizing some of the more important dimensions of the social life of schools and classrooms constitutes the chief task of this book, it seems well to give consideration to some of the difficulties created by present modes of conceptualization.

N. L. Gage suggests that there are two basic types of teaching theories.

First, such a theory can undertake to explain why teachers behave the way they do in their roles as teachers; the teacher's
behavior is a dependent variable in such a scheme. . . .

A second kind of theory of teaching would attempt to explain how it is that the behavior of one person, a teacher, can
influence the behavior or learning of another person, a student. . . .[33]

As a general description of the status of modern theories of
teaching, Gage's propositions are accurate enough. But as a
prescription for the kinds of issues to which teaching theories
should be addressed, and for how theories of instruction should
be oriented, there are a number of problems with his point of
view.

To summarize Gage's position, it would seem that it is possible to ask "What causes teacher behavior?" and then turn to
some theory of personality or theory of social motives for possible
hypotheses. It is a theory of teaching because teachers are the
subjects under study. Alternatively, or as a supplement, one
might ask, "How does teacher behavior affect the behavior or
learning of children?" In this regard, however, Gage would
limit consideration to those kinds of influences Gage labels as
"psychological." He writes: "Influence by one person on another
can take many forms other than teaching. Just as not all changes
in behavior reflect learning, so not all influences on another's
behavior reflect teaching. . . . The kind of force through which
a teacher can, by definition, influence a pupil must rather be
psychological (perceptual, cognitive or affective) forces."[34] One
must assume that social theories of motivation and concepts of
organizational power, thus, would have no place in what
Gage would consider a proper theory of instruction. By definition, Gage has excluded social theory as a basis for developing
theories about the effects of teaching, although social theory
could serve as a source of explanation about the motives of
teacher behavior. Apparently, however, when the researcher has
developed a social theory of teacher behavior he cannot apply
that theory to the relationships between teachers and students.

At least such applications would be prohibited if the researcher found that teachers behave as they do as the result of social—as opposed to psychological—influences. Such exclusion of social theory from theories addressed *to teaching effects* makes it quite unlikely that intelligent discussion of teaching effects or effectiveness is apt to be forthcoming.

Gage and most other educational researchers fail to give sufficient attention to the distinction between teaching as a social act and learning as a psychological process. It is true that teaching has never occurred without a *learner* being present. It is not true that teaching has never occurred without *learning* taking place. Teaching does not depend on learning, any more than learning depends on teaching. *Teaching is the role-related behavior of those individuals who occupy the position of teacher.* As educational psychologists are quick to point out, much learning occurs without the benefit of teaching. What some seem unwilling to acknowledge, or at least to take seriously, is that teaching can take place without the consequence being learning— at least the intended learning.

Teaching is the act of inducing students to behave in ways that are *assumed* to lead to learning, including *attempts* to induce students to so behave.[35] Whether students do, in fact, behave the way the teacher attempts to induce them to behave is a question for empirical study. Whether the behavior induced by the teacher leads to the intended learning outcome, some unintended learning outcome, or no learning at all is a question for mental measurement. The results of such measurement might be useful to both learning theorists and teaching theorists, but measures of mental processes, achievement, and attitude are not the alpha and omega of theories of teaching and instruction.

Appropriate questions for teaching theory[36] are questions like: What are the conditions under which a particular kind of teacher behavior has the effect of inducing students to behave in ways which the teacher expects them to behave? Under what conditions do students respond to the behavior of teachers in ways that are not expected by the teacher? What are the effects upon the teacher's behavior of these unanticipated student re-

sponses? To what extent is the teacher controlled by student behavior? Is teacher behavior independent of student behavior or
are they woven together in the social structure of the school and
the classroom in such a way that they become interdependent?
Can a teacher "change" his behavior *even if* the social system of
the classroom is not designed to accommodate that change?
More directly, is the social system of the classroom largely dependent on the behavior of the teacher, or are its sources more
diffuse? To what extent are the social system of the classroom
and the behavior of participants therein independent of factors
outside the classroom and outside the consciousness of individuals
in the classrooms? To what extent are the social system of the
classroom and the behavior of participants shaped by such outside factors as reference groups, peer groups, departmental loyalties, and class schedules? Indeed, to what extent is the classroom
a social system?

Another way of stating the matter is that teaching has to do
with what occurs between self and other. What the teacher does is
not dependent on the teacher's will alone. In part, at least, what
the teacher does depends on the influence structure of the classroom and the schools. What teacher has not been compelled to
change his intended course of action because a student or students refused to comply with his requests? Theories of instruction, including theories of teacher influence, must take into
account these competing—at times reinforcing—sources of inducement for student and teacher behavior. One should never
succumb to the illusion that linear cause-and-effect models will
accurately reflect the complexity of schools or classrooms. The
idea that researchers can somehow reduce these classroom complexities into rather simple models of causality by factor analysis
and multivariate analysis is quite seductive, but the researcher
must be alert to the prospect that that which is a cause in one
instance may become an effect in the next. In the classroom,
assumed effects are as likely to have impact on assumed causes
as are assumed causes to have impact on effects. Few researchers
would suggest, for example, that evidence that a student has
successfully learned what the teacher desires him to learn will

have no effect on the teacher's future behavior toward that student.[37]   The purpose of assuming that the behavior of teachers is a cause and the learning of students is an effect is to make it possible to convert the overwhelming complexity of the classroom into something bordering on manageable proportions.   Simplified models protect the researcher from being overwhelmed by the complexity of classroom data.   Without such models there would be little likelihood that tested propositions about the effects of teaching and school could ever be generated.   But the difficulty lies not in the fact that simplifying models are needed from which to study schools and classrooms, nor even in the assumption that cause-and-effect models are appropriate to theories of teaching.   Rather, the difficulty lies in selecting analytic units upon which to build such paradigms.

How teachers behave is one sort of question.   What influences this behavior is another sort of question, and the effect of teaching behavior on students is yet another.   An adequate theory of instruction must address at least these questions.   In addition, a theory of instruction must consider how the social system of the school and the classroom affects all the participants, teachers and students alike.   It is in the dynamic interaction between self and other, between the person and the social structure, that the conditions of learning are established and the limits of effects determined.   The background characteristics of students and teachers may determine the potentialities and/or limitations of individuals, and these personal characteristics may even shape the way teachers and students are likely to behave.   But one must look to the social structure of schools and classrooms in order to interpret the effects and meanings of teacher and student behavior.

One of the fundamental difficulties with existing modes of thought about teaching is the insistence that the appropriate units of analysis are the behavior of individuals and idiosyncratic psychological change.   The tendency toward psychological interpretation only partially accounts for this insistence.   Another factor is the close connection between behavior and learning. Some would even go so far as to insist that this connection is so

close that it is pointless to try to separate them, that unless behavioral changes occur, learning has not occurred.[38] Whatever
its sources, however, insistence upon individual behavior and
learning as the basic units for the construction of instructional
theories creates many problems for the theoretician. Whether
or not behavioral change is a necessary *consequent* of learning,
behavior is an *antecedent* to learning. In the terms of a tired
cliché, "learning is an active process." The learner must be
actively "behaving" before the process of learning can occur.
This is the case whether one argues that learning occurs as the
result of some form of association between stimulus and response, or that learning results from some interruption to habitual
patterns of response and subsequent reordering of the cognitive
field. It is the business of teaching to induce those behaviors
which are assumed to be *antecedent* to learning, learning being
the desired consequence of the behavior. Only indirectly can
teaching be conceived as a cause of learning. The cause, if one
chooses to use the term, is more appropriately located with the
learner himself. Teachers can "cause" students to behave in
particular ways, or at least attempt to cause them to so behave.
It is the effort to direct the behavior of students in ways that
seem likely to influence learning that constitutes—ideally at
least—the business of teaching.[39] Furthermore, teachers can attempt to arrange the social and physical environment of the
classroom in such a way that students will be induced to behave
in ways that will lead to learning, even though the teacher is
only indirectly involved in the process of inducement.[40]

Teacher or student behavior, per se, is a relatively useless
unit of analysis if one's purpose is to understand how one person
gains compliance to his directions from another person. For
example, threats, screaming, and shouting are coercive only if the
person who is doing the threatening, screaming, or shouting has
some ability to act on his threats or, *under some circumstances*,
if he is perceived to have such ability. A teacher whose authority
has been undermined by the informal peer-group structures of
a classroom may be much less coercive than a teacher who has
consolidated and maintained his institutionally bestowed power

to control the lives of children. This might be the case even when the subverted teacher shows more overt behaviors that suggest "authoritarianism" than does his colleague. Behavior that takes into account "others" is, by definition, social. Social behavior can be properly understood only in the context of social relationships. Given the fact that teaching so clearly has to do with what goes on between self and others, it is difficult to imagine an adequate theory of instruction that *does not* take social theory as its starting point. And any theory of instruction based on social theory that fails to consider social relationships and social action[41] as key concepts will be as inadequate as theories based on more clinical perspectives. If useful theories of instruction are ever to be developed, educators must come to recognize that the behaviors of *individual* teachers or students are not the relevant units for analysis. The basic unit for study must be the social relationships and social roles out of which and through which these behaviors are enacted.

THE CONCEPT OF LEADERSHIP

Leadership is a central concept in educational research, theory, and practice. The literature on education, particularly that literature related to school administration and management, is jaded with references to leadership styles, leadership ability, and the selection, retention, and training of educational leaders. Though discussions of teaching are less apt to be couched in the explicit terminology of leadership theory, the idea of leadership is clearly central to many considerations of classroom phenomena. For example, some of the studies by Flanders,[42] Amidon,[43] and Good and Brophy[44] may be profitably conceived as attempts to gather data relevant to the testing of propositions about leadership effects and effectiveness.

The troubles that plague leadership studies in education are not unlike those that bother researchers in other fields such as industrial sociology. Katz and Kahn summarize the general situation this way:

> Leadership appears in social science literature with three major meanings: as the attribute of a position, as the characteristic of a person, and as a category of behavior. To be a foreman is to occupy a position of leadership, and to be a company president is to occupy a position of greater leadership. Yet it may be said that a certain foreman exercises considerable leadership, and that the presidents of some companies exercise very little. Moreover, leadership is a relational concept implying two terms: the influencing agent and the persons influenced. Without followers there can be no leader. Hence, leadership conceived of as an ability is a slippery concept, since it depends too much on properties of the situation and of the people to be "led." If the powerfully leading foreman were catapulted into the president's office, would his leadership abilities still be manifest? And if he could not lead as president, what would have become of his leadership abilities?[45]

Unlike the general field of leadership research and theory, however, research on educational leadership has not been subjected to particularly searching criticism, at least not until quite recently. Consequently research on leadership in schools has proceeded on assumptions that have long ago been discarded by most social scientists as irrelevant or nonproductive. For example, studies of leadership "traits" are now viewed by most social scientists as inadequate bases for explanations of leadership behavior; yet there persist in education unremitting efforts to relate "teacher traits" to teacher effects and effectiveness.

In addition to ambiguity about the concept of leadership *per se,* there exists in educational research considerable ambiguity in teachers' leadership functions. On the one hand, in the hierarchical arrangement of most schools the leadership potential of the position of teacher is limited by subordinate relationship to the positions of principal, supervisor, and superintendent. Thus, from the perspective of many administrators and some administrative theorists, leadership logically resides in those who occupy more commanding positions in the administrative structure. On the other hand, the fact that one of the prime functions of teachers is to influence students to behave in organizationally desired ways forces the impression that teaching is somehow a leadership function. This impression, however, is not without its difficulties.

Many who study leadership insist that leadership is more than routine role performance. If all the teacher does is that which is organizationally expected or required, then the teacher is not exercising leadership, even in the classroom. For some, at least, the exercise of leadership involves going beyond required performance and developing the potential of a given position for organizational influence. Katz and Kahn write:

> *we consider the essence of organizational leadership to be the influential increment over and above mechanical compliance with the routine directives of the organization.* Such an influential increment derives from the fact that human beings rather than computers are in positions of authority and power.[46]

Others, like Johnson,[47] go so far as to exclude position-related authority and power from any definition of leadership, and insist that leadership be defined in much more personalistic terms. Johnson seems to prefer the conception that "leadership constitutes an influence relationship between two or more persons who depend upon one another for the attainment of mutual goals within a group situation."[48] The fundamental difficulties with such a personalistic interpretation of leadership are that it places tremendous emphasis on mutualism and limits the study of leadership to relatively small groups in nonorganizational settings. The definition excludes all means of influencing the behavior of others that rely on other than consensual authority— at least within the group—and overlooks the possibility that coercion and manipulation are possible leadership strategies. Whether or not such strategies are desirable is a question of ethics and effect, not a question of definition. Of course, it could be argued that the teacher's need to get a task done, and the student's need to avoid psychological or physical pain, constitutes sufficient mutual interest to make coercive influence strategies conceivable as leadership phenomena, but this is a tautological argument. It seems fair to say that many who study leadership in classrooms would insist that teaching behavior can only be considered leadership behavior when the unique qualities of the teacher are manifest in a way that sets him apart from the routine of organizational life, and when the influence the teacher exercises over students is based upon shared or mutual goals. Such a definition of teacher leadership may be a useful description of how teachers ought to behave in schools organized on democratic principles, but it is hardly a useful way of describing how teachers do exercise leadership in classroom settings. The fact that the legitimate power of the teacher and the legitimate power of students are so obviously distorted in favor of the teacher has led some to the view that to recognize position-related authority as a basis for teacher leadership would be directly contrary to "democratic theories of classroom behavior." Therefore, to some theorists, any acceptable definition of teacher as leader must exclude position-related authority and power, or be considered undemocratic.

There may be ideological appeal in the semantic argument that when teachers exercise authority based on other than mutualism and common goals they are really not behaving as leaders, but as managers, controllers, directors, or organizational functionaries; however, this argument is not very useful in terms of analysis. The desire for more democratic arrangement in schools and classrooms is a noble one, and not to be disparaged. Too many schools are organized on principles that are probably antithetical to the needs of democratic society. But one should not substitute ideological preferences for analytic precision. The facts are clear enough. One of the most significant cleavages in the school is the bimodal distribution of the relatively young and the relatively old. While age may not be as much a source of authority and influence in American culture as it is in some primitive tribes, age differences should not be discounted as bases of influence. Second, from the student's point of view at least, teachers are appointed over them, not elected by them.[49] Though one may argue that community control over schools assures the long-run possibility of democratic responsibility in the classroom, in the short run the organizational relationship is clearly one of teacher dominance, with or without the consent of the dominated. To accept a definition of the teacher as leader that includes position-related power and authority could very well challenge democratic preferences, but the acceptance of such a definition may serve as a valuable source of criticism of the undemocratic—indeed antidemocratic—arrangements of some schools. Even more important than ideological preferences is the fact that any definition of teaching that excludes the institutional components of leadership makes it difficult to assess the relative effectiveness of teachers and the relative impact of schools. As Johnson so rightly observes:

> all teachers are created equal in regard to the legitimate power of their position and the rewards and sanctions that they can use to influence students. They do not, however, remain equal. Some teachers show strong leadership; others do not. Some teachers use their position power more effectively than others; one may use it to maximize his influence in the classroom and school whereas another may fail to use it appropriately and thereby decrease his influence. . . .[50]

One of the basic questions of teacher effects and effectiveness is the degree to which the teacher *uses* the legitimate power of his position to influence students, and the interrelationships of particular usages of power and influence. Any formulation of the leadership role of teachers that excludes the power potentials *and limitations* of alternative structurings of the teacher's role must eventually fall back on some form of psychological reductionism; i.e., all human behavior has its inherent source in the primal makeup of the individual. An adequate formulation of the leadership role of the teacher must include both those properties that are largely attributable to the nature of the school organization and those properties that are largely due to the teacher's unique enactment of his classroom role. That institutional leadership is central to the teaching process, just as is personal leadership, seems so obvious that it is difficult to understand why institutional leadership of teachers has been so little studied. Even when institutional leadership performance is studied, the studies usually take the form of inquiries into "classroom management" and "discipline," with little attention to how the teacher's exercise of institutional leadership interacts with the ability to exercise personal leadership.

Over forty years ago Willard Waller distinguished between teaching as institutionalized leadership and teaching as personal leadership. From Waller's perspective:

> Personal leadership arises from the interaction of personalities. It is an effect of personal gradients among the parts of a social whole. Personal interchange is at its height in personal leadership; there are no barriers shutting off one person from communion with another. In institutional leadership, personalities must be strained through the sieve of the social pattern before they can come into contact with each other.[51]

One source of the lack of attention given to institutional leadership must be the predilection of educators to look for psychological explanations. Another source is the implicit preference for "democratic" solutions and tendency toward naive views about the nature of democracy. Particularly distracting is the tendency to confuse behaviors often associated with democratic relationships, such as responsiveness, openness to suggestion, and willingness to compromise, with the existence of a democratic relationship. A democratic relationship is one in which there is some degree of responsibility of the leader to the led, because of or *in spite of* the leader's peculiar tendencies and proclivities. A teacher may choose, or learn, to behave in a responsive fashion, and the teacher who is indirect in approach may be superior to one who is not so indirect, but this does not change the structure of the relationship between the teachers and the students in schools. The typical student-teacher relationship remains a superordinate-subordinate one, with the teacher establishing most of the limits within which reciprocal roles will be enacted.[52]

CONCLUDING REMARKS

In this chapter the purpose has been to demonstrate the dependence of educational research and theory on individualistic, personalistic, and psychologically oriented explanations of the social realities of schools. Implicit and explicit in this argument is the assumption that a sociological perspective might make it possible to develop more useful and adequate theories of instruction because the units of analysis with which such a theory would begin (social relationships and social actions) would be more directly appropriate to understanding what goes on between and among students, teachers, and schools.

In this chapter the groundwork for the task that lies ahead has been established, the task being the development of outlines for a theory of instruction based on a social conception of teaching. The extent to which this task can be successfully managed will certainly depend on the imagination and rigor with which the would-be theorist approaches his work. But, in no small measure, success will also depend on the willingness of professional educators to consider perspectives not commonly brought to bear on the task of teaching.

NOTES

1. Willard Waller, *The Sociology of Teaching* (New York: John Wiley & Sons, Inc., 1932, reprinted 1967), p. 192. Reprinted by permission of the publisher.
2. Philip W. Jackson, *Life in Classrooms* (New York: Holt, Rinehart and Winston, Inc., 1968), especially pp. 113–117.

3. Ibid., particularly chapter 5.

4. William James, *Talks to Teachers on Psychology: And to Students on Some of Life's Ideas* (New York: Henry Holt and Company, 1939), pp. 11–12.

5. Though no systematic survey of the matter was undertaken, a number of colleagues who have knowledge of teacher education have confirmed the view that psychology plays a dominant role in professional education courses. In addition, the curricula of nine leading teacher education institutions were examined, and in no case is any other discipline nearly so prominent as is psychology.

6. There is some controversy over the quality of the psychological knowledge available in teacher education programs. See, for example, James D. Koerner, *The Mis-education of American Teachers* (Baltimore: Penguin Books, 1963). Whatever the case, to the extent that any academic discipline serves as a basis for inquiries in education, that discipline is likely to be psychology.

7. The distinction between social facts and psychological facts is an important one and should be given careful consideration by educational researchers. A classic discussion of many of the issues involved can be found in Emile Durkheim, *The Rules of Sociological Method* (New York: Free Press, 1966). Although the trained sociologist may find it difficult to understand, there are those who seriously maintain that the way a teacher *behaves* in the classroom is almost *exclusively* a function of personality. Among other things, such a view ignores the compelling nature of social roles, peer group pressure, and the hierarchy of school authority. Nonetheless, the view persists, particularly among teacher educators, that the classroom behavior of teachers is largely independent of the social structure of schools and classrooms and is basically dependent on the background characteristics and personality structures of teachers.

8. Many of these studies have been reviewed in J. W. Getzels and P. W. Jackson, "The Teacher's Personality and Characteristics," in *Handbook of Research on Teaching*, ed. N. L. Gage (Chicago: Rand McNally & Company, 1963), pp. 506–582. For bibliographies of work prior to 1950 see A. S. Barr, "The Measurement and Prediction of Teaching Efficiency: Summary of Investigations," *Journal of Experimental Education*, 16 (June, 1948), 203–283; S. J. Domas and D. V. Tiedman, "Teacher Competence: An Annotated Bibliography," *Journal of Experimental Education*, 19 (Dec., 1950), 101–218.

9. David G. Ryans, *Characteristics of Teachers: Their Description, Comparison, and Appraisal: A Research Study* (Washington, D.C.: American Council on Education, 1960).

10. J. W. Getzels and P. W. Jackson, "The Teacher's Personality and Characteristics," p. 574.

11. Ryans, *Characteristics of Teachers.*

12. Ned A. Flanders, *Teacher Influence, Pupil Attitudes and Achievements,* U.S. Department of Health, Education and Welfare, Office of Education, Cooperative Research Monograph No. 12, 1960.

13. Ryans, *Characteristics of Teachers.*

14. Some researchers have attempted to develop ways of studying reciprocal relationships in classrooms, e.g. student influence of teachers *and* teacher influence of students, but the procedures involved are unusually cumbersome and of dubious theoretical significance. See A. Simon and E. Boyer (eds.), *Mirrors For Behavior: An Anthology of Observation Instruments* (Philadelphia: Research for Better Schools, Inc., 1970), for a comprehensive view of some of the procedures used in the study of classroom behavior.

15. There are a number of exceptions to this proposition. Ryans (*Characteristics of Teachers*), in fact, touched on the matter, although the variables he dealt with were not clearly organizational in nature. Recently, a suggestive study was reported by Ralph W. Larkin, "Contextual Influences on Teacher Leadership Styles," *Sociology of Education,* 46 (1973), 471–479.

16. These conclusions are based on a review of the instruments presented in Simon and Boyer, *Mirrors For Behavior.*

17. Everett K. Wilson, *Sociology: Rules, Roles and Relationships* (Homewood, Ill.: Dorsey Press, 1966), p. 449. Wilson, a professional sociologist, was, for a number of years, the sociologist-in-chief for a National Sciences Foundation–sponsored curriculum project, *Sociological Resources for the Social Studies,* which was designed to bring together educationists and sociologists in a joint effort to produce useful curricular materials.

18. *Review of Educational Research,* Vol. 42, No. 4 (1972).

19. Ibid., 411.

20. Sarane S. Boocock, *An Introduction to the Sociology of Learning* (Boston: Houghton Mifflin Company, 1972), p. 129. Copyright 1972 by Houghton Mifflin Company. Reprinted by permission of the publisher.

21. Wilson, *Sociology,* pp. 692–693.

22. John P. DeCecco, *The Psychology of Learning and Instruction: Educational Psychology* (Englewood Cliffs, N.J.: Prentice-Hall, Inc., 1968), p. 8.

23. On this topic Jackson writes: "The separation of teaching and learning, even in the interest of intellectual speculation, is likely to arouse protests from professionals and laymen alike. If the teacher is not chiefly concerned with learning, with what is he concerned?" *Life in Classrooms*, pp. 161–162.

24. Ibid., p. 159.

25. Ibid., p. 176.

26. See for example Edmund Amidon and Elizabeth Hunter, *Improving Teaching: The Analysis of Classroom Verbal Interaction* (New York: Holt, Rinehart and Winston, Inc., 1966).

27. Merton defines an empirical generalization as "an isolated proposition summarizing observed uniformities of relationships between two or more variables." Robert K. Merton, *Social Theory and Social Structure* (New York: Free Press, 1968), enlarged edition, p. 149.

28. There are those who would label studies involving verbal interaction "theoretically based." For the most part these studies yield only empirical generalization based upon observed co-variance of patterns of teacher "influence" and mean achievement or attitude scores. So far, there is nothing approaching a "theory" of teaching involving verbal interaction. Perhaps some of the empirical generalizations produced by researchers like Flanders will be useful to future theoreticians, but as these propositions now stand, they are almost totally devoid of theoretical content. Indeed, much of the research on classroom behavior is strikingly similar to what C. Wright Mills has called "abstracted empiricism." See C. Wright Mills, *The Sociological Imagination* (New York: Oxford University Press, 1959), Evergreen edition, 1961.

29. Elizabeth G. Cohen, "Sociology and the Classroom: Setting the Conditions for Teacher-Student Interaction," *Review of Educational Research*, Vol. 42, No. 4 (1972), 441–451.

30. Ibid., 450.

31. Merton, *Social Theory and Social Structure*, pp. 39–40. In fairness to Cohen it should be said that what she has in mind seems not dramatically different from Merton's "theories of the middle range," but the tone of her argument could lead to the conclusion that deductions from empirical generalizations were theories. The disagreement with Cohen is, therefore, more one of style than of substance.

32. From *Life in Classrooms* by Philip W. Jackson. Copyright © 1968 by Holt, Rinehart and Winston, Inc. Reprinted by permission of Holt, Rinehart and Winston, Publishers.

33. N. L. Gage, "Paradigms for Research on Teaching," in *Handbook of Research on Teaching*, ed. N. L. Gage (Chicago: Rand McNally & Company, 1963), p. 134.

34. Gage's conceptualization is the position typically held by educational researchers and theoreticians, although some are neither as thoughtful nor as articulate as Gage. The idea that teacher behavior is the "cause" and student learning is the "effect" is the basic model out of which much educational research is done. N. L. Gage, "Paradigms for Research on Teaching," p. 134.

35. One of the things that may account for the failure of so many teaching strategies is that they do not induce the behavior that is the necessary antecedent to learning. There is also the possibility that the behaviors educators *assume* will lead to learning are not always those behaviors that *do* lead to the intended learning outcome.

36. As will become more clear shortly, there is reason to prefer the broader term *instruction* when speaking about theories related to classroom and school effects. Thus, while the term *teaching* will be used interchangeably with *instruction*, teaching is conceptualized in much broader terms than the *overt* behavior of teachers.

37. Educational researchers, including Gage, do recognize that linear cause-and-effect models do not accurately reflect the complex interactions of social and psychological variables in the classroom. What some fail to take into account, however, is that by locating the probable cause of social events in the psychological makeup and individual background characteristics of the participants, researchers limit the explanatory power available to them. To take the behavior of teachers and students as the essential limit relieves the matter only slightly. Behavior, without reference to the social system in which it is enacted, is no more amenable to social explanation than is *individual* personality structure.

38. This reasoning has led to the movement toward behaviorally stated instructional programs and assessment, the idea being that the only reasonable basis for inferring that learning has occurred is evidence of behavioral change.

39. Though the matter has been mentioned before, it bears repeating that one of the major arguments of Philip Jackson's work is that teachers are more concerned with immediate behavioral "feed-

back" than with long-run learning outcomes (Jackson, *Life in Classrooms*).

40. It is the recognition of this possibility that leads to a preference for the term *instructional theory*, rather than *teaching theory*.

41. "Action is social in so far as, by virtue of the subjective meaning attached to it by the acting individual (or individuals) it takes account of the behavior of others and is thereby oriented in its course." Max Weber, *The Theory of Social and Economic Organization*, trans. A. M. Henderson and Talcott Parsons (New York: Oxford University Press, 1947), p. 88.

42. Flanders, *Teacher Influence, Pupil Attitudes and Achievements*.

43. Amidon and Hunter, *Improving Teaching*.

44. Thomas L. Good and Jere E. Brophy, *Looking in Classrooms* (New York: Harper & Row, Publishers, Inc., 1973).

45. Daniel Katz and Robert L. Kahn, *The Social Psychology of Organizations* (New York: John Wiley & Sons, Inc., 1966), p. 301. Reprinted by permission of the publisher.

46. Ibid., p. 302.

47. David W. Johnson, *The Social Psychology of Education* (New York: Holt, Rinehart and Winston, Inc., 1970).

48. Ibid., p. 125.

49. The significance of this point is made very clear in Jacob W. Getzels and Herbert A. Thelen, "The Classroom Group as a Unique Social System," in *The Dynamics of Instructional Groups: The Sociopsychological Aspects of Teaching and Learning*, ed. N. B. Henry (Chicago: University of Chicago Press, 1960).

50. Johnson, *The Social Psychology of Education*, p. 125.

51. Waller, *The Sociology of Teaching*, p. 189.

52. Educators often point to the classic study of Lewin, Lippitt, and White for experimental evidence that "democratic" teaching is better. What is often overlooked is that the study was of volunteer boys' clubs, not schools and classrooms. See K. R. Lewin, Ronald Lippitt, and R. K. White, "Patterns of Aggressive Behavior in Experimentally Created 'Social Climates,'" *Journal of Social Psychology*, 10 (1939), 271–299.

3

A Sociological Perspective

Schools are complex social organizations. That the organizational characteristics of schools have implications for what occurs in classrooms, and consequently for school learning, is not a new insight. As Corwin notes:

> Since the writings of Dewey, it has been apparent to some sociologists and educators alike that the way schools are organized plays an important role in the way people learn—progressive education was a reaction to scholasticism and authoritarian methods employed at the turn of the century. Now, organizational theory promises to germinate an *organizational theory of learning*, a theory in which the premises are organizational principles rather than psychological ones.[1]

Directly, or by implication, a number of scholars have attempted to move toward an organizational theory of learning. For example, Coleman's[2] study of adolescent society, Gordon's[3] study of the American high school, and McDill and Rigsby's[4] studies of academic climates and student achievement represent efforts to apply dimensions of organizational theory to the task of understanding school learning. Yet, as late as 1972 Sarane Boocock wrote:

> In the course of trying to formulate a theoretical rationale for instructional gaming, . . . I turned to the literature of educational

43

sociology for some kind of overview of the social factors related to learning.

I did not find what I was looking for. There were descriptions of the school and classroom as social environments and a multitude of studies on the relationship of one or more social indicators to indicators of academic success, but no discussion pulled the bits and pieces of evidence together in a comprehensive way. Waller's *The Sociology of Teaching*, published in 1932, remained the most comprehensive treatment of the subject.[5]

In spite of the recognized promise to make a contribution to educational theory, sociology, particularly organizational theory, has yet to make its long-awaited contribution. Much has been done to lay the groundwork for a social theory of instruction, but little has been done to systematically advance the development of such a theory. What Feldmesser says of Boocock's book could as well be a commentary on the status of the field:

> Except for a few simple concepts, like the "nested" environments, . . . Boocock still sticks very closely to a literal, not to say unimaginative, description of research findings. . . . Yet, it is precisely a theory that is implied by "a sociology" of learning. This book does not take us very far toward that goal, though it is part of the preparation that is required.[6]

A part of the explanation for the slow development of a sociological theory of instruction lies in the professional educator's preference for personalistic and psychologically based explanations. Another part of the answer lies, perhaps, in what Hansen[7] has called "the uncomfortable relation" of sociology and education. Until recent years American sociologists have been peculiarly reticent, actually sometimes a bit snobbish, in working with educators. Many have almost disdained working on matters that promised to have practical implications for teachers, perhaps in the fear of being labeled "educationists." The preferences of educators and the less pleasant aspects of academic rivalries and status concerns do not, however, explain all that must be explained. To explain why a sociologically based theory of instruction seems always just beyond reach, one must also give attention to conditions in the fields of sociology of education and educational sociology.

SOCIOLOGY OF EDUCATION AND EDUCATIONAL SOCIOLOGY

A number of writers have attempted to distinguish between the fields of educational sociology and the sociology of education.[8] In the fields of both education and sociology there is some feeling that the type of sociology of interest to educators may be distinguishable from the type of sociology of *most* interest to sociologists. Hansen, for example, suggests that it is important to distinguish between sociology of education and educational sociology on the basis of the type of inquiry engaged in, and the theoretical bases of that inquiry. For Hansen, the essential distinction between educational sociology and the sociology of education is that educational sociology has its basis in normative theories, whereas sociology of education takes its direction from empirical theories. Hansen's more general statement of the situation is of sufficient importance to be quoted at length. He writes:

The essential hiatus in the relation of education and sociology is, in fact, not between the two disciplines, but rather between two basic modes in the study of man and society. The modes differ in criteria, each imposing restrictions and demands on problem selection and specification, each contributing to the establishment of differing types of theory. The distinction is between normative and empirical inquiry.

Empirical theory is dedicated to the establishment of verified knowledge, internally consistent, cogent, and adequate to its subject. In such inquiry and from such theory emerge statements of what is, what has been, what is possible and what is likely. In contrast, normative inquiry is dedicated to the establishment of imperatives for the development of policies, programs, and actions, and to the establishment of normative theory; that is, to an internally consistent and cogent body of prescription, adequate to the realization of desired goals and consistent with a valid ethic.[9]

Hansen's argument has considerable appeal. One could, perhaps, quarrel with his use of the terms normative and empirical. Certainly the words do not always convey what is intended by the author. For example, Hansen does not mean that normative research and theory is without empirical bases or referents, at least in the sense that social scientists commonly use the word empirical. In spite of this difficulty, Hansen's insistence that educational sociologists are more consciously concerned with questions of policy, programs, and actions than is the sociologist of education does seem to have merit. At the very least, the kinds of questions the educational sociologist would find compelling might be of only passing interest to the sociologist of education. Conversely, the concern of the sociologist of education that research somehow feed back into some systematic social theory or theories might find a less sympathetic audience among educational sociologists.

Conventional distinctions between educational sociology and sociology of education, including Hansen's, often conceal nearly as much as is revealed. There is another distinction that cuts across the fields of educational sociology and sociology of education, which is equally as important as the normative-empirical distinction; *that is the distinction between the sociology of learning and the sociology of teaching.* Hansen is correct in his observation that "the essential hiatus in the relationship of education and sociology is, in fact, . . . between two basic modes in the study of man and society,"[10] but he is incorrect to suggest that the hiatus is between sociology and education. The problem centers as well on some unresolved issues within the discipline of sociology. When the sociologist turns his attention to inquiries in education, these issues come sharply into focus.

Sociologists have still to develop an adequate formulation of the relationship between social structure and personality. So long as sociological analysis is maintained at the macro level, this deficiency in sociological theory causes only minor discomfort. Most social theorists have had, eventually, to come to grips with the major issues involved. So long as the units of analysis are societal in scope, however, the need for precision of construction is not sufficiently great to force the theorists to precise expressions of the dynamic relationship between self and social structure, social structure and self. When the sociologist begins to deal with units smaller than total societies, even units like industrial plants and military organizations, the problems become pronounced. When the sociologist begins to deal with small groups the issues become acute. The sociologist who deals with schools (whether with social units as large as school systems, or social units as small as behavioral dyads in classrooms) nearly always confronts the issues inherent in the analysis of the relationships between character and social structure. Psychological change, learning, is so obviously central in the business of schooling that those who study schools must confront the relationship between self and social structure.[11] How sociologists decide to deal with these issues largely determines whether their attention will be centered on the sociology of teaching or on the sociology of learning.

SOCIOLOGY OF LEARNING

By far the most common form of sociological inquiry into education is the mode typified by the label *sociology of learning*. For the sociologist interested in learning, the basic questions are related to the selection and measurement of independent variables. The dependent variable, learning, is already established and agreed upon. There are certainly many ways of defining learning, and some (e.g., Boocock[12]) would include both cognitive and attitudinal changes under the heading of learning. The assessment of learning does present many technical problems, but if there is a field of human measurement where the limits are known and the procedures generally defined, it is the field of mental measurement. Though one might argue that too many sociologists of learning are naive about or cavalier toward the definitional and measurement problems connected with the assessment of learning, there is relatively little controversy within the sociological fraternity about mental measurement per se.[13] Controversies among sociologists of learning are more frequently related to issues of statistical analysis (e.g., the use of a regression model in the analysis of the Coleman data[14]) or to issues of conceptualization of independent measures (e.g., what are the appropriate indicators of social class or socioeconomic status).

The sociologist of learning shares much in common with the educational psychologist. Frequently, the measurement instruments appropriate for use by educational psychologists will be used by sociologists of learning, and quite often educational psychologists and sociologists of learning have occasion to exchange information and points of view. It is not uncommon to find educational psychologists and sociologists of education working side by side, dealing with the same basic questions and using much the same data. This is not surprising, for the educational psychologist and most sociologists of learning agree upon the important dependent variables and the kinds of data needed to assess these variables, that is, to assess learning outcomes. Where the perspective of the sociologist of learning and the educational psychologist will differ is in the sources to which they look for explanations of variance in learning. The psychologist will tend to look to individual characteristics for explanations, for example, differences in intelligence, attitudes, personal values, or open-mindedness. The sociologist will look to social factors like class size and socioeconomic status (often expressed as resource variables) for answers to his questions about variances in learning. But even here, the educational psychologist and the sociologist of learning do not differ all that much. Typically, the educational psychologist will take social factors into account, in that he will control for them. Conversely, the sociologist of learning usually tries to control for idiosyncratic variables.[15] The educational psychologist may begin his analysis by observing human behavior. If so, his behavioral observations are then used as a basis for inferences about individual processes. Whether the behavioral observation takes the form of administering a test and inspecting the results, or the direct observation of children at play, the purpose of such observations is to shed light on what kinds of mental processes may be occurring "within" the human organism. The educational psychologist *is* interested in the transactions that take place between the individual and his environment. It is only by understanding these dynamic transactions that it is even *remotely* possible that the educational psychologist will one day be able to make statements like "if this child behaves in manner A the likely outcome will be that the child will learn B." It is, after all, the search for such relative certainties about individual psychological processes that leads to the construction, refinement, and rejection of alternative theories of learning.

The sociologist of learning shares with the psychologist the assumption that the prime mechanism through which learning is transmitted is the behavior of the learner. Many sociologists, like many psychologists who concern themselves with the effects of school and schooling, have failed to adequately distinguish between that behavior which is antecedent to learning and that behavior which may be a consequent of learning. Thus, some of the research done by sociologists of learning suffers from the same conceptual flaws as does some of the research done by psychologically oriented educational researchers. There are, in addition, other conceptual difficulties that typify the research in the sociology of learning. Combined with other conditions in the field of educational research (e.g., the psychological bias) these conceptual problems have needlessly limited the development of a sociologically based theory of instruction.

As noted earlier, sociologists have yet to work out a satisfactory formulation to account for the relationship between personality and social structure. These unresolved issues bear peculiar fruit when the sociologist turns his attention to the study of school life. Broadly speaking, the sociologist of education deals with three kinds of variables: structural variables, behavioral variables, and learning variables. The primary link between the social structure of schools and the learning of students *is* the behavior of students. More than that it is the *social behavior* of students. Any attempt to use random or idiosyncratic behavior as a link between social structure and learning would be a foolish and meaningless task. The only behavior that can conceivably provide a linkage between the individual psychological processes of students and the social properties of schools is behavior that is systematically related to the structural qualities of schools. Unfortunately, many sociologists of learning have disregarded the behavioral linkage between social structure and personality, or have not fully come to grips with the basic theoretical and methodological issues involved.[16] The resulting research has not been impressive. Spady sums it up as follows:

> The crude and deceptive measures of supposedly relevant resource variables [is a problem]. The resources tapped in the majority of studies are selected on an ad hoc basis, are tangible or structural, are crudely and even unreliably measured, stress quantity or mere presence over quality or mode or degree of utilization, and are recognized as proxies for presumably more important process variables that remain unmeasured. A statistical relation between school resource A and student outcome B, for example, may provide few clues as to *why* the relation exists, often because the mechanisms linking the two remain unspecified.[17]

Proceeding from the dual assumptions that differences in social structures will result in differences in behavior patterns and that differences in patterns of behavior will result in systematic differences in learning, sociologists of learning attempt to *link directly* differences in social structures and differences in learning. Few, however, demonstrate that the *assumed* differences in behavior patterns are in fact present. Certainly, there can be little justification for using a structural variable as an independent variable in a design that holds learning or other psychological change as dependent until it is reasonably demonstrated that the structural variable relates to behavior. Learning is directly *dependent* on the behavior of students, and the only way learning can be conceived as dependent on other variables, including structural ones, is to demonstrate that these variables have an impact on student behavior. To assume that particular structural variables *should* affect behavior is not adequate. The researcher who attempts to relate particular structural variables to learning has an obligation to demonstrate that the assumed linkage between the structural variables and student behavior exists in other than postulate form. As indicated by Spady[18] and by Herriot and Muse,[19] there are both methodological and conceptual reasons that explain the confusion that surrounds the effects of schools. The sociology of learning has clearly contributed its share to the confusion.

There is one further area where sociologists of learning do not shed as much light as might be expected, namely, in the area of measuring school outcomes. As indicated earlier, to the extent that measures of school outcomes are limited to mental measurement, the limits of the field are relatively well known, and the problems, while profound, are basically problems of technique. Perhaps because sociologists have not thought as much as they might about the nature of learning, many have been willing to accept the general proposition that the most valid and reliable means of measuring learning is through some process of "testing" for cognitive development. Spady describes the matter as follows:

> the bulk of the research dealing with school resource variables is limited and conservative in the outcomes selected for study. Although cognitive development is one of the universally accepted missions of public schooling, the nearly monolithic focus on standardized achievement measures in research betrays a lack of imagination within the educational research community. There are, of course, studies that also investigate variability in student educational goals and plans, but the validity and reliability of these variables are also problematic. One must generally look beyond this literature to studies on classroom interaction, ability grouping, and research on the college experience to find more

broadly defined evidence on the differential impacts of schooling on students. This suggests that kinds of impact may exist that have been ignored by researchers, both within and outside the cognitive domain.[20]

In industrial sociology it was long ago recognized that "production" is only one indicator of organizational effect and effectiveness. Other indicators of effectiveness *are available,* and from a sociological perspective would seem to have more appeal than do measures of central tendency on achievement tests. Among the types of indicators of school-related differences that are possible measures of school effects are the number of students who actually enter college, the number of students who graduate from college, the number of students who find satisfactory employment in the first year out of school, the number of students who are brought before criminal courts and convicted, the television viewing patterns of students, the kinds of books students read *on their own,* dropout rates, absenteeism, and even the evaluation by students some five to ten years after being out of school. One of the basic goals of American schools *is* academic achievement, and it can be argued that all other effects are beside the point. One does not have to be opposed to academic achievement, however, to recognize that public education in America is intended to do much more than improve the students' ability to score well on achievement tests—even though scoring well on an achievement test is not to be disdained. What sociologists of learning should do is apply the collective "sociological imagination" to the conceptualization of appropriate social measures of school outcomes. At the same time, more attention must be given to the development of defensible indicators of the structural characteristics assumed to be related to those measures. It is only in this way that teaching and learning can be conceptually united in a fashion that will make practical sense to teachers, as well as theoretical sense to sociologists. As things now stand, little is known about the kinds of impacts schools have. This is partly because there is little that can be said about what differences in schools might make a difference, and partly because measures of school outcomes are generally not very creative. But there is still another reason. Many sociologists, like many educators, apparently find it discomforting to separate teaching from learning. Until such a separation is accomplished, sociology will not make its full contribution to either theories of teaching or the understanding of the social basis of learning.

SOCIOLOGY OF TEACHING

Most sociologists would agree that Willard Waller's *Sociology of Teaching*[21] is a classic model of sociological inquiry in education. Sociologists of learning (e.g., Boocock[22]) often point to Waller as an illustration of what sociology might do for education if the science were properly applied. What many overlook when they consider Waller's work is that he paid very little attention to learning. Waller was interested in the social processes that occur in schools, how these processes relate to each other, and their sources and consequences. He was most interested in giving coherent meaning to the patterns of human behavior he observed in schools. He attempted to relate these patterns to the social relationships and social structures that constitute the social life of the school. In Waller's own words his task was:

(1) To describe with all possible care and competence the social life of human beings in and about the school.
(2) To analyze the descriptive materials (particularly from the standpoints of sociology and social psychology).
(3) To attempt to isolate causal mechanisms involved in those interactions of human beings having their locus in the institution of the school. . . .[23]

The extent to which Waller was successful in accomplishing his task was suggested in chapter 1 of this book. More important than paying deserved homage to Waller, however, is to observe that, by concentrating on a carefully *limited task*, Waller produced what Boocock has called "the most comprehensive treatment of the subject."[24]   Interestingly, the "subject" to which Boocock refers is that of "social factors related to learning." *One can read and reread Waller and find little that directly relates social factors to student learning*—at least as the learning is commonly measured.   This is said not to discredit either Waller or Boocock, but only to point out the possibility that sociologists may be able to contribute substantially to the understanding of school learning without directly addressing themselves to learning processes as expressed by measurable psychological change.

The key, it would seem, is summed up in Waller's third statement of his task.   He clearly sees that the sociologists' basic unit of analysis must be human interactions, not psychological effects.   He also notes that such a conception places considerable limits on the kinds of data to be considered. Once human interactions are accepted as the basic unit for analysis, one must look to social factors for sources of causal mechanisms.   This means that idiosyncratic and personalistic data must be foregone. Waller limited *his* inquiry even further.   He insisted that his intent was to look only for those causal mechanisms that have their locus in the institution of the school.   Waller's view of the matter was necessarily restrictive, and therefore he overlooked—or looked past—many factors commonly assumed to be central to the analysis of school effects, such as individual characteristics, library holdings, financial resources, and mean achievement scores.   Yet, Waller's analysis bore directly on many of these matters, though from a very different perspective than is common among educational researchers.   For example, in his discussion of the teacher's inability to maintain the "learner's attitude," he points to G. Stanley Hall as an exception and writes:

> Now G. Stanley Hall was one of those rare teachers who keep the learner's attitude to the extent of being anxious to learn from their students, and this was surely not unconnected with the creativeness of his intelligence.[25]

One given to psychological explanations might suggest that G. Stanley Hall was responsive to students *because* he was creative and intelligent. Waller's kind of analysis suggests other sources of explanation. For Waller, much of Hall's creativity and intelligence was a *consequence* of his relationship with students. In understanding Waller's mode of explanation, one comes to the nub of the differences between theories of teaching based on sociological premises, and psychologically based theories of teaching. It is not that sociologically based theories of teaching discount personal characteristics, for they do not. Waller would not suggest that "just anybody" could be as creative as G. Stanley Hall, even if one maintained the "attitude of the learner." What is the case is that sociologically based theories of instruction would take individual variations *as givens,* and then ask, What is it in the nature of the social relationships in schools that contributes to, or accounts for, any particular manifestation of those characteristics? Even more pointedly, a sociologically based theory of teaching might ask, To what extent do the structures of social relationships in schools offset, or enhance, the manifestations of unique and idiosyncratic phenomena? For example, how much of what a teacher does is done because the teacher occupies a particular social position, and how much is attributable to something unique or special about the person of the teacher?

The sociology of teaching takes both the structure of personalities and the social structures of larger communities as givens. Community structures and personality structures are factors to be taken into account, but they are not the causal mechanisms of immediate concern. Rather, the sociology of teaching seeks causal mechanisms that "have their locus in the institution of the school." Furthermore, the dependent variables for which causal explanations are sought are human interactions, especially interaction patterns that occur in schools.[26] That variations in school-related interactions may (indeed, probably do) relate to learning is assumed, but it is not for the sociology of teaching to make that connection. That connection is more likely within the purview of sociologists of learning, educational psychologists, and learning theorists.

A further bifurcation of an already divided field may seem arbitrary, even presumptuous. Given the tendency for educa-

tional theoreticians to think in terms of psychological explanations, the distinction does, however, seem necessary, particularly
if a socially based theory of instruction is to be developed. Any
effort to develop a socially based theory of instruction that does
not consciously distinguish between teaching and learning will
probably fall into the traps of psychological reductionism. Given
the nature of the field, it is very easy to have attention deflected
"from relationships *between* self and other to those *within:* emotional, cognitive, neurological."[27] The task of a sociology of
teaching is to call attention *to* the relationships between self and
other which occur in school settings. It is the sociology of teaching rather than the sociology of learning that promises to serve
as a basis for an organizational theory of instruction.

NOTES

1. Ronald G. Corwin, "Education and the Sociology of Complex Organizations," in *On Education: Sociological Perspectives*, ed. Donald A. Hansen and Joel E. Gerstl (New York: John Wiley & Sons,
   Inc., 1967), pp. 165–166.

2. James S. Coleman, *The Adolescent Society: The Social Life of the
   Teenager and Its Impact on Education* (New York: The Free
   Press, 1961).

3. C. Wayne Gordon, *The Social System of the High School: A Study
   in the Sociology of Adolescence* (Glencoe, Ill.: The Free Press of
   Glencoe, 1957).

4. Edward L. McDill and Leo C. Rigsby, *Structure and Process in
   Secondary Schools: The Academic Impact of Educational Climates*
   (Baltimore: Johns Hopkins University Press, 1973).

5. Sarane S. Boocock, *An Introduction to the Sociology of Learning*
   (Boston: Houghton Mifflin Company, 1972), p. ix.

6. Robert A. Feldmesser, a review of Sarane S. Boocock's *An Introduction to the Sociology of Learning*, in *Contemporary Sociology:
   A Journal of Reviews*, 2 (1973), 649.

7. Donald Hansen, "The Uncomfortable Relation of Sociology and
   Education," in *On Education: Sociological Perspectives*, ed. Han-
   sen and Gerstl, pp. 3–35. Reprinted by permission of John Wiley
   & Sons, Inc.

8. A useful distinction between sociology of education and educational sociology is provided by Wilbur B. Brookover, "Sociology of Education: A Definition," *American Sociological Review*, 14 (June, 1949), 407–415.

9. Hansen, "The Uncomfortable Relation of Sociology and Education," p. 16.

10. Ibid.

11. Although the study of personality is usually thought of as distinct from the study of cognitive processes, it seems logical to assume that whatever difficulties there are in relating personality to social structure would surely hold for efforts to relate learning to social structure.

12. Boocock, *Introduction to the Sociology of Learning*, pp. 4–5.

13. When it comes to the issues of assessing achievement, sociologists of learning seem somewhat less astute than their colleagues in educational psychology. Mental measurement is a very tricky undertaking, and questions of validity are peculiarly bothersome. One of the criticisms of much of the research on school and teacher effects is that the dependent measures are often of dubious validity.

14. See, for example, Samuel Bowles, "Towards Equality of Educational Opportunity," *Harvard Educational Review*, Vol. 38, No. 1, 1968, 89–99.

15. In practice, there is a growing affinity between the sociologist of learning and the educational psychologist, frequently under the umbrella of social psychology. Both sociologist and psychologist recognize that a phenomenon as complex as learning cannot be explained from the necessarily simplistic frame of reference of either of the separate disciplines. Therefore, it seems sensible that the disciplines join forces under the heading of social psychology, whether by some formal agreements or by encouraging free exchanges of views and criticisms back and forth across discipline boundaries. The number of sociologists being offered, and accepting, faculty appointments in departments or schools of education seems to be increasing. It is not at all unusual that sociologists who find themselves on the faculty of a department of education will also be a part of the same organizational unit that "houses" educational psychologists.

16. Whether one can link structural variables to personality structures without specific attention to behavior is an issue of considerable controversy in the field of sociology. There are indeed many sociologists who would maintain that to attempt to link structural variables to individual behavior is to blur necessary distinctions

between the subject matter of sociology and the subject matter of psychology.

17. William G. Spady, "The Impact of School Resources on Students," in *Review of Research in Education* I, ed. Fred N. Kerlinger (Itasca, Ill.: F. E. Peacock Publishers, Inc., 1973), pp. 136–137. Copyright 1973, American Educational Research Association, Washington, D.C.

18. Ibid.

19. Robert E. Herriot and Donald N. Muse, "Methodological Issues in the Study of School Effects," in *Review of Research in Education* I, pp. 209–235.

20. Spady, "The Impact of School Resources on Students," p. 137.

21. Willard Waller, *The Sociology of Teaching* (New York: John Wiley & Sons, Inc., 1932, reprinted 1967).

22. Boocock, *Introduction to the Sociology of Learning*, p. ix.

23. Waller, *Sociology of Teaching*, p. 2.

24. Boocock, *Introduction to the Sociology of Learning*, p. ix.

25. Waller, *Sociology of Teaching*, p. 394.

26. At the very least such a perspective would shed light on questions of concern to those who are coming to the view that schools and teachers have no independent effects on students. By concentrating on questions related to possible causal mechanisms in schools, as opposed to causal mechanisms in the community at large or the psychological makeup of the child, researchers might find out if schools do or can make a difference. If the answers are negative, so be it. There would be some comfort, at least, in knowing that these answers derive from analysis that is appropriate both to the questions and to the data under consideration.

27. Everett K. Wilson, *Sociology: Rules, Roles and Relationships* (Homewood, Ill.: Dorsey Press, 1966), p. 693.

4

The Study of
School Organizations

Organizational theory has seldom been applied to the practical concerns of classroom teachers. In part, this is because of the difficulty of articulating organizational propositions in ways that are relevant to the concerns of teachers. In a larger measure, however, organizational theory has not been applied to classroom matters because few scholars have been interested in the subject. Most educational researchers who are knowledgeable about organizational theory are more concerned with issues related to school administration than with issues related to the social structure of classrooms. What goes on in the classroom is related to what goes on in the larger school system, but there are few precise statements about how this is so.[1] By studying the roles of teachers and students in the decision-making process, administrative theorists do sometimes bring classroom variables into their reckoning.

Administrative theorists have recently become intrigued with the potential of "systems analysis" for understanding schools, although the term *system* is frequently used by educational theorists in ways that are quite different from the more classic uses of the term found in sociological theory. Indeed, one must make reference to a specific theorist and his unique formulations before speaking with assurance about how the term is being used. The most common connotation of the term systems analysis, at least as it is used in the literature of educational administration, is that of a computer model, with considerable attention to variations in input, output, and throughput. In spite of the fact that systems terminology is often used imprecisely, and sometimes naively, the general frame of reference has led administrative theorists to re-examine the role of teachers and students in their formulations. Among other things, researchers have had to consider whether students constitute a resource variable and are therefore input, or an object to be "worked on" by the system and therefore throughput.[2] Systems analysis, although often simplistically applied, has made some educational researchers more conscious of the need to more clearly specify the relationships between classroom variables and school system variables.

Sociologists who study schools as a special instance of a more general class of organizational phenomena have been somewhat more sensitive to the manner in which they have formulated the structure of relationships between classroom social structures and the larger school system. Sensitivity to the interlocking mechanisms of classroom phenomena and structural variables in the larger school culture is clearly evident in the work of Coleman,[3] Gordon,[4] and Corwin.[5] Others, like Parsons,[6] have related classroom and school social structures to social structures that are well beyond the organizational boundaries of the schools. Indeed, Parsons attempts to develop a linkage at a societal level. Most sociologists, even sociologists of education, are not overly concerned with the practical implications of the relationships between classrooms and schools. Rather, their concern centers on the development and expansion of organizational theories. Although sociologists—at least some of them—do not disdain efforts at practical application of their findings, most do not find such applications central to their analysis. Corwin,[7] one of the more thoughtful students of school organizations, was one of the first sociologists to suggest the possibility of developing a comparative typology of schools. His reasons for developing such a typology, however, give some indication as to why sociologists of school organizations have contributed so little that has direct relation to normative theories of instruction.

Once schools have been differentiated among themselves by use of such profiles, hopefully the typology can be extended to non-educational systems. Within the guidelines of such a typology, sociological studies of educational organizations can benefit from the growing theory and research on a wide variety of organiza- . tions. And this field, in turn, can contribute more systematically to the development of a theory of complex organizations.[8]

Putting the case in a direct fashion: it seems that those who, by inclination or training, view the schools as complex social organizations have not found it necessary to look with precision at the classroom. For the most part it has been sufficient for them to observe that the classroom constitutes a potentially distinct social subsystem. Scholars concerned with the organization of schools, whether administrative theorists or sociologists, have not gone into much detail about the nature of the social relationships that might exist in that subsystem.

The lack of concern that students of social organization have shown toward classroom phenomena is, unfortunately, complemented by the disinterest that students of classroom behavior have shown toward factors in the general social life of the school. Aside from the need to control for such obvious factors as race, sex, socioeconomic status, and sometimes peer group affiliations, those who study classrooms often seem quite insensitive to the larger social system of the school. For some, the complexities of the classroom are quite enough to manage in one conceptual model, and the difficulties of developing an adequate definition of classroom social systems seems an overwhelming task.

CLASSROOMS AS SOCIAL SYSTEMS

There have been a number of thoughtful and provocative statements on the idea of treating the classroom as a distinct social system within the context of the larger school organization.[9] There are at least two reasons given by scholars for conceptualizing classrooms in this manner: (1) to better understand the relationship of the schooling process to larger social structures (e.g., to understand more clearly the function of the school in socializing the young for future adult roles, or the function of schools in the allocation of human resources in adult society),[10] and (2) to provide a conceptual model or framework to "give meaning and order to observations already made and . . . specify areas where observations still need to be made."[11] That the classroom can be usefully conceived as a social system for these purposes has been demonstrated by a number of researchers and theoreticians.[12] What some overlook, however, is that the declaration that the classroom is a distinct social system does not make it so. The concept of social system carries with it the idea of interdependent human relationships woven together in a network that clearly sets the social unit under examination apart from other social structures. This "setting apart" *need* not be physical. It is never simply physical. There are many collectivities of human beings that do not constitute social systems but are physically set apart from others (e.g., a crowd on an elevator). There are other human arrangements that exist in the midst of other human collectivities that take on systemic qualities. For example, families may be dispersed from one end of a nation to another, yet the network of relationships is still sufficiently compelling that members will behave in predictable ways in times of celebration or tragedy. In sum, the concept of social system contains the idea of an overlapping and interlocking group life, a form of social existence where participants must take into consideration the existence and expectations of others in the system.

Whether it is useful or conceptually accurate to define the classroom *a priori* as a group *or* distinct social system is debatable. There is, for example, a point early in the history of a class—if only the first day of school—when the behavior that occurs in the classroom is the behavior of a collectivity of individuals under the direction of a recognized institutional authority. Sometimes slowly, sometimes quickly, and perhaps never, the collectivity of individuals assigned to the classroom begin to function in ways that suggest the development of group life. Statuses are designated, roles are assigned, and shared expectations begin to emerge. Whether the classroom does become a distinct social system, how such a development comes about, what its consequences seem to be—these are questions for empirical examination, not *a priori* definition. Indeed, to define the classroom *a priori* as a group or social system may distract attention from some of the more important sources of variance among classrooms.

As an illustration, most of the research in elementary classrooms is based on the implicit assumption that classroom life is a special form of group life. In most elementary schools such an *a priori* definition of the classroom causes few difficulties, for given the nature of most elementary schools, the social life of the classroom usually comes to manifest the group characteristics researchers impose on it.[13] Some students come to dominate, others to submit; some clean the erasers and others are expected to always have the "right answer" to the teacher's question. In many secondary schools, and certainly most colleges, concepts of group and social system would need to be stretched to the breaking point to make them applicable to classroom situations. There is, indeed, some wisdom in the convention of talking about *the* student role. In many classes, whatever group life there is would be more accurately described in terms of behavioral dyads, each one having the teacher as a referent point. Perhaps this explains why research done in elementary classrooms is seldom applicable at the high school and college levels.

The existence of people in close physical proximity, even when they are following common directives or responding to common stimuli, is not evidence of the existence of a group or a social system. For example, a crowd at a football game responding to the exhortations of cheerleaders does not constitute a group. Such behavior is system-related but the social system to which it is related is located well beyond the athletic arena. The researcher would need to look to larger societal structures, including leisure institutions, vestiges of tribalism in the academic setting, and the ritual life of communities, for appropriate explanations of behavior at football games. The structure of some classrooms resembles the football arena, with the teacher as cheerleader. Classrooms frequently seem more adequately described as collectivities of individuals working independently together than as social systems. At other times, classrooms take on the characteristics of loose coalitions of a number of tightly knit social systems (and in this way have more of a systemic quality than a collection of individuals), and at still other times, the classroom seems to be twenty or thirty behavioral dyads, with the teacher involved in each dyad.

One of the most important variables in classroom life may be after all the degree to which the behavior of the participants is built into a system of interlocking roles, expectations, and rewards. Locating the source of sanctions, role expectations, and the like may be among the most important inquiries in the construction of adequate theories of instruction. Whether the causal mechanisms that account for student and teacher behavior are located in the systemic qualities of the classroom *or* in the larger school system may make a great deal of difference in how teacher effects and teacher effectiveness are assessed. To insist on imposing *a priori* social definitions on the structure of classrooms or other school units makes much that should be investigated a part of the assumptions from which inquiry proceeds. Of basic concern should be the degree to which there is empirical evidence that the social units (e.g., classrooms) under study have distinct social boundaries that set them apart from the larger organization. If such boundaries do exist, it may be both useful and defensible to think in terms of distinct social systems, but where some degree of "separateness" cannot be demonstrated, it is doubtful that the concept of classroom social system is a useful one for understanding life in classrooms. Indeed, it may be that one of the greatest shortcomings of some classrooms is that there is no identifiable social system other than that which centers on the teacher as a representative of the larger social system of the school.

ORGANIZATIONALLY RELEVANT GROUPS

"A complex organization consists of (1) stable patterns of interaction, (2) among coalitions of groups having a collective identity

*(e.g., a name and location(s), (3) pursuing interests and accom-
plishing given tasks, and (4) coordinated by power and authority
structures.*"[14] The centrality of groups in the structure of complex
organizations cannot be overemphasized. Complex organizations
are more than systems that coordinate the activities of individuals
and direct these activities toward given tasks. Even more basic
is the coordination and direction of the activities of *groups*. In
organizational analysis, the pattern of relationships between and
among groups is at least as important as the pattern of relationships between and among individuals. The energies and activities of individuals may carry out the task of the organization,
but it is through the coordination of groups and within the
structure of groups that these energies and activities are mobilized
and given direction.[15]

One of the most perplexing problems confronting the organizational analyst is the development of procedures to locate
and isolate groups within the organization that are relevant to
those aspects of organizational life the analyst is trying to interpret. On the one hand, there are features of organizations
that seem to imply the existence of structured social life (e.g.,
departments), which may be of minor significance when the
social analyst looks beyond flow charts, administrative handbooks,
and official statements. On the other hand, there may be features of group life that are central to the operation of the organization which fail to appear on superficial inspection of the more
"public" descriptions of organizational features. Words like
formal and informal, official and unofficial have been used by
scholars to convey that there is indeed a complex network
of relationships among the various group structures that the
organization comprises.

There are no hard and fast rules for locating relevant social
groups, either in schools or in other organizations, but there are
some general guidelines that seem to have served relatively well.
These guidelines do not, however, appear in any one handbook.
Rather, they emerge from examination of the methods employed
by students of complex organizations as they go about their
craft. Three of the most important of these guidelines are described here. (1) The researcher must be clear about the level

of analysis and should indicate with as much precision as possible the level at which he or she is working. (2) Once a level of analysis is settled on, a systematic search for potentially relevant social units should begin. (3) After potentially relevant social units have been identified, the boundaries of these units should be clearly specified and defined. Only after these three things have been accomplished is the researcher or the theoretician in a position to engage in the difficult task of interpreting the sources, directions, and consequences of patterns of human interaction in schools.

Levels of Analysis

It is useful to think of school organizations at three distinct levels of abstraction; the classroom level, the school building level, and the district level. There is much that goes on below the level of the classroom that is significant for purposes of analysis, but the classroom is the lowest level at which relevant organizational analysis seems likely. It is not always true that classrooms represent distinct social systems in schools, but it is usually the case that the classroom is where the social structure of the school presses most directly on the behavior of students. Writing about the school class, Parsons says: "it [the school class] is recognized both by the school system and by the individual pupil as the place where the 'business' of formal education actually takes place."[16]

The school building clearly represents an identifiable level in the school organization, larger in scope than the classroom, yet not as all-encompassing as the school district. It is perplexing that educational theorists and researchers (with the possible exception of those who are specifically concerned with the role of the building principal) have been quite casual about the significance of the building level unit. In the literature of education, the phrase *school system* has come to represent both building level considerations and district concerns. Frequently researchers disregard completely the distinction between building level analysis and district level analysis. For some purposes this may be appropriate, but there is the potential that findings will be distorted by such a procedure. As Herriot and Muse observe:

> If the available data are at a system level higher than that of interest (e.g. one is studying schools, but measures of important variables are available only at the level of the school district) a problem of *disaggregation* known to sociologists as the "ecological fallacy" (Robinson, 1950) or the "aggregative fallacy" (Riley, 1964) may be encountered. In the classic statement of this problem, Robinson demonstrated that observed statistical associations at the analytic level of aggregated populations can differ in the magnitude and direction from those at the level of the individuals being aggregated.[17]

Though something of a high-blown statement, Herriot and Muse's point is well taken. There is, for example, considerable evidence that school districts make quite different allocations of resources to school buildings attended by children of the affluent and those attended by children of the poor.[18] Yet, many of the studies that attempt to relate school resources to achievement derive their data from district level averages. Clearly, such disregard of levels of analysis can be a source of serious error in interpretation.

In addition to the possibility of gross differences in resource allocations at the building level, there are other reasons to think of the school building as a distinct level for analysis. In spite of administrative centralization, many school buildings maintain features that set them apart from other schools in the district, as well as from the district itself. School buildings usually have their own athletic teams, bands, parent organizations, and departments of instruction. In some large city systems, central office supervisors must obtain the building principal's authorization *before* visiting teachers, *and* the building principal may have the authority to exclude supervisors altogether. With increasing attention to deconsolidation, neighborhood schools, and community control, it is likely that the building level will become an increasingly important location for both operation and analysis.

Understanding district level operations has been one of the main preoccupations of administrative theorists. Questions related to management, budget, personnel recruitment, resource allocation, and interorganizational relationships are most frequently located at the district level. The outer limits of what is school and what is not school are located and described at the district level. If the classroom is the place where students are most apt to come face to face with the school organization, it is at the district level that the school is most likely to come face to face with the outside world. To be sure, there is considerable interaction between the local community and building level units (e.g., the office of the principal). Sometimes these interactions can be accurately interpreted without reference to any level beyond the building. More frequently, however, community relations—even when they appear to center on the building—have their motive force and essential form located in the structure of the larger school organization. For example, building principals may have considerable autonomy as to how they will relate to parent-teacher organizations, but whether or not such organizations will exist usually is a decision made at the district level.

The web of relationships that hold together the classroom units, building level units, and district level units is difficult to locate and describe. Often decisions made in the central office seem to be only remotely related to the routine life of the classroom, and sometimes these decisions do have little significant effect on teachers and students. Frequently, however, these decisions have more impact on the routine life of classrooms than is ordinarily recognized, even by those who make the decisions. For example, a central office decision that, in the interest of conserving energy, football games will be played on Friday afternoon rather than Friday night will probably alter the atmosphere of all classes held late in the afternoon on Friday. The main reason for thinking of school organizations as three distinct levels of analysis is to be found, however, in the injunction by C. Wright Mills that "every self-conscious thinker must at all times be aware of—and hence be able to control—the levels of abstraction at which he is working."[19]   The classroom may be the most pervasive reality in the practice of teachers, but structural realities at the level of the building and the district often shape and mold the nature of classroom relationships, perhaps even more than teachers and researchers realize.

Locating Relevant Social Units

There are many social and organizational features in schools that do not manifest the characteristics of group life. These features may, however, have an impact on the way groups are formed and on how people interact. More importantly, these features provide strong clues as to where the most vital and relevant aspects of the social life of the organization may be located. Chief among these features are administrative units, structurally relevant categories, and proximate collectivities. School districts, school buildings, and classrooms are typically organized in terms of recognizable *administrative units,* such as departments, offices, and reading groups. Certain ways of *categorizing* human beings become the basis for the development of some structural features of school organizations. All schools, for example, recognize sex as a relevant structural category in everything from the designation of restroom facilities to the assigning of physical education classes and instructors. Many times accidents of scheduling, or mere physical presence, become the source (sometimes the consequence) of peculiar groupings of individuals and unique patterns of interaction. Individuals who are in close physical proximity to one another have increased opportunity to develop common bonds and distinct patterns of interaction, even though they may not come to do so. Thus, *proximate collectivities* (individuals who share a common seating area, locker assignments, or hall duty) are often useful leads to the location of the group life of the organization. At each level of analysis (the classroom, building, and district levels), attention to organizational features like administrative units, structural categories, and proximate collectivities is the first order of business in developing a description of group life in schools.

The purposes of the researcher will influence the level of analysis at which the inquiry will proceed. The researcher's intentions will also narrow the range of organizational features that need to be taken into account. In addition, if findings are to be generalizable, it is necessary that other criteria be applied. (1) The features studied should be organizationally relevant. Categorizing children according to the color of their eyes, for example, would probably not be a useful procedure. Schools do not take eye color into account when structural features are determined, although some schools do categorize according to the color of one's skin. (2) The features examined should be conceptualized in a way that makes it possible to locate equivalent features in most schools. Some schools do not have teacher work rooms but all schools have places where teachers meet outside of the presence of students. Whether or not these places are "officially" designated may be of considerable importance, but the function they serve is more important than what they are called. (3) There should be empirical or theoretical reasons to believe that the features under consideration are likely to be related to the social life of the school and, furthermore, that the particular aspect of the school's social life that is affected seems likely to be related to the particular subject of study. For example, if one intends to study the sources and consequences of particular patterns of classroom interaction, one might well want to consider the teacher's relationship to the local teachers' college or university. It might also be of interest if the superintendent were in the habit of "dropping in" on the teacher's classroom. It is doubtful, however, that the researcher interested in the classroom would need to be interested in the superintendent's pattern of relationship with the board of education.

In terms of present inquiry, it will be useful to limit discussion to those organizational features which seem likely to have some bearing on the way students behave in the classroom. The purpose of this book is to lay the groundwork for an organizational theory of instruction. The business of instruction is largely the business of inducing students to behave in ways that are assumed to affect learning. It is assumed that there is a relationship between the way schools are organized and the means employed to induce students to behave in organizationally required or expected ways. The search for the causal mechanisms through which and by which student behavior is directed, motivated, and controlled within the classroom is the central concern. The level of analysis at which the inquiry will be located will be determined, by and large, by the requirements of the questions asked. When operating at the classroom level, attention will be centered on features like seating arrangements, reading groups, and work groups. When the level of analysis is at the building level, attention will more likely be directed at play groups, peer groups, departmental affiliations, and the like. When the analysis moves to the district level, inquiries will be directed toward characteristics like administrative arrangements, supervisory roles, resource allocations, and school community relationships. Always in the forefront will be the question: "How is it that the patterns of relationship that are observed to exist in particular classrooms come to be as they are, and what in the organizational nature of schools creates, maintains, or influences these patterns?"

Boundary Definitions

To locate the organizational sources of human relationships—a central concern in this book—one must first decide what is inside and what is outside the organization. Past studies of school organizations have not reflected sensitivity to the issues involved in defining the boundaries of social units. Researchers have usually relied on categorical procedures to determine who is inside and who is outside. For example, all students on a class roll may be considered "inside," all others being outside. Those teachers who have regular contracts with the school board may be considered "inside" the teachers group; all others—including substitutes—may be excluded. For some purposes such *a priori* categorical definitions of organizational boundaries are appropriate. For example, interest in the political behavior of a school district might lead a researcher to consider all eligible voters "members" of the district. Categorical definitions of the social boundaries of groups and organizations can, however, be misleading. Some participants in group life are more "inside" than are others. Clearly, the quantity and quality of student and teacher participation in the life of the school differ both between categories and within categories. Some teachers, for example, seem much more a part of the organization than do other teachers, if for no other reasons than that they spend more time in the school building, attend more school functions, and represent the school at more activities than do other teachers.

Researchers generally have been inconsistent in the boundary labels they have applied to teachers and students. Sometimes students are referred to as members (insiders), at other times as clients (outsiders). With the advent of systems analysis, students have come to be labeled (somewhat less appealingly) inputs, outputs, and throughputs. Teachers, while seldom conceived of as outside the school organization, have been variously described as employees, staff, faculty members, subordinates, lower level participants, and work force. Teachers are often viewed as a "class" much in the way that factory workers are often viewed as a "class" in industrial sociology. The position teachers are perceived to hold "inside" the school is, in addition, one of the chief determinants of whether students will be defined as insiders or outsiders. If the teacher is thought of as an employee, students are likely to be defined as outside the school— perhaps as clients or as something to be processed by the system. It is only when the level of analysis moves to the classroom that there is relative assurance that most students will be defined as "insiders."

There is considerable variance between and among teachers and students in regard to the performance required, the commitment they have toward the school, and the degree to which the school controls their lives.[20] For example, coaches are expected and required to stay after school for practice, whereas most teachers leave shortly after the final school bell. Some students attend school only because they are forced to by their parents or by compulsory attendance laws. Other students attend school because they want to go to college, or because they find life in schools personally satisfying. Some teachers and some students seem to be more under the "control" of the school than do others. Nontenured faculty are often more careful in what they say about school officials than are tenured faculty. All of these variances in performance expectations, involvement, and subordination bear directly on the relationship between teachers and students in classrooms. The teacher who feels more system control may be less willing to innovate, less willing to step away from organizationally prescribed forms and so on. The student who is in school only because he is coerced by the law or his parents to be there will probably not respond in the same way as will a student who is positively committed to the school.

Given the centrality of organizational boundaries in the determination of the relationships between and among teachers, students, and schools, it is essential that organizational boundaries be defined in ways that (a) reflect the social dynamics involved in the relationships of teachers and students and school boundaries, and (b) permit one to view the boundary position of teachers and students as problematic and a source of variance within and among school units. Whether students and teachers are to be thought of as insiders or outsiders, employees, staff, clients, members, or products is more usefully conceived of as a question for empirical determination than as a problem of definition. The boundaries of schools and groups within schools are determined, maintained, expanded, and contracted in the dynamic interplay between the school and its social environments. Thus, any conception of the social boundaries of schools that is limited to geographic lines and categorical lists will miss much that is important in the social life of the school and will also miss much that relates to the behavior of teachers and students in classrooms.

Perhaps the greatest source of difficulty in locating and defining group boundaries is the tendency to think of groups as collections of individuals engaged in interaction. Certainly groups are that, but they are both more and less than that. No single group commands all the loyalty or attention of any individual. Individuals do not belong to *a* group; individuals are members of many groups. The individual's claim to membership in a group is that he accepts the group's definition of social reality, at least insofar as he has dealings with other members of the group. As Wilson puts it: "The newcomer must understand and accept the group's goals and agreed-upon means for achieving them."[21] In short, to be a member of a group, an individual surrenders some of his idiosyncratic definitions and comes to accept the subjective meanings supported by the group. When the individual behaves toward another member of the group or when, *as a group member*, he behaves toward outsiders, he must accept the group's definition of the meaning of that behavior. The prospective group member who is unable or unwilling to share the group's meanings may never gain admission to the group. Members who reject those meanings may suffer exclusion. New teachers, for example, may find that they are not fully accepted into the "established teachers" group until they come to "understand" that wearing ties and other badges of authority is indeed an obligation to the group.

Groups attempt to control the behavior of individuals in those areas where the behavior is considered relevant to the goals and activities of the group. The boundaries of the group are defined by (a) the social behavior over which the group attempts to exercise control or exert influence and (b) the degree to which social behavior defined as relevant to the group is successfully controlled and influenced by the group. Group boundaries are not, however, determined by individual choices.[22] Sometimes an individual will act on the commandments of one group over another only to find himself literally expelled from the group whose authority he spurned.[23]

To develop a dynamic definition of boundaries it is necessary to acknowledge the centrality of *control* and *exclusion* in the life of groups.[24] For a group to effectively impose its subjective meanings on the actions of group members, the group must positively influence the behavior of participants, and it must

74

exclude interference from any other source. The military recognizes this by denying access to civilians during the early stages of boot training. Schools recognize it by making access to areas of vital concern (e.g., classrooms) cumbersome and sometimes impossible. The social boundaries of organizations are determined by the degree to which cooperation is obtained (i.e., the degree to which participants do that which the group expects or requires of them—including the acceptance of subjective meanings) and the degree to which interference is resisted.

It is useful to think of both control and exclusion in more precise terms than is commonly the case, for one of the more significant sources of variance between and within schools lies along these two dimensions (i.e., variations in the ability of the school to control relevant social behavior and to exclude influences that interfere with that control). Some concepts that hold promise of giving precision to the general ideas of control and exclusion are the ideas of cohesiveness, extensiveness, scope, pervasiveness, and permeability.[25]

Cohesiveness has to do with the recognition of group solidarity, the acceptance of a common identity, including actions designed to exclude others from the group. Cohesiveness is a relative concept and when applied to groups it is usually stated in terms of more or less. Small groups tend to be more cohesive than larger groups, but some large groups—including some organizations—are more cohesive than are others. Group cohesiveness has both a controlling function and an excluding function. Cohesive groups tend to exercise more control over members, at least in the behavioral areas of interest to the group, precisely because the conditions that lead to cohesion also develop control. At the same time the solidarity that exists within the group tends to become institutionalized in terms of rites of passage, clear identification of members, and so on; this in turn helps to exclude influence from outside sources. Among the indicators of group cohesion are high rates of task-oriented and person-oriented interactions. Though group cohesion is not entirely dependent on high rates of interaction, significant interaction does foster cohesion. Cohesive groups will also frequently evidence a high degree of person-oriented interactions, in addition to those interactions related to organizational tasks. For example, a highly cohesive department would be more likely to have department-related friendship cliques, as well as a high rate of task-related activities. A department low on cohesion would be less likely to manifest these characteristics.

Extensiveness refers to the number of identifiable social units (including individual actors) who participate in the activities of the group. Extensiveness is an indicator of both size and complexity: size, because one of the indicators is the number of social units involved; complexity, because this number will vary, not only with the number of individuals involved, but also with the number of identifiable groups that make up the coalition under study. Typically, social units that exceed the size of small groups (two to eight people) will break into subunits. The larger unit may be socially identifiable as "unitary," but within its boundaries other social units have established behavioral claims. If, for example, one wanted a measure of extensiveness in a classroom setting, one would surely count the number of students involved. In addition, one would attempt to determine how many relevant subunits were operating in the situation (e.g., friendship cliques and reading groups), and how many social units exert some form of influence on the behavior setting of the classroom. In some cases it might be useful to think of all the school beyond the classroom door as a single unit. At other times it might be useful to conceive of a number of district or "building level" units (e.g., departments and grade levels). Increased extensiveness tends to increase problems of control, since greater extensiveness increases the likelihood that external influences will enter the life of the group. For example, a classroom made up of four or five highly cohesive and clearly identifiable friendship cliques constitutes quite a different behavioral setting than does a classroom of thirty individuals working independently *together*. The teacher of the class with the tight clique structure must be aware that any instructions or comments made to one student (even privately) are apt to circulate throughout the student's circle of friends. Additionally, the teacher can be assured that interactions with a student, if the student is a clique member, will be interpreted differently by that student's circle of friends than it will by the other students. Indeed, between-group rivalries may lead one group to approve of the teacher's performance and another group to disapprove.

Scope has to do with the number of activities the group or organization attempts to control, as well as the number of activities that are successfully controlled. It might be useful, depending on the purposes of the researcher, to distinguish between scope as defined by the group control efforts, and scope as defined by the group's effective control.[26] Clearly, it is important to know what the organization attempts to control, as well as what the organization is successful in controlling.

That there is a wide variance in the scope of schools is easily demonstrated by reference to variances in dress codes. Some schools take it upon themselves to regulate dress; others leave dress entirely up to personal choice, current fads, family practices, and so on. Other illustrations of variances in scope include variations in regulations with regard to the use of school facilities like bathrooms, pencil sharpeners, and telephones. Some schools have no regulations at all about "bathroom going," other schools require a hall pass, and still others issue "demerits" for going to the restroom during class time.[27] It would be interesting to determine if variances in organizational scope are related to student morale, the incidence of discipline "problems," or the mental health of building principals and classroom teachers.

Pervasiveness has reference to the degree to which those actions that are under the control of the group are directly regulated or, conversely, to the degree to which individual variations in performance are permitted. In some schools the central office establishes a policy that teachers will submit grades each six weeks (an indication of scope). In other schools teachers are required to submit grades each six weeks, *and the precise method by which grades will be derived and computed is specified* (an indication of pervasiveness). Pervasiveness—if it is high—serves both to control behavior and to exclude outside influence. It is particularly important that highly pervasive organizations tend to foster evasions of official expectations. Indeed, if evasions do not emerge, the organization may become totally unresponsive to its environment.

Permeability has to do with the degree to which the control claims of an organization or a group are successfully countered by the claims of other social units, including those social units often thought of categorically as "inside." One of the first indications of a shift in group boundaries is the inability of the group to uphold traditional norms. When one teacher comes to school with a low-cut neckline or without a tie, the group may be able to bring the recalcitrant one into line by some form of internal sanctioning such as humor. If the situation is sufficiently grave, the deviating teacher may be excluded from the group. If, however, enough teachers begin to violate the traditional dress code, the teachers will need to accommodate the new behavior or create a condition where the outcast teachers will form a competing social group. In either case, there will be a change in group boundaries.

Highly permeable organizations must share with other interfering or competing units many of what the group defines as its "legitimate" decision areas. Organizations that are low on permeability would be able to exercise effective control in most areas where control efforts are made, and there would be little evidence of interference with those control efforts.

An Illustration

Perhaps it would be well to end this discussion with an illustration of two kinds of schools, one high on the boundary dimensions of cohesiveness, pervasiveness, scope, and extensiveness and low on permeability, the other high on permeability and low on the other four dimensions.

School A (high on cohesiveness, pervasiveness, scope, and extensiveness, low on permeability) might typify some of the eastern boarding academies that specialize in preparing the children of the affluent for entry into Ivy League schools. These academies often have powerful boards of trustees, but these boards usually consist of former graduates who have a vested interest in maintaining the traditions of the academy. Consequently, the permeability of the organization to unwanted outside interference is kept low. The cohesiveness of such organizations is reflected in many ways—the trafficking between selected academies and selected Ivy League institutions and the interlocking network of old grads, new faculty, and future students. That these schools are wide in scope and high in pervasiveness is reflected in all manners of social behavior, down to stereotypes of accents, political leanings, and religious preferences. That the organization is extensive is testified to by its interlocking relationships with institutions of higher learning, alumni groups, and so on.

School B, high in permeability, and low in the other four dimensions, may well be typical of public school systems in small towns with a university constituency. The faculties in these public schools are often quite unstable because of the attractions of graduate study, or the fact that graduate student husbands eventually move, taking their teacher-wives with them. Even the student body has more of an "in and out" quality because of the mobility of various segments of the population. Thus, it is probably difficult to develop cohesive action. Indeed, the more locally oriented students and faculty in university town public schools often complain of the "lack of school spirit and solidarity." Even the football team cannot stir great pride, particularly when the skills of its players pale beside the more professional performances of the college team.

Given the plurality of values inherent in university communities, it is difficult for the school to lay effective claim to areas of influence outside the most narrow definition of "academic," and even in these areas the teachers and administrators may receive—and be forced to act upon—more advice than they find necessary or desirable. The typical school in the university community is, indeed, likely to be low in pervasiveness and scope, and is certainly likely to be highly permeable. Even the graduate advisors of teachers who are part-time graduate students have direct access to curricular decisions, textbook selections, and disciplinary policy.

This illustration is based on stereotypes. Yet, stereotypes and fiction have a way of pointing to reality. The fact that boundary concepts are so useful in describing "stereotypic" differences between schools suggests, at least, that the utility of these concepts should be tested on the real world of public schools.

NOTES

1. Waller, of course, stands as an exception. Willard Waller, *The Sociology of Teaching* (New York: John Wiley & Sons, Inc., 1932, reprinted 1967). A number of other works bear on the issues involved. Representative of these works are: Robert S. Dreeben, *On What Is Learned in School* (Reading, Mass.: Addison-Wesley Publishing Company, 1968); Talcott Parsons, "The School Class as a Social System: Some of Its Functions in American Society," *Harvard Educational Review*, Vol. 29 (1959), 297–318; and Jacob W. Getzels and Herbert A. Thelen, "The Classroom Group as a Unique Social System," in *The Dynamics of Instructional Groups: Socio-Psychological Aspects of Teaching and Learning*, ed. N. S. Henry (Chicago: University of Chicago Press, 1960), pp. 53–82.

2. Robert E. Herriot and Donald N. Muse, "Methodological Issues in the Study of School Effects," in *Review of Research in Education*, ed. Fred N. Kerlinger (Itasca, Ill.: F. E. Peacock Publishers, Inc., 1973), pp. 209–235. Copyright 1973, American Educational Research Association, Washington, D.C.

3. James S. Coleman, *The Adolescent Society: The Social Life of the Teenager and Its Impact on Education* (New York: Free Press, 1961).

4. C. Wayne Gordon, *The Social System of the High School: A Study in the Sociology of Adolescence* (Glencoe, Ill.: The Free Press of Glencoe, 1957).

5. Ronald G. Corwin, *A Sociology of Education: Emerging Patterns of Class, Status, and Power in the Public Schools* (New York: Appleton-Century-Crofts, 1965).

6. Parsons, "The School Class."

7. Ronald G. Corwin, "Education and the Sociology of Complex Organizations," in *On Education: Sociological Perspectives,* ed. Donald Hansen and Joel Gerstl (New York: John Wiley & Sons, Inc., 1967).

8. Ibid., p. 218.

9. Parsons, "The School Class," and Getzels and Thelen, "The Classroom Group."

10. For example, Parsons, "The School Class."

11. Getzels and Thelen, "The Classroom Group," p. 64.

12. Ibid.; also Parsons, "The School Class."

13. It is not suggested that classes take on group characteristics *because* researchers define them as groups. Rather, classes do frequently—and elementary classes usually—become amenable to analysis as a group because of the nature of classroom life. This convenient coincidence between the researcher's preconception and the realities of some classrooms should not, however, be used to justify designating the classroom as a group or social system *a priori.*

14. Corwin, "Education and the Sociology of Complex Organizations," p. 161.

15. For a classic study of the significance of the human group in organizational life see George C. Homan's *The Human Group* (New York: Harcourt, Brace & World, 1950).

16. Parsons, "The School Class," 297.

17. Robert E. Herriot and Donald N. Muse, "Methodological Issues in the Study of School Effects," in *Review of Research in Education* I, ed. Fred N. Kerlinger (Itasca, Ill.: F. E. Peacock Publishers, Inc., 1973), pp. 217–218. Copyright 1973, American Educational Research Association, Washington, D.C. M. W. Riley, Sources and Types of Sociological Data," in *Handbook of Modern Sociology,* ed. R. Faris (Chicago: Rand McNally & Company, 1964). W. S. Robinson, "Ecological Correlations and the Behavior of Individuals," *American Sociological Review,* 1950, 15, 351–357.

18. See, for example, Patricia C. Sexton, *Education and Income: Inequalities of Educational Opportunity in Our Public Schools* (New York: Viking Press, 1961).

19. C. Wright Mills, *The Sociological Imagination* (New York: Oxford University Press, 1959), Evergreen edition, 1961, p. 34.

20. The basic conceptualization for this discussion comes from Amitai Etzioni, *A Comparative Analysis of Complex Organizations: On*

Power, Involvement, and Their Correlates (New York: The Free Press of Glencoe, Inc., 1961), especially pp. 16–21.

21. Everett K. Wilson, *Sociology: Rules, Roles and Relationships* (Homewood, Ill.: Dorsey Press, 1966), p. 41.

22. The word *choice* connotes a more rational and logical process than that which is usually involved in reconciling group pressures. Seldom does an individual consciously choose which group to use as a point of reference. Rather, the process is more one of drift and thrust, pull and haul, act and react. In the dynamics of accommodation and assimilation, group boundaries come to be defined.

23. The number of group members may be diminished by expulsion, but the number of group members is not the only—or even the most significant—determinant of social boundaries. So long as the group maintains its claim to control social behavior in the area of interest, the boundaries have not been substantially modified by individual expulsion.

24. Much of the following discussion closely parallels Corwin's discussion of boundaries. See Corwin, "Education and the Sociology of Complex Organizations," pp. 198–209. Many of the concepts have been substantially modified, however, and in some instances (e.g., pervasiveness) have been fundamentally recast. See also Etzioni, *Comparative Analysis of Complex Organizations*.

25. All of these concepts appear in Corwin's discussion.

26. Organizations frequently attempt to control activities that they are unable to control. Schools, for example, frequently attempt to intervene in the personal hygiene habits of students. On the school ground the efforts seem effective, but every teacher has an anecdote about some child who seldom bathes or brushes his or her teeth, and the anecdote usually demonstrates the futility of school intervention into matters deeply rooted in family patterns.

27. It is literally true that one school in the author's experience issues demerits—routinely—for getting a drink of water or going to the restroom during class time. Students are, however, permitted ten demerits before it affects their "conduct" grade. The scope of this school is great indeed.

5

The Framework
of a Typology of Schools

The development of an organizational theory of instruction depends upon the creation of a theoretically consistent means to compare structural differences in schools. Without such a conceptual framework, progress toward describing the impact of organizational variables on the classroom behavior of teachers and students is seriously compromised, if not prohibited. Indeed, the lack of such a comparative system is one of the chief reasons that an organizational theory of instruction has yet to emerge. The intent of the present chapter is to present the broad outlines of a framework that may lead to a more practically useful and theoretically relevant means of comparing differences between and among schools.

There currently exists no adequate description or formulation of the structural characteristics of schools. There *are*, however, a number of excellent sources from which to begin the formulation of an empirical theory of school organizations. Indeed, the entire field of sociological study of complex social organizations is an invaluable resource for the construction of such empirical theories of school organization. Through argument by analogy, comparative study, and informed speculation, a theoretician can begin to develop the necessary formulations out of which an organizational theory of instruction might arise.

In writing this chapter, the intent has been to compare

variables that are organizational in nature, not variables that are attributable to some characteristic of participants (e.g., perceptions) or some quality of the clients served (e.g., socioeconomic status of students or race). Since the intent is to study, describe, explain, and predict relationships between organizational variables and classroom behavior, it is essential that the independent variables studied, that is, organizational variables, be conceptually distinguished from the dependent variables, that is, the behavior of individuals. Without this distinction, research and theory generated by the framework would likely be tautological in nature.

DEVELOPING A TYPOLOGY OF SCHOOLS

The remainder of this book proceeds from the assumption that schools can be usefully categorized in terms of two broad features of the school organization: the mode of organization that prevails in the school and the position students occupy *vis-à-vis* the boundaries of the schools.

Mode of organization[1] may be thought of as consisting of two elements: (1) the degree to which bureaucratic and professional expectations are present and effective and (2) the degree to which classrooms reflect structural looseness or structural tightness. The *position of students* in the school can be conceptualized in terms of (1) the degree to which students are identified as products, clients, and members and (2) the extent to which students are alienative, calculative, or moral in their involvement. Placing these variables on a two-dimensional matrix results in thirty-six distinct cells, each cell reflecting a different combination of boundary and expectational variance (see Table 1). For example, cell 1 is a school (or subunit in a school) characterized by bureaucratic expectations, structural tightness, and a morally involved student body who are defined as members. Cell 36 suggests a school (or subunit in a school) characterized by professional expectations, structural looseness, and an alienated student body identified as products.

TABLE 1. A Typology of Schools Based on Variance in Social Boundaries and Mode of Organization*

MODE OF ORGANIZATION

POSITION OF STUDENT		Bureaucratic		Professional	
		Tight	Loose	Tight	Loose
Member	Moral	1	2	3	4
	Calculative	5	6	7	8
	Alienative	9	10	11	12
Client	Moral	13	14	15	16
	Calculative	17	18	19	20
	Alienative	21	22	23	24
Product	Moral	25	26	27	28
	Calculative	29	30	31	32
	Alienative	33	34	35	36

*An "ideal type" sketch of each of the thirty-six types of schools is included in the appendix.

EMPLOYEE EXPECTATIONS—
BUREAUCRATS AND PROFESSIONALS

The nature of teachers' roles in school and in society has had considerable discussion in past years, but much of the discussion has lacked precision and clarity. Some, for example, do not distinguish between teacher role expectations that have their locus in the larger society and those role expectations that more clearly have their locus in the organizational structure of the school.[2] Unfortunately, many who study teachers' classroom roles disregard the fact that the teachers' role performance in the classroom may be interpretable only if one refers to the expectation structure within the school building or school district.[3]

The typology developed in the present chapter leans heavily on Corwin's[4] conceptualization of the differences between bureaucratic and professional modes of school organizations (see Table 2). The framework provided by Corwin assumes that whatever else the teacher is, the teacher is an employee of the school system. Teachers are not individual entrepreneurs, nor do they engage in private practice, although there is a compelling set of norms to uphold the teachers' freedom of action and freedom of decision making.[5] In school there is considerable allegiance to the idea that the teacher, by virtue of training and calling, should behave as and be treated as a professional. However, if the teacher is a professional, he is a professional in a bureaucratic setting. Expectations of the teacher as a professional have considerable significance in some schools and with some teachers, but in other schools and with other teachers it is clear that the dominant expectations are those of the teacher as bureaucrat.[6] Corwin notes, however, "An association (school) may be simultaneously organized around contradictory employee and professional principles. . . ."[7]

By way of example, consider the expectation of loyalty to one's superiors as compared with loyalty to clients. According to Corwin, a professional mode of organization would be high on loyalty to clients, but a bureaucratic organization would be high on loyalty to superiors.[8] In the short run it may be possible

TABLE 2. Contrasting Characteristics of Professional and Employee Modes of Organization*

Continuum	Bureaucratic-Employee Expectations		Professional Expectations	
	High	*Low*	*High*	*Low*
Standardization	Stress on uniformity of clients' problems		Stress on uniqueness of clients' problems	
	Routine of Work			
	Stress on records and files		Stress on research and change	
	Continuity of Procedure			
	Rules stated as universals or rules specific		Rules stated as alternatives or rules diffuse	
Specialization	*Specificity of Rules*			
	Stress on efficiency of technique. Task orientation		Stress on achievement of goals. Client orientation	
	Specialization on the Basis of Function			
	Skill based primarily on practice		Skill based primarily on knowledge	
	Monopoly of Knowledge			
	Decisions concerning application of rules to routine problems		Decisions concerning professional policy and unique problems	
Authority	*Responsibility for Decision Making*			
	Punishment-centered administration		Representative administration	
	Centralization of Authority			
	Rules sanctioned by the public		Rules sanctioned by powerful and legally sanctioned professions	
	Loyalty to the organization and to superiors; authority from office		Loyalty to professional associations and clients; authority from personal competence	
	BASIS OF AUTHORITY			

* Adapted from Ronald G. Corwin, *A Sociology of Education: Emerging Patterns of Class, Status, and Power in the Public Schools* (New York: Appleton-Century-Crofts, 1965), p. 232,© 1965. Reprinted by permission of Prentice-Hall, Inc., Englewood Cliffs, N.J.

to uphold both sets of expectations. So long as administrators do not require actions that violate the teacher's view of what is "good for students," there is no reason for the teacher to behave in a way that is "disloyal" to superiors.

The question, therefore, is not simply one of whether the teacher is more or less loyal to superiors or students. It is also a question of whether those in authority hold the same expectation for students as does the teacher; what will happen if the teacher acts in a way that contradicts the commands of the principal; and how one comes to know which orientation is the appropriate one to apply in a given situation. In the situation where teachers hold the expectation that they should be loyal to their students and systematically behave in a manner that reflects this loyalty, the critical question of whether—on the dimension of loyalty—the school is bureaucratic or professional hinges on three facts. (1) Do administrative superiors of the teacher share the teacher's definition of the situation? (2) If they do not, do they attempt to enforce their own expectations through the systematic application of sanctions? (3) If they do apply sanctions, are they successful in inducing more conformity to their (the administrators') expectations? Schools in which administrators have bureaucratic expectations and are successful in gaining conformity to them are best typified as bureaucratic. Where administrators hold the view that teachers should be expected to behave as professionals, the key lies in the degree to which teachers conform to these expectations. If teachers insist on bureaucratic performance and are successful in their resistance to professional demands, the school continues to be best typified as a bureaucracy. On the other hand, if teachers share professional expectations with the administration, the school would be more appropriately categorized as professional.

Critical to the distinction of the school as a bureaucracy or a professional organization is the degree to which bureaucratic and professional expectations effectively regulate the school and classroom behavior of teachers. Schools can be typified as bureaucratic even when administrators make sincere efforts to create an environment in which the teachers will uphold professional expectations.[9]   Conversely, teachers may well perceive themselves as professionals, develop elaborate evasion strategies to avoid bureaucratic expectations, perhaps engage in systematic and extreme forms of nonconformity (e.g., strikes), yet continue to behave as and be treated as bureaucratic employees.

STRUCTURAL LOOSENESS AND TIGHTNESS

The concept of structural looseness, as it is used here, means the degree to which the social unit under consideration (e.g., classroom or building) is characterized by autonomy of action.

Elementary school classrooms evidence a great deal more "structural looseness"[10] than do high school classrooms, or so it seems.   But the degree to which classrooms are autonomous units within schools and school buildings varies not only with grade levels but from school to school.   Some high schools may be more like some elementary schools (in terms of structural tightness and looseness) than they are like other high schools.

Bureaucratic modes of organization probably create conditions that are more conducive to structural tightness than structural looseness; however, the fact that a school is bureaucratic in its organizational form does not predetermine the existence of a structurally tight arrangement.   Bidwell, for example, points out three ways in which routinization can be accomplished, only one of which necessarily results in a structurally tight bureaucratic arrangement.   The first means identified by Bidwell is "the interweaving of staff orientations with professional norms and local school system policies, thus maximizing the commitment of teachers and school principals with such commitments."[11]

In this case the situation suggested here could be either "loose" or "tight," depending upon the degree to which professional norms were upheld by external as opposed to internalized sources of control.   In some schools, the orientation of teachers may be such that they seek out bureaucratic authority and react with frustration when they do not feel that it is sufficiently present.[12]   In these situations, whatever professional expectations permeate the classroom are more likely to be the result of outside enforcement of professional norms than the internalization of those norms within the classroom.

Because the concept of autonomy is so often used in conjunction with the idea of professionalism, it may be difficult to imagine a situation in which a professional mode of organization could exist in conjunction with structural tightness.   On the surface, at least, the idea of structural tightness seems antithetical to professionalism.   Yet, there is a sense in which this is not so.

Professionalism is not necessarily synonymous with "every one doing his own thing."   Professionalism does not mean the absence of rules, sanctions, and norms for performance.   Rather, it means that the rules, sanctions, and norms derive from some assumed basis of knowledge and expertise instead of being allocated to particular positions within the organization.   The professional is autonomous only insofar as the norms, values, and performance standards of the profession are not violated.   For example, a modern physician who insisted on continuing the practice of "bleeding" patients would—hopefully—quickly lose the right to practice.

In the school setting it is possible to conceive of situations in which the activities of any particular classroom might be carefully monitored and regulated by "outsiders," yet in which professional norms were rigorously upheld.   Such a situation would be most likely to arise when a pattern of differentiated staffing had developed as a result of genuine and demonstrable differences in competence and training.   In such a situation it would be likely that paraprofessionals might carry the bulk of the responsibility for implementing decisions at the classroom level, but at the same time these individuals would be only peripherally involved in making the critical decisions concerning what actions should be taken.   Such situations—though probably rare—would fall into the professional–structurally tight category.

The second and third means identified by Bidwell by which schools can establish and maintain routine performance are more typically bureaucratic in nature.   These are the following:

(a) the establishment of standards of student accomplishment prerequisite to movement from grade to grade, that is examinations which constrain the performance of teachers as well as of students;

(b) and the bureaucratization of school and classroom activities by rules of procedure which restrict the discretionary autonomy of classroom teachers or school staffs.[13]

Clearly, when bureaucratization of routines proceeds to the point that the discretionary autonomy of classroom teachers or school staffs is severely limited, the situation is best described as structurally tight. Yet, it is possible to bureaucratize most of the activities of schools without directly intervening in the activities of the classroom. Perhaps the most common way of bureaucratizing routines and maintaining structural looseness is by giving careful and systematic attention to "output" measures such as standardized examination scores and routine promotion policies. Bureaucratization probably tends to push schools toward structural tightness, but there are many other factors in schools (e.g., the professional orientations of teachers) that work to maintain structural looseness, even in bureaucratic environments.

STUDENTS—PRODUCTS, CLIENTS, AND MEMBERS

The position the student holds in relation to the organizational boundaries of the school is frequently discussed as a matter of philosophic preference or categorical definition. The present discussion proceeds from the assumption that students' boundary positions are determined by social definitions that obtain in the classroom, the school building, and/or the school district. Few schools consider very young children to be members of the school organization. The idea of membership carries with it some recognition of moral commitment, reciprocal obligations, shared goals, and a sense of belonging or community. (Very young children do not belong to the school; they belong to their family.)

Very soon, often on the first day of school, some of the child's loyalty to the family is shifted to the teacher.[14] Indeed, some families begin the process of transferring the loyalties of children to school authorities, particularly teachers, long before children enter school. The process by which this is accomplished varies, but many have observed the tendency of middle class parents to take opportunities to point out to preschool children how nice, how good, and how right teachers are. "In a sense, parents are particularly occupied with forcing the child to develop so that he can leave the family."[15] The process that families start (shifting loyalties from home) is continued by the teacher. Using the loyalty students come to feel toward them as adult authorities, primary school teachers set about the delicate task of encouraging children to become loyal to ever more abstract symbols, beliefs, and customs.[16]

Student *membership* in school organizations is symbolized quite early in the lives of school children. Some children are given positions of "responsibility" (e.g., hall monitors, school patrol, and lunch money collection); others are not. As time goes on, some students become more and more integrated into the grain and fiber of the school, and they come to be viewed as members of the school community. However, many students never really become morally committed to the school and are therefore unwilling to take up the responsibility and obligations of membership.[17] Furthermore, in later school years schools become increasingly task and performance oriented, and the inclusion of all students as members may have dysfunctional consequences. Thus, both students and schools differentiate between students who are members and those who are not.

Membership is a reciprocal notion. The member accepts obligations and responsibilities to be sure, but the group also has obligations and responsibilities to the member. Students, as members of the school or the class, are in a position to make demands on the system, and they are also in a position of moral obligation to the system. Membership provides privileges as well as obligations. Privilege subverts control. Thus, as the control needs of the school increase and as the personal authority of teachers diminishes, the definition of student membership in school becomes increasingly restrictive. Students who were treated as members of their third grade class (and thus indirectly as members of the school) find themselves defined by the school as "outsiders." Certainly, some students retain their membership rights very late in their school careers. In most schools, however, the student position as member becomes an increasingly restricted category and significantly more demanding on those who would occupy it.

For example, in early school years about all that membership requires is that one passively submit to the teacher's authority and where the larger school intervenes, one must recognize the authority of those in charge (e.g., the principal). By junior high school, passive submission is not enough. Active performance and supporting actions are required. Students who do only that which is expected or required of all students are seldom seen as members of schools. To qualify for membership in later school years, students must show more than routine performance in academic matters. Students must also be actively involved in functions the school provides, such as clubs, athletics, and perhaps student government, and they must indicate a willingness to serve the interest of the school *even at some personal sacrifice*.[18]

Among the things students may be called on to sacrifice are the allegiances, friendships, and loyalties developed in earlier school years. As performance and task become more important, so does impersonal and objective evaluation. For example, the boy who, in the sixth grade, could well be designated a school boy patrolman because he was mature and responsible—even if only a C student—may, in high school, be excluded from office in student government because his grade point does not meet the required 2.5 average. It is not improbable that this young man (and there are many such) will see a friend[19] (perhaps from his old neighborhood elementary school) encouraged to seek student office while he (the C student) is discouraged or prohibited from doing so. Eventually, those who are members of the school organization will find themselves in the same clubs, the same classes—indeed at the same parties and in the same student hangouts.[20]   Those who are not members may also find a common base of group action, and most will come to accept the fact that they are "outsiders."

The idea of the student as client of the school has almost as much support in the ideology and traditions of educators as does the idea of student as member.   The need for teachers to identify themselves as professionals makes a clients view a comfortable one.   However, whether one is a client of an organization is not determined by one's own definition of reality or even one's commitment to the organization.   Rather, clientship has to do with the way categories of participants are defined by the organization.   Members are inside the organization and clients are outside, but clients can and do have claims on the organization.

The basic distinctions between students as members and students as clients are to be found in differences on the boundary dimensions of scope, pervasiveness, permeability, and cohesiveness.   In relative terms, for students who are members, the scope of the organization is likely to be wide.   The number of social actions over which the school exercises some control—or attempts to exercise some control—will be relatively great.   For the client, the scope of the organization will be more restricted.   For example, athletic squad members often find that their dating, eating, and sleeping habits are regulated by the school; students who are not involved in athletics are not likely to be so regulated.   For the client, the pervasiveness of the school organization is likely to be low.   The client is unlikely to be given much direction about how to proceed to use the services extended.   Rather, the services will be offered, and it is up to the client to use them.   For members, on the other hand, performance expectations are more likely to be specified.   It is accepted that members should do certain things in certain ways, and it is the responsibility of the organization to assure that this is done.   If a member's performance falls below the expected level, it is a reflection on the organization as well as the member.   On the other hand, students classified as clients are often told that "an education is here for you if you want to do what we suggest, but we cannot make you do it." Members are likely to get more positive direction. If a client fails, it is likely to be considered the fault of the client; if a member fails, *particularly if a significant number of members fail*, the teacher or school may begin serious appraisal to locate the organizational source of the problem. Furthermore, members, even low-level members, are likely to have more impact on the behavioral expectations applied in a given situation than are clients. School boundaries and classroom boundaries are more permeable through students considered as members than through students considered as clients. When students who are defined as clients attempt to influence areas the school considers within its boundaries, the matter is likely to be treated as a boundary threat and counteraction will be taken. When student members attempt to influence or change policy, the action is more likely to be considered a legitimate part of the organizational process. For example, the student council—with the approval of the advisor—may make recommendations about dress codes that will be positively received by the administration. (The students may indeed be congratulated and assured that this is the way democracy really works.) On the other hand, students identified as clients would probably be less likely to receive positive responses from "insiders." More likely, their suggestions would be treated as unwarranted invasions of boundaries.

The degree to which student members are likely to interact with each other outside school (a measure of cohesiveness) probably will be higher than is the case for clients. Clients are likely to have more diffuse peer groups, at least diffuse in terms of the particular population from which membership is drawn. Almost by definition, members will have more task-related interactions than will clients.

In addition to the student as member and client, there is a third category into which schools sometimes place students. That is the category of product. The most significant boundary dimension for distinguishing products from clients and members is pervasiveness. The degree to which the behavior of student *as product* is monitored, checked, and controlled is very high. Students as products find that those areas considered within the scope of the school are narrowly proscribed and prescribed. The range of deviation tolerated is small, the standards are explicit, and the performance required is generally known throughout the system. Frequently, a product orientation is reflected in the attention to individualization of instruction, diagnostic testing, and reliance on behavior modification techniques. Indeed, the language of behavior modification (reinforcement schedules, contingency plans, and criterion referenced instruction) gives attention to the uniformity of the end result.[21] For example, in addressing themselves to the utility of defining teachers in training as products, Howsam and Houston write:

> In a competency-based program, the emphasis is placed on exit rather than entrance requirements. With this approach, the possibility is opened for admitting a wider variety of persons to the group entering the program. Continual assessment of progress, optional choices of learning experiences and performance criteria within the program make entrance requirements far less crucial than they are in traditional programs. Many who previously would have been precluded from entrance by their cultural development or by their previous educational choices and performance safely can be admitted to the competency-based program. Many of these students may be expected to enter and to complete successfully such a program. The result can be a wholesome diversity of backgrounds in the teaching profession.[22]

Though contradictions and paradoxes are apparent in such thinking, Houston and Howsam's statement represents a mode of thought that is coming to dominate teacher education. Whether these human engineers will supplant diversity of means as they have already supplanted diversity of ends is a subject that needs to be given serious thought by educators who value democracy as much as efficiency and accountability. It is difficult to understand how treating students as products and people as things can be nearly as humanizing and liberating as those like Houston and Howsam claim it to be.

STUDENT COMMITMENT—ALIENATIVE, CALCULATIVE, AND MORAL

Involvement or commitment reflects the degree to which participants in the life of organizations define their position *vis-à-vis* the organization in terms of a positive affinity toward the organization or a negative orientation toward it.

In regard to involvement Etzioni writes: "The intensity of involvement ranges from high to low. The direction is either positive or negative."[23] Etzioni then goes on to define three types of involvement, each type representing a zone on a continuum from high-positive to low-negative involvement. Etzioni writes:

> Alienative involvement designates an intense negative orientation; it is predominant in relations among hostile foreigners. . . . Inmates in prisons, prisoners of war, people in concentration camps, enlisted men in basic training, all tend to be alienated from their respective organizations. . . .
>
> Calculative involvement designates either a negative or a positive orientation of low intensity. Calculative orientations are predominant in relationships of merchants who have continuous business contracts. . . .
>
> Moral involvement designates a positive orientation of high intensity. The involvement of the parishioner in his church, the devoted member to his party, and the loyal follower in his leader are all "moral." . . .
>
> . . . Pure moral commitments are based on internalization of norms and identification with authority (like Riesman's inner-directed "mode of conformity").[24]

Student commitment to the school organization and to subunits within the school (e.g., classrooms, athletic teams, and so on) can be characterized as alienative, calculative, and moral. There is, furthermore, considerable utility in such a classification of students. This classification permits one to consider student orientation toward school as a significant independent variable.

It also opens up new avenues through which motivation and control may be studied, for as Etzioni makes clear, the type of involvement participants have in an organization is directly related to the kinds of power and authority that will be effective with them. In later chapters this will be explored in detail.

USING THE TYPOLOGY: HOW AND WHERE IT MIGHT BE APPLIED

Rather than precise descriptions of reality, typologies are ways of organizing reality into manageable proportions. Typologies necessarily ignore some differences in order to point up selected common features. Those who employ typologies must be conscious of what is being looked at and what is being ignored. Two considerations are paramount in the use of any typology: (1) the level at which the typology is to be applied, and (2) the criterion or criteria appropriate to inclusions or exclusion from any of the categories upon which the typology is based.

The typology suggested here lends itself to application at the building level and at the district level. With some modification and cautions, it can also be applied to units within school buildings, such as classrooms and student organizations. When the building level is the unit of analysis, the determination of structural tightness and looseness is made with reference to the degree of autonomy of action at the classroom level. If school units other than classrooms are of interest, then determinations about structural tightness are made in terms of the units under study. For example, if the interest is to compare behavior in various student government arrangements, one might characterize the student government in terms of structural looseness and tightness in much the same way as the classroom is characterized. For example, to what extent is the decision making within the governmental framework autonomous from other parts of the school structure, and to what extent is it dependent on the approval of "outside" authority?

The determination of participants would be all of those who are high on at least one of three dimensions—commitment, performance, and subordination.[25] Students, by definition, are always participants in the life of the school and the classroom, for they will always be high on subordination if not on the other two variables. Whether students are best categorized as products, clients, or members is determined by the way in which students are related to the social boundaries of the unit under study. As elementary classrooms take on social system characteristics, some students will clearly be "within" that system, and others outside, perhaps either as an audience or as potentially interfering groups. In classrooms with system qualities, all students who are defined as in the system are also members of the school.

At the high school level, however, the situation may be quite different. Students in a particular classroom may reflect relational patterns that characterize the group as having distinct and separate qualities from the school. Indeed, the student group may be related to the school in a way that suggests either a client or a product orientation. For example, students in a special education class may come to develop recognizable in-group loyalties, and relate to other students in the school in terms of those loyalties. But *as a group,* the special education students might be systematically defined as "nonmembers" of the school organization, at least as indicated by measures of scope, pervasiveness, cohesiveness, and permeability. Thus, if the unit of analysis is a classroom, it might be well to include some students as members who would not be viewed as members at the school or district level.

Alienative, calculative, and moral involvement has to do with the degree of commitment of students to the behavioral expectations that have their locus at the organizational level under study. For example, students committed to school organizations like athletic squads would, by definition, be less alienated from school (more positively committed) than students who have no unit in the school system to which they feel a positive commitment. Highly committed students would be characterized as morally involved while mildly alienated, or mildly committed, students would be categorized as calculative.

In general, then, determinations about the boundary dimensions of the typology are measured in terms of scope, pervasiveness, permeability, and cohesiveness. Indicators of expectational dimensions (e.g., bureaucratic or professional) are measures of variance in distribution, enforcement transmission, and conformity.

PLACING SCHOOLS

Making determinations about the correct placement of empirical illustrations of each of the thirty-six types of schools is a matter that stands in need of considerable attention. At present all that exists are some commonsense guidelines. (1) Whatever determination is made, judgments about the placement of the school unit must be made in terms of all the participants of the unit being studied (e.g., one could not use the typology at the building level and then exclude, *a priori*, some students who attend the school). (2) Most schools will represent "mixed" types rather than pure reflections of the typology. For example, schools where most students could be categorized as members will be likely to have some student participants who are alienated. (3) Alternative measures should be employed, depending on the purposes of using the category system. For example, in regard to student involvement, it may be useful to consider categorization from several perspectives. One means of categorizing students would be to develop a measure of involvement that would run from alienation to strong positive (moral) commitment. All student participants could be assessed in terms of commitment and the school judged to be alienative, calculative, or moral on the basis of some mean score of "involvement." An alternative means would be to categorize students into one of the three groups (alienative, calculative, and moral) and consider the category with the greatest participant representation to be the category that best typifies the organizational mode of the school.

Perhaps the most important guideline to placing schools is to remember that the function of ideal types and typologies is to illuminate reality and to facilitate generalization. It is neither useful nor necessary that a typology describe *precisely* any single occurrence.

SUMMARY

To summarize, it has been suggested that by assessing variances between schools on the dimensions of employee expectations (bureaucratic and professional), structured tightness and structured looseness, student position (product, client, and member), and student involvement (alienative, calculative, and moral), it is possible to distinguish thirty-six types of schools. Each of those dimensions is organizational in nature; therefore, the typology that emerges is relevant to comparison of structural difference between and among schools. The implications of these differences for the practical concerns of educators are the subject of much of the remainder of this book.

NOTES

1. The basic concepts upon which the typology is based (i.e., the ideas of bureaucratic and professional expectations, structural tightness and looseness, the student as product, client, and member and the student as alienative, calculative, or morally involved) will be elaborated and developed in the pages that follow.
2. Robert J. Havighurst and Bernice L. Neugarten, *Society and Education*, ed. 4 (Boston: Allyn and Bacon, Inc., 1975), chapters 19 and 20. Havighurst and Neugarten present one of the more useful discussions of teacher roles, but their discussion is limited to description and does not move to a level of precise analysis.
3. One of the limitations of most of the work done by Flanders and those who have followed his lead is that little attention has been given to factors outside the classroom—but within the school—

that might account for some of the variances he has reported in teacher classroom behavior. See, for example, E. J. Amidon and N. A. Flanders, *The Role of the Teacher in the Classroom* (Minneapolis: Paul Amidon and Associates, 1963).

4. Ronald G. Corwin, *A Sociology of Education: Emerging Patterns of Class, Status, and Power in the Public Schools* (New York: Appleton-Century-Crofts, 1965).

5. See Charles E. Bidwell, "The School as a Formal Organization," in *Handbook of Organizations*, ed. James G. March (Chicago: Rand McNally & Company, 1965), especially pp. 972–978.

6. Ibid.

7. Corwin, *A Sociology of Education*, p. 230.

8. Ibid.

9. On the basis of some research findings one could reasonably infer that some teachers might resist professional expectations on the grounds that the latitude of decision making creates too much ambiguity and thus a feeling of powerlessness and frustration. See, for example, Gerald H. Moeller, "Bureaucracy and Teachers' Sense of Power," *Administrators Notebook*, November 11, 1962.

10. Bidwell, "The School as a Formal Organization," develops the concept of structural looseness and applies it to schools (pp. 972–1022).

11. Ibid., p. 976.

12. See the earlier reference to Moeller, "Bureaucracy and Teachers' Sense of Power."

13. Bidwell, "The School as a Formal Organization."

14. See Robert S. Dreeben, *On What Is Learned in School* (Reading, Mass.: Addison-Wesley Publishing Co., 1968).

15. William J. Goode, *The Family* (Englewood Cliffs, N.J.: Prentice-Hall, Inc., 1964), p. 73.

16. Dreeben, *On What Is Learned in School*.

17. Dreeben (see preceding note) suggests that teachers often overestimate the extent to which students have internalized the reward structure of the school.

18. Waller's discussion of the role of martyrs in the life of schools, though perhaps overdrawn, is instructive. See Willard Waller, *The Sociology of Teaching* (New York: John Wiley & Sons, Inc., 1932, reprinted 1967), p. 129.

19. There is something quite sad about the ways school organizations disrupt loyalties and friendships established in the neighborhood

school. Perhaps such disruptions are necessary to the socialization and educative process, but it is only the callous who fail to see pathos in the plight of the child who finds a friend moving away from him simply because one is a C student. Yet, C students do not participate in the organizational life of the school the way A students do. Perhaps "hard nosed" educators are correct when they say "that's the way it is in real life," but that is a debatable point.

20. David H. Hargreaves, *Social Relations in a Secondary School* (New York: Humanities Publishing Company, 1967).

21. The "systems approach" to school administration and curriculum development, with emphasis on input, output, and throughput, is often found in conjunction with performance contracting, competency-based programs, and behavior modification techniques.

22. Robert B. Howsam and W. Robert Houston, "Change and Challenge," in *Competency-Based Teacher Education: Progress, Problems and Prospects*, ed. Houston and Howsam (Chicago: Science Research Associates, Inc., 1972), p. 9.

23. Amitai Etzioni, *A Comparative Analysis of Complex Organizations: On Power, Involvement, and Their Correlates.* Copyright © 1961 by The Free Press of Glencoe, Inc., p. 9.

24. Ibid., pp. 10–11. Etzioni makes a distinction between pure moral commitment and social moral commitment. The distinction is not made here, as much of the distinction is picked up in the discussion of social exchange strategies and psychological strategies, which follows shortly.

25. This closely parallels Etzioni, *Comparative Analysis of Complex Organizations.*

6

Behavioral Expectations and Variance among Schools

Patterns of exclusion and control effectively describe the boundaries of group and organizational life. The content and process of life within those boundaries must, however, be described in terms of the relationships that provide the internal structure for organizational behavior. Among the more important of these are the relationships among the behavioral expectations typical of the organization and the social behavior of the participants in the life of schools.

THE SOCIAL NATURE OF EXPECTATIONS

Groups have their structure and origin in human interaction. Over time, participants in the life of a group come to expect certain kinds of performances from some group members and other performances from other group members. As the group takes on more formal characteristics, these expectations often become institutionalized into roles.[1] Individuals who occupy particular positions in the organizations are expected and often required to carry out tasks related to those positions in prescribed ways. Expectations generated in interaction take on patterns

105

and become structured. These expectations come to have a life of their own, different both in kind and in degree from the perceptions and expectations of individual group members. Indeed, when outsiders attempt to gain entry to the group, they must first learn the expectations of the group. The new group member must learn those expectations that apply to his own performance and, equally important, he must learn what is appropriate to expect of others.

Group expectations vary in content (i.e., what is expected); they also vary in process (who knows about the expectation, to whom does it apply, how are violations treated, and so on). Most research on teacher expectations has concentrated on the content of expectations (does the teacher expect much more or little). Little systematic attention has been given to the processes through which these expectations are enacted in the classroom (e.g., is the teacher's expectation of a student reinforced by the expectations of the student's peers?). To understand the significance of behavioral expectations, it is necessary to have a clear understanding of the nature and sources of variance in the structure of expectations. This necessity holds whether the analysis is at the level of the classroom, the building, or the district. Four sources of variance[2] that seem crucial to understanding the structural and behavioral differences in schools and classrooms are: (1) the distribution of expectations; (2) the enforcement of expectations; (3) the process by which expectations are transmitted; and (4) the nature and types of conformity to these expectations.

THE DISTRIBUTION OF BEHAVIORAL EXPECTATIONS

Who knows about a particular expectation? Which and how many of the participants accept or agree with these expectations? To whom do the expectations apply? Do they apply in all circumstances or only under special conditions? Each of these questions pertains to the distribution of social and behavioral expectations. Variances in the answers to these questions may suggest important differences among schools and classrooms.

One of the assumptions underlying projects like *Upward Bound* is that children born to poor parents are often unaware of the kinds of expectations they will be required to meet if they are to succeed in higher education. Sometimes—whether by accident or design—those who are in positions of authority do not permit those "under them" to know precisely what is expected of them or what they should expect of each other. Apparently, some teachers use knowledge of expectations as a means of maintaining their authority in the classroom. By keeping students uncertain about what is expected and required, the teacher is in a position to justify a wide range of evaluations and actions that might otherwise be challenged. By keeping expectations unclear, teachers can keep approval always just beyond reach.[3]

When those in authority become explicit about their expectations, they establish both goals and limits for the group. For example, the teacher who *grades on the curve* has, in effect, announced to the class how many students will pass and how many will fail—regardless of individual performance levels. Thus, there is a great deal of pressure applied to intensify the "competition between and among class members, at least competition to stay off the bottom."[4] Those at the top, however, are under considerable pressure not to be "rate-busters." The goal then becomes to stay off the bottom of the group, but not necessarily to produce maximum performance. There are, in fact, social motives for high achievers to limit their performance.

The fact that a teacher announces (overtly or covertly) what is expected is no indication that those expectations are accepted by all group members. The concept of self-fulfilling prophecy[5] has recently come to be used in conjunction with teacher expectations, perhaps on the assumption that since the teacher seems so central to classroom life, the teacher must be central to the establishment and maintenance of the structure of behavioral expectations in the classroom. There is some basis for this assumption, but it is also true that teachers seldom, beyond the first or second grade, confront classes that are totally lacking in group history. Each fall, new students come in and some students move out, but it is seldom the case that a "new" class will be made up of total strangers.[6] In past interactions (in other classes, in the halls, and on the streets) some students have taken up certain roles in the group life of children. Some have been labeled dumb, some bright, some handy, some clumsy; some emerge as dominant, others subordinate.[7] Whether these labels are accurate and how much they have to do with the behavior of prior teachers are questions for study, but that these labels and differentiated roles do exist is beyond doubt. The existence of these student expectation structures suggests that students do have firm expectations of each other—and perhaps of themselves—and, further, that these expectations may be independent of the teacher. The idea that the expectations and actions of a single teacher can dramatically alter expectations that have become imbedded in the structure of group life seems (depending on one's view) unusually hopeful or unusually pessimistic. That teachers' expectations are important is certainly true, and in the long run these expectations may change the expectations of other participants in the class. It is likely, however, that in those situations where the teacher's expectations have a direct and immediate effect on the self-concept of a child, the child will be very young or have very loose ties with his peers and classmates.[8] Teachers are significant actors in the classroom, but they are not the only actors. Indeed, the longer children go to school, the less important the behavior of a single teacher may be, for the nature of groups and group expectations has a way of offsetting individual perceptions and behaviors—even the perceptions and behaviors of so powerful a figure as the teacher.[9]

Some behavioral expectations apply only to certain categories of students or teachers. Female students are expected to be neat; boys are not expected to be so neat. Male teachers are expected to be willing to (physically) discipline students, whereas female teachers may not be expected to do so. It is not unusual for female teachers to request the man next door to "do the honors" when a paddling seems in order.[10] Variations in the applicability of behavioral expectations suggest much about the school. A few examples will illustrate this point. Some students are exempt from many of the routine expectations (procuring hall passes, bringing notes of excuse upon absence), while others must follow the rules to the letter. Some teachers will suffer severe reprimand from the principal if they are absent from the classroom for any reason; other teachers seem free to stay away from the "charges" for considerable lengths of time without major difficulty.[11]

Certain kinds of expectations apply only under special circumstances, whereas others apply routinely. For example, students are frequently encouraged to work together on projects, but cooperation is replaced with competition at test time. Indeed, cooperation on a test—or sometimes on an outside project— is often labeled cheating. At the faculty level, when the accrediting team from the regional accrediting agency is about to appear in the school, faculties are expected to be knowledgeable about the "school's philosophy," the overall curriculum design, and so on. At other times this expectation does not apply. As another instance, teachers may be expected to be gate attendants at athletic events, but not at school functions like plays and concerts. Teachers may be required to attend the autumn meeting of the PTA, but thereafter attendance is voluntary.

Variations in the distribution of expectations in classrooms, at the building level, and at the district level suggest much about the effective location of power, influence, and authority. It also indicates the possible sources of prestige, status, and disrepute. Knowledge of the distribution of behavioral expectations would not tell all there is to know about the social fabric of schools. However, it would certainly suggest much about the variety of human relationships that exist in schools, and how these relationships impinge upon the lives of teachers and students.

ENFORCEMENT OF BEHAVIORAL EXPECTATIONS

The ways in which group and organizational expectations come to be enforced is a second important source of variance in schools. Williams suggests six different ways enforcement can vary: (1) punishment vs. reward; (2) severity of punishment; (3) the enforcing agency; (4) consistency of enforcement; (5) source of authority for enforcement; and (6) internal vs. external enforcement.[12]

Schools are typically punishment centered, relying heavily on relative deprivation as the chief vehicle for sanctioning.[13] In schools, all students may begin equal, but some students quickly become less than equal. A few students may become more than equal. The idea of the "average" student tends to conceal the fact that few students meet the official expectations of the school. Furthermore, it is assumed that few *can* meet those expectations. The superior student is the one who does what all students should do, if all students were to meet the official expectations of the school. Usually, schools are evaluated in terms of the number of superior students they produce. No school would be proud of a record that indicated all of its students were "just average." Each school expects maximum performance from each student, but assumes that relatively few will perform at the level required for the school to achieve the goal of "producing superior students." Those who perform at a level evaluated as superior get relatively more of what the system has to offer than do other students. It is in the dominance of less over more, in fact, that the punitive nature of school enforcement becomes so clear, for the reward structure of the school is based on scarcity. More for some students means less for others.

Most schools, indeed, operate on the assumption of the mythical "normal curve." According to this myth, if enough instances of a phenomenon were recorded, they would eventually be distributed along a line in a way that would represent a bell-shaped curve, with mean, median, and mode convergent on the same point. Student performance relative to school expectations is assumed to conform to this model. But schools neither respect nor reward "normalcy"; they expect and reward abnormality. Students who deviate—in a positive direction—from "normal" get more rewards than those who stay within more "normal ranges" of performance. A's are not given to average or normal students; they are given to extremely abnormal ones. It is *assumed* that no school or classroom could be made up of all "positively" abnormal students. A teacher who gives all A's to his students is not likely to be congratulated for creating such unusual conditions in his classroom that all students meet the peak expectations of the system. Rather, the teacher's standards for passing out rewards will become suspect. He is giving too many A's. For a student to receive a C may not be punishment, but it is certainly not a reward. C's procure few scholarships; A's purchase admission to college. Schools make A's relatively scarce and thus deprive all but the selected few of them. Students may avoid punishment (an F) by being normal, but they cannot procure rewards for routine performance. Indeed, the grading practices of schools often create a peculiar paradox. If normal performance is the official expectation of the school, there are few—if any—rewards for meeting the official expectations. The only motivation grades provide for most students is the assurance that their normal performance will help them be somewhat less deprived than some of their colleagues and peers.

Reliance on grades as an organizational reward leads to certain distortions in the nature of the reward structure of schools. There are other rewards in schools than those symbolized by grades. But most of the rewards that are organizational in nature are interlocked with grades. One cannot play football, be in the band, join clubs, or be in student government unless one has a particular grade average (at least in most schools). The recommendations school officials write for students are tied to grades. Few prospective employers or college admissions officers would be impressed, for example, by a statement to the effect that "this student is quite normal, average, and routine. He never does more or less than is required of him; he is as punctual as need be, as attentive as necessary, and as thorough as he is instructed to be." In school, students are expected to do more than is *required* to get rewards.

The relative scarcity of organizational rewards in schools, and the tendency to distribute these rewards only for outstanding performance, makes it difficult to use rewards as a means of upholding, maintaining, and enforcing routine behavioral expectations. (By definition *most* behavioral expectations have a routine quality about them.) Thus, the use of punitive measures becomes central to the structure of most schools. Students are denied hall passes; they do not "earn" them. Students are denied the right to be on student council; they do not earn the right. Certainly, the language used to describe these acts of relative deprivation suggests that a reward is offered. Words like "hall passes are privileges to be earned" are seldom followed, however, by guidelines for positive performance. Students earn hall passes by *not* behaving in a way the school defines as inappropriate.

Those who do have access to rewards, and the authority to distribute these rewards, are in a position to generate considerable influence over the actions of the groups in which they participate. For example, teachers often find that the allocation of personal status and prestige within the faculty group depends on the approval of particular faculty members. The new teacher learns that the few prestige and status rewards available within the faculty group are allocated only with the approval and consent of a particular cluster of teachers. The teacher who values his colleagues' esteem may, therefore, become very sensitive to the behavioral expectations and evaluative comments of this powerful group of teachers. Similarly, students may find that peer status and prestige depend upon gaining the approval of particular cliques, gangs, or organizations within the school.

Whether behavioral expectations are upheld by rewards or by punishments indicates important dimensions of the social structures of schools and classrooms. The severity of the punishment and the magnitude of the reward suggest still other dimensions of that structure. For example, some behaviors are disapproved as much by the failure of the group to take them into account as by overt sanctions. Very little punishment—or reward—may be involved in the teacher's refusal to call on a student whose hand waves wildly in his face. Frequently, however, schools and teachers develop elaborate schedules of rewards and punishments and publish them in student and faculty handbooks. One school within the author's experience, for example, has a student handbook that spells out an elaborate system of merits and demerits for students. Something of the values of the school and the mentality of those responsible for the construction of this book is reflected in the fact that a student will receive *ten* demerits for showing disrespect to a teacher, but only *five* demerits for bringing a loaded gun to school.

The scarcity of positive rewards available in schools tends to support the equalitarian sympathies of educators. Because few rewards exist in school, it is difficult for school officials to treat students or teachers in vastly disparate ways—at least in regard to *positive* rewards. For example, a teacher whose performance is evaluated as exceptional may gain high regard and differential status among students, parents, and colleagues. But the salary the teacher receives and the organizational perquisites (e.g., sabbaticals and travel allowances) will be only as great—or as little—as those of most other teachers.

Unlike rewards, the punishments available to the school vary quite dramatically, and often this variance is not a simple continuum from "light punishment to extreme punishment." Frequently, the punishments available to schools rest at the extremes of no action or severe reprisals. It is often difficult for the school to administer mild punishment for relatively minor infractions of rules and expectations. If the behavior of teachers and administrators often appears capricious and arbitrary, it may be because the nature of the school organizations makes it so. Frequently, extreme punishment is the only form of available sanction even if the infraction is only minor. Short of dismissing a teacher, or refusing to grant the teacher tenure, for example, there is little official action schools can take to apply punitive sanctions to teachers. Some minor irritations, like scheduling a full day of study halls, giving an inordinate amount of hall duty, and assigning the teacher to undesirable classes, are available and *may* be used, but few schools can require an individual teacher to undergo retraining, though they may require all teachers to do so. Schools cannot furlough teachers as a disciplinary measure, schools cannot withhold salary, nor can teachers be demoted. Teachers are teachers are teachers, so long as they are on the payroll. These facts are mentioned not to advocate that it should be otherwise, but to point out that, because of the nature of the relationships between the teacher and the school system, sometimes the only available negative response to a teaching performance judged inadequate is an extremely punitive one. Among the more obvious consequences of this situation are: (a) administrators committed to teacher accountability may engage in arbitrary dismissals, since dismissal is the only option open for sanctioning unsatisfactory performance; (b) unsatisfactory performance will pass without action until the performance becomes so poor that a case clearly calls for dismissal; (c) *threats* of dismissal will become the basic "punitive" measure used by administrators. Furthermore, these threats often result in petty bickering. Unless the teacher's performance is unusually poor, there is considerable assurance that dismissal would not be approved by the school board, parents, or teachers. Many marginal teachers know this as well as does the administrator. Thus the struggle between the principal and the teacher may degenerate to petty retribution and bickering rather than a clarification of issues and positions.

The nature of the enforcing agency can be a clear indication of the organizational level at which the behavioral expectation has its locus, although this is not always the case. At times, teachers are expected to enforce school rules even though the rules may be disruptive of classroom routines. For example, schools may insist that teachers not permit students to go to the library during class hours, and the teacher may be obliged to uphold such rules, even though students may need access to the library. There are some behavioral violations that are not even in the purview of the teacher, and if the teacher observes these violations, he is required to report them to the principal.

For example, students caught smoking are usually sent to the principal. Students who physically attack the teacher are dealt with by the principal. Students who persistently refuse to comply with the expectation that they will subordinate themselves to the commands of teachers may be sent to the principal.

Specific expectations may be so much a part of the life of the group that they become internalized and enforcement is diffuse throughout the group. The sanctioning process that supports the group expectation is shared in by all group members as opposed to being assigned to individuals. Sometimes, for example, students will support a teacher in maintaining silence by "shushing" their peers. Frequently, teachers and students cooperate in maintaining good discipline when dignitaries are in schools, or when outsiders are in the classroom. Much of school life indeed conforms to what Goffman[14] describes as a *team effort,* played to an audience of perceived outsiders with mutually reinforced group sanctions.

Consistency of enforcement is a subject about which teachers and students *seem* remarkably agreed. Concepts of equity, fairness, and the like permeate schools and classrooms. Teachers do not like to be seen, especially by their colleagues, as arbitrary. Rather, they prefer to be viewed as evenhanded. It is a widely shared belief in the teaching fraternity that students respect teachers who are firm and consistent. School administrators often pride themselves on the fact that "rules are rules, and exceptions cannot be made." Yet, for all the talk about consistency, schools can be amazingly inconsistent places, and the inconsistency does not result simply from capricious or arbitrary behavior. Indeed, inconsistency seldom results from conscious efforts at all. In the classroom, for example, teachers may announce that they expect students to appear promptly before the bell, but then only enforce the expectation in an episodic fashion. These episodes may evolve from single individuals' deviating more and more from the expectation (e.g., a student who is routinely tardy becomes even later in his arrival). Periodic enforcement episodes may arise because more and more individuals deviate a little from the expectation. (The number of tardy students increases.) There are some expectations, however, that are never to be violated; the slightest indication of violation will result in reprimand. Many teachers and administrators, for example, insist that students refrain from making insidious remarks about other teachers. Vulgar language is not tolerated. Faculty-student sexual encounters are virtually taboo, as are overt indications of sexual interest between teachers. Even unmarried teachers find it difficult to pursue the type of flirting behavior one might find between peers in other organizational settings. (Schools are notably asexual.)

Inconsistency of enforcement is often the result of change. Sometimes the customs of the student body or the faculty have undergone subtle drifts, but the official rules have not been "updated" to keep up with these changes. The clashes over dress codes that typified student protests in the 1960's resulted from shifts in the student culture that were more dramatic than the schools were able to accommodate. Some schools tried to avoid clashes by inconsistent and half-hearted efforts to uphold the old standards. Other schools were more rigid in their approach and permitted clashes over dress code enforcement to lead to student dismissals, expulsion, and sometimes strikes. Many schools yielded to the pressures of the times and abolished or altered dress codes.

Other sources of inconsistent enforcement are found in the competing and contradictory expectations emanating from various levels of schools and various groups within those levels. School board policies, for example, may directly clash with what the teacher sees as the best interest of the class. Thus, the teacher may support the policy in only the most public aspects of his job. Sometimes particular student groups (e.g., athletes) find it difficult to meet the expectations of both the athletic field and the classroom. Some teachers may be sympathetic to their plight and make it a practice to avoid rigid interpretations of certain performance expectations during the football season.

The authority for enforcement of expectations varies with the expectations and the location from which it emanates. Some school rules, for example, are justified on the grounds of rationality, expedience, or necessity. Other rules are justified on the basis of "the wisdom of the elders," teachers' prerogatives, the wishes of the community, the inherent superiority of the group, and the values of belonging and togetherness. In bureaucratically organized schools, authority is rationalized and assigned to positions. Teachers often claim their authority is based on superior knowledge, but frequently they derive their authority from being "teachers."

The rules that govern school life are more internalized by teachers *and* students than most discussions of schools (including this one) would lead one to believe. Students, teachers, and administrators generally do not need external regulators to keep them in line. They behave as they are required because they believe the expectations to be right, good, and justified. Though there is much talk of student alienation, the evidence is that most students believe in the benevolent paternalism of the system.[15] The social web of schools, the woof and warp of human relationships in schools, is held together because participants in schools find it difficult to imagine other ways of behaving. At least they find it difficult to imagine patterns that would be more satisfying. Even the dissatisfactions pointed to by students and teachers become stylized, routinized, and expected. Students complain about irrelevant assignments, but when asked for suggestions of relevant assignments, they are often quite as confused as their mentors. Indeed, one of the indications that norms are internalized is that group members come to sanctify the illogical dimensions of expectations with qualities of moral goodness. As comedians like Bill Cosby make clear, there is much in the life of schools that is illogical and still considered good.[16]

THE TRANSMISSION OF BEHAVIORAL EXPECTATIONS

Educational philosophers and psychologists often speak of students "learning how to learn." This is indeed a critical aspect of school learning, and probably a great source of variance between schools. The ways in which expectations are transmitted—expectations about what should be learned, as well as expectations about how one goes about behaving in the context of the school—are major sources of school variance. If students learn to go to school *in school*, and if teachers learn to teach in school, what are the mechanisms through which the learnings are transmitted? If one learns the behavioral expectations that apply to one's self, as well as the expectations that apply to others, is the process the same for all schools, and all expectations? Do schools differ in the ways they transmit behavioral expectations? Within schools are some kinds of expectations transmitted in one fashion and others in another? How does one learn how one is supposed to learn in school? Perhaps, most important, what is the child supposed to learn in school?

Some students learn what is expected in school from older students and friends. Some expectations—like the teacher is boss—come to middle class children almost with their first teeth. Other expectations must be more or less formally taught, for example, teaching children the correct procedure for going to the restroom in the first grade. (In some classes one asks to be excused; in others, one raises one's hand; in others, one or two fingers continue as the appropriate sign.)[17] Frequently, however, less explicit instruction is given. Beginning teachers are told to "observe" more experienced teachers, and sometimes new teachers are exposed to a series of orientation programs. Observation and imitation are among the basic sources of transmission in schools.

How particular expectations are learned (whether from intimate groups, family, or friends, or whether from other teachers, classmates, and formal orientations) may be significantly related to the impact these expectations will have on behavior and human relationships in schools. Expectations transmitted in the informal banter of the teacher's lounge may have a very different impact on behavior from the expectations transmitted in the formal orientation sessions. Expectations that have the support of one's work mates or classmates may be more compelling than board policy, school policy, or even the policy of the teacher.

Another source of variance in the transmission of behavioral expectations has to do with the degree to which there is a common connection between the source that transmits the expectation and the enforcing agency. Sometimes expectations are transmitted by groups that do not support the expectation, as a means of alerting a new member of potential dangers from outside inter- ference. For example, teachers will commonly report to one another what the "principal expects" as much to protect one another from sanctioning (thereby meeting yet another group expectation) as to gain the compliance of the teacher to the ex- pectations of the principal. There are instances when the source that transmits the expectation also transmits information as to how the expectations can be avoided. (Tax lawyers do this regularly for their clients, and teachers do it for students prepar- ing for regents examinations, college boards, and so on.) When the enforcing agency is also the transmitting agency, it is likely that the behavioral significance of expectations will be consider- ably different than would otherwise be the case. For example, teachers are likely to be more consistent in the enforcement of rules they have generated than in the enforcement of rules imposed from the top down.

CONFORMITY TO EXPECTATIONS

The fact that expectations exist, that people know about them, and that effective sanctions are available to uphold them does not guarantee conformity. Some expectations are so heroic that few make a serious effort to meet the expectation. The reward for conforming to the expectation may not be sufficiently com- pelling, or the punishment not sufficiently severe, to encourage many to consider the behavioral effort worthwhile. The previous illustration of grades provides a useful example. If one assumes that each grade (A, B, C, D, E) represents a certain level of performance, and that rewards are distributed in accordance with that performance, it is clear that few students conform with the expectations implicit in the grade A. Probably many students do not try, for they find the standard too heroic; other students do not try because they find the reward less than compelling. In academic work, most students find the gray world of neither punishment nor reward (C) an acceptable lot. Another example is found in athletics. In schools, it is often expected that every young man should "try" to make the athletic squads, though most will never play on the team. Many never really try, for they know they cannot meet the standards imposed. Other students make only ritual efforts, perhaps for appearance' sake. These students then revert to some other set of expectations they find more comfortable, such as the athletic boosters' club.[18]

In some instances, expectations are seldom violated, and there is little need to call sanctions into play. This is usually the case when expectations have become internalized and generalized throughout the group or organization. For example, students seldom stay in the building after the fire drill alarm is sounded. In other instances, however, expectations are more frequently noticed in the breach than in the observance. In some schools, for example, there may be rules against teachers "moonlighting" (taking jobs outside of school), yet the practice of moonlighting persists. Indeed, schools in which moonlighting is not a persistent problem seldom have rules against the practice.

The extent to which behavioral expectations are violated, avoided, or deviated from varies from minor infractions of rules (e.g., hair that is just a little long, a dress that is a little short) to patterned evasions of expectations (the use of crib notes, cram sessions, and ponies)[19] to systematic and drastic violations of the expectations. For example, some teachers find themselves victimized by students who decide—for good or ill-advised reasons—that the teacher must *go*. In such instances, students sometimes consciously plan how they will sabotage the teacher's plans, disobey his requests, and subvert his authority. At the building level, students may make an "art form" out of smoking in off-limits areas, passing around test questions, and disrupting study halls. Teachers also engage in systematic and drastic violations of official expectations. For instance, many teachers openly flaunt the authority of the principal and defy him to apply sanctions to them for discussing controversial issues in the classroom, assigning "banned books," or joining unions. And sometimes these systematic violations have the effect of reshaping official expectations or relocating the source and forms of authority. All in all, variations in behavioral expectations go far to explain some of the more perplexing realities of school life.

NOTES

1. Some of the more provocative work on the emergence and institutionalization of roles in group life and the nature of role differentiation in small groups has been done under the supervision, direction, or inspiration of R. F. Bales. See, for example, R. F. Bales, "Task Roles and Social Roles in Problem Solving Groups," in *Readings in Social Psychology*, ed. 3, ed. E. E. Maccoby, T. M. Newcomb, and E. L. Hartley (New York: Holt, Rinehart and Winston, Inc., 1958), pp. 437–447. See also Bruce Biddle and Edwin J. Thomas, eds., *Role Theory: Concepts and Research* (New York: John Wiley & Sons, Inc., 1966).

2. This framework is suggested by Robin M. Williams, Jr., as a means for studying variances in cultural norms. The framework for the discussion in this chapter follows closely the basic outline provided by Williams; Williams, in turn, freely adopted much that was developed by Richard T. Morris, "A Typology of Norms," *American Sociological Review*, Vol. 21, No. 5 (1956), 610–613. Robin M. Williams, Jr., *American Society: A Sociological Interpretation*, ed. 2 (New York: Alfred A. Knopf, Inc., 1960), pp. 25–35.

3. Though there are many legitimate criticisms of behaviorally stated objectives, one of the more interesting objections was voiced by a teacher-graduate student. This teacher said, "The main thing I have against behavioral objectives is that once students know what is expected, they don't have to work as hard."

4. James S. Coleman, "Reward Structure and Allocation of Effort," in *Mathematical Methods in Small Group Processes*, ed. J. H. Criswell et al. (Stanford: Stanford University Press, 1962).

5. The concept received its greatest impetus (in educational circles) with the publication: Robert Rosenthal and Lenore Jacobson, *Pygmalion in the Classroom* (New York: Holt, Rinehart and Winston, Inc., 1968).

6. One of the more interesting characteristics of the population in the Rosenthal and Jacobson study was the high degree of student transiency; about 30 percent of the student population transferred in or out during the school year. The relative fluidity in student peer-structures may give teacher expectations inordinate impact in such a situation. New students have yet to establish peer-referents, and teachers are such obvious features in the "topography" of classrooms that they are easy referents to the uninitiated.

7. See, for example, Muzafer Sherif et al., *Intergroup Conflict and Cooperation: The Robbers Cave Experiment* (Norman, Okla.: University Book Exchange, University of Oklahoma, 1961).

8. A study reported by Flanders and Havumaki is certainly suggestive along these lines. Their data suggest that teachers can more easily gain compliance to their expectations in situations where group interaction is minimized. Ned A. Flanders and Sulo Havumaki, "Group Compliance to Dominative Teacher Influence," *Human Relations*, 13 (1960), 67–82.

9. One study, at least, suggested that interpersonal friendship is a critical link between the structure of the school and student college plans. See Ernest Q. Campbell and C. Norman Alexander, "Structural Effects and Interpersonal Relations," *American Journal of Sociology*, 71 (1965), 284–289.

10. Though some states have made corporal punishment illegal, other states have laws which prohibit school boards from having policies that exclude the use of physical punishment in schools.

11. Coaches, for example, are often permitted to leave their rooms to report early for practice, but regular teachers seldom are permitted such latitude.

12. Williams, *American Society*, pp. 26–27.

13. See, for example, Sarane S. Boocock, *An Introduction to the Sociology of Learning* (Boston: Houghton Mifflin Company, 1972), pp. 164–168.

14. Erving Goffman, *The Presentation of Self in Everyday Life* (Garden City, N.Y.: Doubleday & Company, Inc., Anchor Books, 1959).

15. Charles E. Silberman, *Crisis in the Classroom: The Remaking of American Education* (New York: Random House, 1970), p. 157.

16. Bill Cosby, *Why Is There Air?* Warner Brothers Recording, particularly "Kindergarten," "Personal Hygiene," and "Shop."

17. Bill Cosby has a particularly funny routine he has developed describing the child's plight with learning the correct procedures for school bathroom going. (See preceding note.)

18. With no disrespect to student managers of athletic teams, one cannot help but wonder how many managers receive their position for heroic efforts to "make the team" but ability limitations so great as to make continued effort embarrassing for peers and coaches alike.

19. For a particularly lucid discussion of "institutional variations and the evasion of normative patterns" see Williams, *American Society*, chapter 10, p. 372.

7

Power, Influence, Commitment, and Adaptation

Chief among the tasks of schools is the motivation, direction, and control of students. A secondary task is the motivation, direction, and control of other participants (e.g., teachers). Unlike many other organizations, schools have few recognizable goals beyond those of encouraging participants to behave in ways in which it seems good for them to behave.[1] Schools do not produce automobiles, gasoline, or widgets. The long-run aim of schools is to "produce" learning, but learning is extremely difficult to measure and impossible to observe directly. If schools produce anything (and there is reason to argue that the factory model is inappropriate to the study of schools)[2] they produce behavior—behavior that is an antecedent to learning. As Jackson[3] makes clear, teachers respond to student behavior, not to student learning. One might argue that schools respond in the same way.

The process of directing others to behave in ways that are organizationally valued or personally desired is sometimes labeled inducement. Inducement refers to *efforts* by one person or group to gain from another person or group acceptance of directives, support of norms, or other actions desired of them by the initiating party.[4] Inducement is an attempt to gain compliance with one's intentions. All inducements are not equally successful. Some forms of inducement are more compelling than are others,

125

and in some settings inducements are more compelling than they are in other settings. For example, appeals to patriotic symbols are usually more compelling in times of war or national calamity than in times of peace and tranquility.

In the process of inducement, people develop strategies for the employment of power and influence. Sometimes these strategies are successful and sometimes they are not successful. The reason for success (or failure) may lie in the way power or influence is exercised (i.e., in the type of strategy employed), or it may lie in the fact that the person employing the strategy called upon power or influence that he did not command. For example, a six year old's physical threats may be less compelling to a teacher than the threats of an armed gangster. Furthermore, the success or failure of inducement strategies is at least in part determined by the ways in which people are related to each other, and the positions they hold in relationship to sources of power and influence. For example, the threat of expulsion or poor grades is effective only with students who value (for whatever reason) school attendance.

The chief activity of the schools involves the inducement of others to behave in ways the schools and teachers define as good for them to behave. Schools, however, are related to sources of power and influence in ways which make the resources available to them to achieve this end both limited and proscribed. Unlike economic organizations, there is little in the way of financial rewards schools can offer (at least directly). Teachers are not given great financial rewards for even vastly different teaching performances, and in most schools, the idea of paying students carries with it the suggestion of moral taint. Schools do have some ability to inflict pain and suffering on participants, but their ability to use punitive measures is limited by law and custom. Though schools are sometimes compared to prisons, the comparison has more utility in the rhetoric of student radicals than in scientific analysis. To a great extent, the ability of the school to influence student behavior depends on the student's (and other participant's) acceptance of the school's definition of the good, the bad, and the desirable.[5]

The kind of involvement participants develop toward the

school will affect the types of inducement strategies that are likely to be used, as well as the extent to which those strategies used will be successful. In chapter 5, three different types of involvement were identified: moral, calculative, and alienative. It is now necessary to distinguish between and among types of inducement strategies also. Among the more important potential strategies of inducement are (1) coercive strategies, (2) remunerative strategies, (3) normative strategies, (4) social exchange strategies, and (5) psychological affective strategies.

COERCIVE STRATEGIES

Coercive power rests on the application, or the threat of application, of physical sanctions such as infliction of pain, deformity, or death; generation of frustration through restriction of movement; or controlling through force the satisfaction of needs such as those for food, sex, comfort and the like.[6]

Certain categories of students may be related to the school organization in ways that make likely the use of coercive inducement strategies. Some students may find life in school quite intolerable, and would not attend if it were not for compulsory attendance laws. For at least some of these students, school attendance alone is a form of coercion.[7] On the other hand, some students (including some who are alienated from school) would continue to attend, even if the laws compelling attendance were removed. For example, the value of peer interaction might be sufficient to induce some students to attend school, even if it were not sufficient to elicit desired performances while in school. Some students might find that family disapproval would be overwhelming, and therefore continue school attendance with or without *legal* compulsion. Compulsory attendance laws *are* coercive *only to some students*.

Compulsory attendance laws are not the only form of coercion available to schools. Corporal punishment is another form of coercion, as are detention, the requirement of hall passes (restricting movement), and specifying times to use restroom facilities (controlling through force, the need for comfort). In school settings the use of coercive strategies often takes on subtle characteristics. The complexity of the reward structure is such that the school is often able to make the absence of coercion something of a positive reward.[8] For example, the satisfaction of basic needs, such as the needs for elimination and water, becomes a privilege extended to those who behave properly. Students who *abuse* these privileges are denied the right to exercise them. By this peculiar logic, students are not denied water; water is a reward for behaving in the expected manner. Students are not denied access to the hall; they gain access to the hall as a privilege earned. By making coercion routine, the withdrawal of coercion becomes a reward.

It is in the nature of coercion, however, that its use tends to create an increasing need for its application. For example, in schools with mildly alienated students, the routine application of group punishment will likely cause more intensive alienation, thus increasing further the need for punitive measures. As Etzioni notes:

> Coercive power is probably the only effective power when the organization is confronted with highly alienated lower participants. If, on the other hand, it is applied to committed or only mildly alienated lower participants, it is likely to affect adversely such matters as morale, recruitment, socialization and communication, and thus to reduce effectiveness.[9]

The school's use of coercion is severely proscribed by both law and custom. Teachers can deny students privileges but few communities would tolerate the routine practice of denying *most* students access to bathrooms and water fountains.[10] Barbarisms applied to a few can be rationalized; barbarisms applied to many must be accounted for by other means. Schools may inflict pain on some, limit the mobility of others, and deny comfort to more, but there is always the danger that the routine application of these measures will escalate to the point that coercion goes beyond the bounds of law and custom. Therefore, even repressive schools must retain a character where (a) coercion is applied only to the few, and (b) the lack of coercion for the many is seen by most participants as a positive reward. If the school fails to retain this character, crisis may be precipitated. Even the most repressive schools are obliged to rely on voluntary compliance for the success of most inducement strategies. Compliance gained by coercive means is accepted as a necessary expedient, but not as a basis for routine practice. And when the coercive practices do become routine, they must be subtly disguised as *rewards*.

REMUNERATIVE STRATEGIES

Remunerative power is based on control over material resources and rewards through allocation of salaries and wages, commissions and contributions, "fringe benefits," services and commodities.[11]

Insofar as students are concerned, there are few ways that schools can use remunerative strategies to induce organizationally expected or required behavior. In the early elementary years, teachers may use small rewards (e.g., pencils, candy bars, and similar items) in ways that might be called remuneration. As children grow older, however, the few material rewards the school has to offer (such as letter sweaters) have more symbolic than material value. Indeed, even in the first grade, material rewards are probably more significant symbolically than they are materially. Some schools—and these are not many—have tried ideas like the token economy[12] as a way of gaining student compliance and performance. Some of the recent efforts in the area of behavior modification are characteristically more remunerative than are other school programs. However, giving students material rewards for exceptional performance (not to mention routine conformity) frequently carries with it connotations of bribery and moral taint. In most school settings it is assumed that students should be *intrinsically* motivated to achieve. To reward achievement with crass material prizes is thought by many to somehow diminish the intrinsic worth of education. Good students are those who learn because they see the inherent value of knowledge or so it is often argued. Even students who turn in outstanding performances on tests, but do so *only for the grade*, are valued less highly than those who do well "just because they should." It is probably significant, therefore, that token economies and behavior modification are more likely to be applied to students found to be difficult for schools to manage without coercion. More often than not, token economies are tried in so-called tough schools and behavior modification is reserved for students in remedial classes or groups.

The scarcity of remunerative power in school settings is also reflected in the relationship of teachers and administrators to school organizations. Until recent years, teachers who were thought to be motivated primarily by economic considerations were suspect to colleagues and superiors alike.[13] Even now there is a prevailing view that teachers should not teach "just for money."[14] The rise of militant professionalism and the growth of teachers unions have somewhat offset the more glaring aspects of this anti-remuneration syndrome. Characteristic dialogue in professional negotiation indicates, however, that many continue to believe that dedicated (and thereby morally preferable) teachers are not so concerned about their own offspring as about the children of others. There are many—in teaching and outside—who continue to feel that teachers should not be overly motivated by remunerative strategies. Indeed, one argument against merit pay for teachers (as opposed to standardized salary schedules) is that teachers will become too mercenary.

There are, however, some kinds of remunerative inducements to which teachers can respond without fear of disapproval. Basketball and football coaches are often given cars if they win state championships. Some communities provide outstanding teacher awards, and many include money with the award, but the recipient of the award would be wise to give thanks more for the honor than for the money. From time to time, administrators are in a position to reward teachers—financially—by providing summer employment, placing them in stipend-producing summer workshops, and similar fringe benefits. These inducements are freely used.

It is routinely accepted that administrators deserve more remuneration than do classroom teachers. This, in turn, induces some classroom teachers to seek administrative positions. In addition, school administrators often find that there are a number of fringe benefits to their own jobs that provide performance inducements. Some schools, for example, provide certain administrators with travel budgets, cars, entertainment allowances, and so on. Indeed, in large city systems, it is often difficult to distinguish between corporate executives and school superintendents. For the most part, however, remunerative power is severely limited in school settings, and school personnel are not likely to develop sophisticated strategies for employing what little remunerative power is available.[15]

NORMATIVE STRATEGIES

Normative power rests on the allocation and manipulation of symbolic rewards and deprivations through the employment of leaders, manipulation of mass media, allocation of esteem and prestige symbols, administration of ritual, and influence over the distribution of "acceptance" and "positive response."[16]

Schools rely heavily on normative power in their relationships with participants and outsiders. The social network of schools is shot through with elaborate mechanisms for manipulating various forms and degrees of normative rewards. Words like good and bad, right and wrong, appropriate and inappropriate dominate the language of the teachers' lounge and the classroom. Evaluative language is the language of schools. Much of the advice supervisors give to teachers, and professors give to student teachers, is advice on the appropriate means of distributing acceptance and positive response. In the classroom, much of the teacher's leadership function is one of allocating and manipulating the symbolic rewards of the system. Who shall get smiling faces and frowning faces on their papers in the first grade is replaced by who shall get A's and who shall get F's in the eighth grade. As Jackson notes, "Schools are basically evaluative settings. . . . It is not only what you do there but what others think of what you do that is important."[17] Though Jackson's attention was on the classroom, he was not mistaken in his use of the word *school*, for students are not the only subjects of evaluation. Teachers and administrators are evaluated almost as persistently as are the students.

Factory workers may be productive or efficient but teachers are good or competent. Foremen may be labeled as harsh or lenient, effective or ineffective, while principals are more likely to be labeled as dogmatic, permissive, democratic or authoritarian. One need be in school only a short while before it is clear that schools are places of moral certainty and rectitude. People are expected to know what is right and make an effort to do it. Those who do not know what is right, or who fail to try to do what is right, are likely to have their character, as well as their performance, assaulted. For instance, students who cannot add a sum of numbers but *try* are better than those who cannot add and refuse to take up pencil and paper. Teachers who have discipline trouble but do not hesitate to use coercion are better than teachers who have problems with classroom control and refuse to use coercive measures. Teachers who respond to threats to their authority by using coercion are tough, whereas those who allow their authority to erode rather than use coercion are soft. It is better to not have discipline trouble than to need to resort to coercion, but it is better to use coercion than to be judged as soft. *It is moral approbation, and the fear of moral approbation, that serves as the chief source of control in schools.* Teachers fear being called unprofessional, principals fear being called "soft," students fear being called bad, and one of the worst things teachers or students can be labeled is a "disruptive influence."

Sometimes young teachers are evaluated as soft, but their softness is attributed to "inexperience" (yet another moral term in an institution that values experience over training and competence) or immaturity. If softness is viewed as something a teacher will outgrow, or overcome with time, the flaw may be forgiven, but the teacher who announces that his refusal to be coercive has philosophical or psychological grounds may find himself losing status, and being denied other symbolic rewards. Students, too, tend to devalue teachers they come to identify as soft. One of the ways a teacher's peer may find out that discipline "problems" are present in the classroom, in fact, is that morally disapproving students report "what is going on."

The ability to uphold expectations through the use of normative strategies is largely dependent on moral integration within the organization. Participants must value and be positively committed to relevant areas of the social life of the school or these strategies will be ineffective.[18]

SOCIAL EXCHANGE STRATEGIES

Those who are in a position to exercise power are also in a position to make judgments about how that power will be exercised, or when to refrain from exercising the power they are legitimately entitled to exercise. For example, a teacher may refrain from sending a student from class for "talking back" even though the teacher might be authorized to expel students from his room for such behavior. The ability to give and not to give organizational rewards and punishments tends to accrue to those in authority still another source of influence: social exchange.[19] By distributing organizational rewards and punishments, an individual comes into a position where he is able to accumulate obligations from others that are of more personal and particularistic nature than are the more organizationally described obligations. *The power an individual has by virtue of position quickly translates into influence by virtue of performance in that position.*

No organization, and especially schools, could run effectively on the basis of the routine and impartial application of organizationally based rewards and punishments. Much that occurs in schools is too subtle and particular in nature to submit easily to the application of impersonal forms of inducement. Normative power has a tendency toward personalization and particularization, but even normative power cannot have the effect that more primary and basic relationships have in inducing one to accept the subtle meanings and covert drift of events that are present in the dynamics of human relations in organizations.

Social scientists generally are aware that there are significant differences between organizational power and personal influence, but the distinctions between the concepts often become blurred in analysis as well as in practice. There is much that goes on between the webbing of organizational life that can never be understood by reference to the formal structure of things. Conversely, however, much that goes on between the formal web of relationships is itself deeply imbedded in the fabric of the organization. For example, teachers have the legitimate right—at least in most schools—to call on any student in the class for an answer to a question, and students are under some obligation to respond. There is also some feeling among educators that teachers should call on all students, and should not be either unusually lenient or unusually demanding of any student. The idea of fairness dominates the thinking of teachers and students alike. Yet, it is clear that teachers do not call on all students in the same manner or to the same extent. Some students are called on more frequently than others, while some students are hardly ever asked a question by the teacher. Some students, when asked a question, may be given but a second to respond; others may be given much longer. Some students who respond inappropriately will be given a second chance; others will be immediately reprimanded or bypassed.[20]

To the uninitiated, all of this asking and not asking, responding and not responding may seem to be haphazard and random, but it is not so. Those who systematically observe classrooms find that predictable patterns of inducement and response occur in the classroom. Some, like Good and Brophy,[21] suggest that how the teachers respond to students may have to do with the teachers' assessment of the students' abilities. Others, while not denying the importance of expectations based on ability, find that simple structural arrangements like seating may have much to do with who gets how much attention.[22]

Some years ago George Homans wrote: "Influence over others is purchased at the price of allowing oneself to be influenced by others."[23] The nonrandom nature of teachers' "calling on" patterns may be attributable to this giving and taking of influence. For instance, the simple matter of where a child is seated may turn out not to be so simple a matter at all. Adams and Biddle[24] report that the action zone of the classroom—those areas of the classroom where students are most likely to initiate interaction or be called on—is confined to a very limited area in the room. "This area extends from the front of the room directly up the center line, diminishing in intensity the further away it is from the point of origin."[25] This area, according to Adams and Biddle, includes nearly all the students who initiate interaction, and all of those who are called on. Though the Adams and Biddle study was limited in scope, it does reinforce what every school boy and teacher have known for a long while: some students can avoid compliance with the demands of the teacher simply by sitting in the right place. Perhaps more important, those who sit in the "action zone" are in a good position to make their compliance and noncompliance more noticeable, especially to the teacher. Therefore, students in the action zone may be able to exert greater influence over the teacher, *in exchange* for submitting to the teacher's influence. Furthermore, those who sit in the action zone and do not comply may find their actions receiving even greater sanctions than will others who are on the periphery of the room.

Given the centrality of control in the classroom, the greatest exchange commodity available is compliance. If teachers lose control, they may lose their jobs. Thus, students who are in a position to determine the extent to which the teacher will control the flow of interaction are also in a position to demand special consideration from the teacher. Teachers and students may not consciously and overtly recognize these exchanges, but they are there and they are real. Furthermore, social exchange is not limited to the immediacy of classroom interaction. Students of good repute in the school are also students who have the respect of other teachers. If a student of good repute objects to a teacher's performance, the prestige loss to the teacher will probably be much greater than if a student with a less sterling reputation lodged a protest. Indeed, students who are held in low esteem by teachers generally might enhance the repute of a particular teacher by complaining about the teacher's classroom performance. Teachers, furthermore, are aware that students may talk about them to other teachers. Indeed, the threat is so great that in many schools, it is considered a breach of professional ethics for a teacher to discuss with students the performance of another teacher.[26] But when enough "good" students become so distressed with a teacher's performance as to lodge formal and informal protests, the teacher's school life is in jeopardy. The exchange influence this situation gives "good" students has not been empirically determined or verified, but it must be considerable.[27]

Given the high value schools place on control and compliance, even the more passive forms of noncompliance (e.g., ritualism) become subject to exchange value. Griffin[28] suggested that the grade of C should stand for confused and compliant. Though the remark was made in jest, it contains more than a bit of truth. Teachers find it much more difficult to penalize passive students than they do students who overtly refuse to comply with the teacher's or school's directives. In this instance, C is neither a reward nor a punishment, perhaps a suiting response to a neutral gesture like ritual performance. If the ritualistic student does not *really* do what is expected, at least he gets credit for making some effort to *appear* to be behaving appropriately.[29]

PSYCHOLOGICAL AFFECTIVE STRATEGIES

Among the most highly regarded and most often discussed inducement strategies in the repertoire of schools and teachers are those referred to here as psychological affective strategies. Psychological affective strategies square well with the view of teaching and school as an individualistic enterprise. Psychological affective strategies are those strategies most often associated with the tutorial model upon which so much teaching theory is based. Most "legitimate" teaching strategies, as Gage so plainly points out,[30] are assumed to be some form of psychological inducement. Students are assumed to respond personally and clinically to the teacher. The teacher is assumed to act toward the student in a personal and clinical fashion.

Psychological affective strategies rest on the assumption that the teacher—as a person—is socially significant to the student. In more general social contexts (e.g., relationships among faculty) the assumption is that there is a person-oriented relationship between the parties of the interaction, and that this relationship is sufficiently strong to make factors like personal loyalty and personal obligation sources of inducement. Psychological affective strategies are limited, almost by definition, to more primary relationships, and are usually not found in hierarchical or vertical relationships. Among other things, the successful application of psychological affective strategies depends on what Etzioni calls social commitment. "Social commitment rests on sensitivity to pressures of primary groups and their members (Riesman's 'other-directed')."[31] Teachers seldom distinguish between psychological affective strategies and normative strategies. There is, however, a subtle, and perhaps important, distinction between the teacher's rewarding a student by calling him a "good boy" as opposed to calling him a "good student." The lack of distinction betwen normative strategies and psychological affective ones, in fact, tends to blur the lines between a teacher's evaluation of a student's *performance* and the evaluation of a student's *character*. Students, like teachers, often become confused about the nature of the student-teacher relationship. This is particularly true in early elementary school. Often students respond to a teacher's normative inducements in a personalistic manner, and to a teacher's psychological affective inducements as if they were normative. This confusion can be deadly for the student and frustrating for the teacher.

By way of illustration, some teachers, even in the early years of grade school, use grades to encourage children to work harder. If the student defines the relationship with the teacher as a personalistic one, however, a low mark is not only a reflection of performance but also a reflection of self. To the teacher who may have thirty students, the significance of a low mark on one six weeks' report card may seem minor. To the first grade student, who has but *one* teacher, it may be the beginning of school failure. Or, the converse may occur. Sometimes teachers do treat youngsters in a special fashion because they develop a special affinity toward them. (For example, in middle class schools, well-meaning teachers may give special consideration to the one poverty-stricken child in class.) The child, however, may define the relationship in more instrumental terms, and respond to the teacher's inducements as normative rather than psychological affective. In this case, the child's failure to respond may be taken *by the teacher* as a personal rejection. Unlike the rejected student, however, the rejected teacher is in a position to become effectively punitive toward the child.

There is evidence that teachers in early elementary schools use many more normative and psychological affective strategies than do teachers in later years. In the very early years, psychological affective and normative strategies are probably the predominant strategies attempted. Could it be that the failures some students have in first and second grades relate to the teacher and students not establishing convergent definitions of the social relationships between them? The possibility is sufficiently interesting to be investigated, and the potential rewards of such investigation are sufficiently compelling to warrant some rather unrestrained speculation.

ADAPTATION[32]

Once an inducement has been emitted, the target group or individual is called on to respond to it. Frequently the response may be a counter inducement. Not only does the target population refuse to behave in the way indicated by the inducer, but the target person or group becomes a source of attempted counter influence. (This often happens when a teacher asks a question; the student asks the teacher to clarify the question, thereby placing the burden back on the teacher. The student *has* indicated willingness to conform, but has made conformity conditional on further action by the teacher.) Eventually, however, one or the other of the parties in the social interchange will adapt to the directives offered or the commands given. The form these adaptations take may vary, all the way from simple conformity (i.e., doing that which the inducer wants done) to rebellion (refusing to do what is required or requested). Both conformity and rebellion are means of adapting to inducements.

The nature of the inducement, its sources, and its direction go far to explain both the nature and consequences of conformity, and the nature and consequences of resistance. The case of conformity is rather clear. If a directive is followed, what will be done is contained in the directive, and those who follow the inducement will be rewarded or escape punishment, whichever the case may be. Rebellion is not so clear as conformity. In some instances rebellion is nothing more than a person in a position of power or influence indicating to those with less power or influence that he is unwilling to take any more direction from them. For example, students may ask the teacher to put a test off until the following day and the teacher may refuse. Rebellion from a teacher—whether momentary or long-term refusal to take influence from students—is in one sense a simple affirmation of authority. Everyone knows that teachers need not take influence from students, and teachers have sufficient power to enforce their intentions (at least in the short run) with or without the willing acceptance of the students. When students refuse to comply with the teacher's directives, however, the matter is quite different. The official structure does not provide students with sufficient authority to command the teacher's performance without some significant alterations in power relationships. Sometimes an individual student may refuse to take direction from the teacher, and though it may present a crisis, teachers can easily deal with such rebellion. At other times, however, students generate enough informal influence over the teacher's actions (e.g., through social exchange obligations or psychological affective strategies) that they come to feel that they are in a position to resist the teacher's directives. (This is not to say that they can or will try to exert positive inducements toward the teacher, for that takes even more power or influence.) For example, a teacher who is on shaky ground with the building principal because of weak discipline may find himself at the mercy of the class, precisely because the failure of students to follow the teacher's directives will be seen as further evidence of lack of control. The students know this as well as the teacher. Thus, the teacher gives a directive and students refuse to conform, perhaps on the assumption that the teacher will not make the resistance a public issue for fear of further jeopardizing his own position *vis à vis* the principal. Student awareness of the principal's judgment that the teacher is ineffective may decrease even further the power and influence available to the teacher. Indeed, students may come to a position where they can resist the teacher's influence. In a matter of time they may generate sufficient influence and form enough coalitions to be able to exert—with real effect—counter inducements against which even teacher resistance will not suffice.[33]

Because of the disproportionate amount of power and influence in the hands of teachers, student rebellion is seldom effective. When it is, it bodes poorly for the system, for it probably indicates an impending crisis of control in the community as well as in the classroom. Teacher rebellion, however, is a different matter. Unlike students, teachers are not temporary residents in the school. Many teachers stay in the same system and the same building for years. As many young principals know, established teachers are often in a position to generate sufficient personal influence to resist any inducements they choose not to follow. It is not that these teachers run the school; they just refuse to permit others to run *their* classrooms. There are many features about schools that contribute to the development of effective teacher resistance. Among the more pronounced of these features are the norm of the closed classroom door, the tendency of classrooms to develop systemlike qualities, and the general impropriety of giving or seeking information about what is going on in a classroom from any source other than the teacher.[34]

Overt rebellion and conformity are the extreme forms of reaction to inducement. Because of the hierarchical distribution of power and authority in schools, however, conformity is the most common mode of response to the requests of superordinates. Overt resistance to requests by superordinates is difficult to sustain in a system where power is so unevenly distributed. There are, however, other forms of resistance that are less dramatic, and perhaps more common in schools. Two of these are ritualism and retreatism. Jackson spells out in considerable detail the ritualistic form of much school behavior, a great deal of form but no content.[35] Students are instructed that all the blanks must be filled in (even if you don't know the right answer); that current events happen on Friday (so cut something out of the newspaper); and that extra papers (even of inferior quality) earn extra credit. Students and teachers learn to go through the forms, neither resisting nor really conforming. While conformity calls for active involvement, ritualism is more passive. The critics of schools—particularly the more shrill critics—complain of the conformist nature of schools. It is often not conformity to which they have reference. It is ritualism.

Teachers (and administrators) also engage in significant amounts of ritual behavior. Averaging grades often takes on a ritual quality, as does the faculty meeting (often more appropriately called the principal's meeting). Even democracy becomes routine and ritualized. In many schools, votes are taken on all matters of policy, but there are never dissenters. As one principal said after long discussion in a faculty meeting, "O.K., democracy time is over; it's time to vote."[36]

Retreatism is another way of resisting inducements. One simply withdraws from the area of social action where unwanted inducements are likely to come into play. Some students, for example, involve themselves as little as possible in school-related events and thus avoid concerning themselves with inducements emanating from school sources.[37]   In the classroom, students learn to sit outside of the action zone (retreat), and when public performance is called for, turn in a ritual performance (e.g., the C student referred to by Griffin).   Teachers, too, learn to withdraw from potential encounters with authority.   Indeed, entire curricula can take on a retreatist quality.   Rather than be controversial to any segment of the community, the curriculum becomes gray, bland, and harmless to all.

SOME ADDITIONAL REMARKS

The thrust of this chapter may make it seem that the school is a place of power brokers, each trading the lives of others—something of a Hobbesian world.   To some extent it is that, but it is also more than that.   The school and classrooms are filled with people, each trying to make life space for themselves, to control the flow of their own lives, or at least the flow of minute-to-minute social behavior, particularly when that behavior impinges on them.   It is not only in matters of discipline (what is commonly called management) that this pull and haul of power, influence, and adaptation occurs.   It is in all areas of school life where the aim is to induce people to behave in ways they would not behave if the inducement were not present.   Thus, power, influence, and adaptation are deeply woven into the academic and intellectual webbing of schools, for the aim of the school is to "produce" learning that would not occur without schools.   In order to accomplish this end it is necessary for teachers and schools to induce students to behave in ways which seem to influence learning.

NOTES

1. Philip W. Jackson, *Life in Classrooms* (New York: Holt, Rinehart and Winston, Inc., 1968), pp. 159–177.

2. Christopher Jencks et al., *Inequality: A Reassessment of the Effect of Family and Schooling in America* (New York: Basic Books, Inc., 1972).

3. Jackson, *Life in Classrooms.*

4. This usage parallels definitions of power found in the literature. See, for example, Amitai Etzioni, *A Comparative Analysis of Complex Organizations: On Power, Involvement, and Their Correlates* (New York: The Free Press of Glencoe, Inc., 1961). Power, however, is usually defined in terms of ability. Inducement, as the term is used here, is an *effort* to use power or influence.

5. In Etzioni's typology of organizations, schools are considered as dual organizations, with the primary characteristics typified as normative, and secondary characteristics as coercive. Ibid., pp. 40–67.

6. Ibid., p. 5. Excerpts from *A Comparative Analysis of Complex Organizations,* copyright © 1961 by The Free Press of Glencoe, Inc., are reprinted by permission of Macmillan Publishing Co., Inc.

7. To use the existence of compulsory school laws as evidence that the relationship between schools and *all* students is coercive is to miss an important point. School laws are effectively coercive only for those students who do not attend school in response to other forms of inducement.

8. Some school officials become quite ingenious in making students feel that they are being rewarded when coercion is withdrawn. Truly repressive school environments have the quality of Orwell's *Animal Farm.*

9. Etzioni, *Comparative Analysis of Complex Organizations,* p. 13.

10. Corwin reports on a particularly caustic note to teachers in which the principal warned teachers that the building was much too noisy and that more careful policing needed to be done. The principal's closing comment is revealing. "For goodness' sake, don't eliminate children's water breaks to cut down on noise. In this kind of weather you must water them." To say the least, the principal's remarks show something of the *Animal Farm* qualities referred to earlier (without, unfortunately, the subtlety of the Orwellian intent). In addition, it shows some sensitivity (if that word is at all appropriate) to the fact that coercion is limited in even repres-

sive environments. See Ronald G. Corwin, *A Sociology of Education: Emerging Patterns of Class, Status, and Power in the Public Schools* (New York: Appleton-Century-Crofts, 1965), pp. 306–307 for a full text of the letter.

11. Etzioni, *Comparative Analysis of Complex Organizations*, p. 5.

12. Token economies have been tried in prisons, schools, and summer camps with mixed success. The idea is that participants receive token rewards for appropriate behavior, which they can then exchange for something of "real value." Recent court decisions probably make the token economy system illegal in prisons, but whether the ruling applies to schools and students is not clear. The ruling referred to had to do with behavior modification programs undertaken in Project START (special treatment and rehabilitative training). These projects were declared unconstitutional. Among other things, the judge suggested that the program constituted cruel and unusual punishment (*New York Times*, Feb. 10, 1974). Behavior modification is *much more widespread* in schools than the more complex token economy systems.

13. For evidence that this was the case—and to some extent remains the case—one need only consult any good history of education text. For example, see R. Freeman Butts and Lawrence A. Cremin, *A History of Education in American Culture* (New York: Holt, Rinehart and Winston, Inc., 1953).

14. Given the salaries most teachers are paid, there is little danger that this norm is likely to be seriously violated.

15. One of the most perplexing things about school reform is that those who run schools are always convinced that what they need is more money and they will do the job better. Yet, when grants come their way, most school administrators find it necessary to hire consultants to tell them how the money should be spent.

16. Etzioni, *Comparative Analysis of Complex Organizations*.

17. Jackson, *Life in Classrooms*, p. 10.

18. Ibid., p. 12.

19. Though this discussion has been influenced by social exchange theory, the concept of exchange is not used in the restrictive fashion that typifies much of the work in this area.

20. Good and Brophy have done extensive research in this area. Much of this research is reported in Thomas L. Good and Jere E. Brophy, *Looking in Classrooms* (New York: Harper & Row, Publishers, Inc., 1973).

21. Ibid.

22. Raymond S. Adams and Bruce J. Biddle, *Realities of Teaching: Explorations with Video Tape* (New York: Holt, Rinehart and Winston, Inc., 1970), p. 49.

23. George C. Homans, *Social Behavior: Its Elementary Forms* (New York: Harcourt, Brace & World, Inc., 1961).

24. Adams and Biddle, *Realities of Teaching*, p. 49.

25. Ibid., p. 50.

26. Corwin, *Sociology of Education*, pp. 301–340.

27. Many astute observers have made observations relevant to this argument, e.g., Willard Waller, *The Sociology of Teaching* (New York: John Wiley & Sons, Inc., 1932, reprinted 1967), and Corwin (see preceding note).

28. Professor Griffin was for many years a member of the faculty of the Department of Education at The Ohio State University. As a teacher of social studies teachers, he spent many hours observing classroom teachers in action.

29. In one classroom visit, a teacher was overheard to remark, "I don't care if you study, but you had better look like it."

30. N. L. Gage, "Paradigms for Research on Teaching," in *Handbook of Research on Teaching*, ed. N. L. Gage (Chicago: Rand McNally & Company, 1963), pp. 94–141.

31. Etzioni, *Comparative Analysis of Complex Organizations*, p. 11.

32. The discussion here roughly follows a line of argument presented by Robert K. Merton, *Social Theory and Social Structure*, 1968 enlarged edition (Glencoe, Ill.: The Free Press of Glencoe, 1968), pp. 193–211.

33. It is interesting that educators seldom consider the reciprocal nature of classroom influence. Teachers lose control; students are never seen as gaining control. One cannot help but wonder why organizations that purport to produce leaders become more repressive when there is evidence that they have been successful.

34. See Corwin, *Sociology of Education*.

35. Jackson, *Life in Classrooms*, especially chapter 1, "The Daily Grind."

36. Personal observation by the author.

37. For some idea of the degree to which students differ in their participation in school life, see Roger G. Barker et al., *Big School— Small School: Studies of the Effects of High School Size upon the Behavior and Experiences of Students* (Midwest Psychological Field Station, University of Kansas, 1962).

8

Organizational Impact
on Classroom Performances

The comparative analysis of schools and the linkage of school social structures to curriculum decisions, inducement strategies, and adaptation lead logically to the formulation of an organizational theory of instruction. The general framework of such a theory is both implicit and explicit in parts of the preceding discussion. In this chapter and the chapters that follow, it is intended that more precise expression be given these formulations. Before proceeding with this task, however, several cautionary remarks seem in order.

First, there is a tendency for a structural view of schools to seem deterministic and mechanistic. It is easy to assume that the demands of social structure leave little room for human variation and individual initiative. Such a view represents what has been called an oversocialized view of man.[1] Individuals can and do act in ways that are contrary to the structural requirements of the systems in which they live. Furthermore, individuals participate in many systems, not just one system (e.g., the child must live in the family as well as in the school). Indeed, it is precisely because human beings participate in many groups, all of which make claims on them, that life in society is as dynamic as it is. Even when the individual behaves in a way which indicates that he is autonomous from the structure, he must take the structure into account. In fact, even in the exercise of autonomy the system shapes and molds how one will act. For example, a teacher in a type 33 school (bureaucratic, alienative, product-oriented, tight) may rebel against the rigidity of the system and attempt to generate the ability to exercise psychological affective influence with students. It is possible for the teacher to do so, but in the process the teacher would become vulnerable to organizational sanctions. Though he may develop elaborate evasion strategies and create a classroom environment that is relatively isolated from the rest of the school, the amount of energy that must be expended in maintaining the boundaries of the classroom may become overwhelming. The tightness of the organization is in itself a constant threat to classroom autonomy, and any student or teacher who objects to the teacher's personal style of leadership can find ready allies in the outer system. So long as the teacher lives in the bureaucratic-tight situation, he must deal with bureaucratic requirements like departmental tests. Thus it is that while individual teachers can make a difference, even in the most oppressive of environments, the social structure of the school will make a difference in how teachers come to have personal contact with their students.

A second cautionary remark is that the theoretical propositions set forth in this book remain yet to be tested empirically. The data now available do not refute the propositions set forth, but little research has been done that is directly addressed to the theoretical propositions set forth here. Thus, while the theory is "verifiable" (i.e., known facts or generalizations do not seem to contradict it), it is not verified in the sense that research specifically generated by the theory has been undertaken.[2]

A final caution is that theories are statements about classes of data and the relationships among them. Theories are not statements about individual incidents or unique instances. It is probably true that no school will fit perfectly into any one category of the typology presented in chapter 7 any more than any one teacher will evidence the precise inducement patterns that seem implicit in those structures. For example, a school that is extremely high in structural tightness and bureaucracy may be only marginally leaning toward a product orientation or student alienation. The function of theory, however, is to account for a range of alternatives. Theory cannot be tied to a specific event. This condition does not detract from theory; rather, it gives it added power, for it is in the ability to generalize that theory serves its basic function.

SOME ASSUMPTIONS

Implicit or explicit in the analysis and discussion that have preceded this chapter are a series of assumptions about the relationship of school organizations to the classroom behavior of teachers and students. An organizational theory of instruction, at least the theoretical formulations presented in this book, must be based on such assumptions. Therefore, it seems appropriate to risk some repetition in order to bring the more relevant of these together in one place. Some of the more central of these assumptions are the following:

1. The school is a complex social organization.
2. The organizational structure of the school, particularly the mode of organization and the students' commitment and boundary position, is systematically related to the patterns of inducement and adaptation that typify a school or classroom.
3. Patterns of inducement and adaptation are among the chief determinants of the social and intellectual environments of schools and classrooms.
4. The social and intellectual environments of school and classrooms place limits on, and provide opportunities for, the attainment of alternative instructional goals.
5. Therefore, the ways in which schools are organized are directly related to patterns of classroom instruction and thus to what can and will be learned in school.

CURRICULAR AND INSTRUCTIONAL GOALS: ORGANIZATIONAL IMPLICATIONS

In the later 1950's and early 1960's the federal government provided funds for the purpose of developing new curricular materials for use in secondary schools. Some of the most impressive of these materials were produced in the areas of biological science (BSCS) and the social sciences—for example, the High School Geography Project (HSGP) and Sociological Resources for the Social Studies (SRSS). Most of these materials have as one of their goals the development—in students—of a scientific attitude toward knowledge, and skill in the use of some of the basic tools and modes of scientific inquiry. The sociological curricular material puts it thus: "Our goal is reliable knowledge—knowledge that holds up against rigorous testing. . . ."[3] In such materials, theoretically at least, the source of authority lies in the data collected or presented. Authority does not reside in a person. Judgments of what is reliable knowledge are submitted to the test of public verification, testing ideas with facts, and so on.

Materials like those produced by SRSS and BSCS, if they are to be properly implemented in the classroom, would require that both the teacher and the students submit themselves to the authority of evidence, and that when opinions, beliefs, or supposed forms of knowledge violate the requirements of evidence, those who hold the contradictory beliefs would be exposed to knowledge-based normative sanctions from others in the classroom. Indeed, in the inquiry-oriented classroom, the most appropriate inducements for both teachers and students would be normative inducements related to the acceptance of the principles of reason, rational argumentation, open inquiry, the right of refutation, and so on—the open classroom atmosphere so vaunted by those committed to reflective examination and inquiry approaches to instruction.

In the bureaucratically organized school, however, authority resides in the office, not in special or superior knowledge. Thus, it is difficult for teachers in the bureaucratically organized school to shift the basis of classroom authority in a fashion that is adequate to meet the requirements of the goals implicit or explicit in some of the inquiry-oriented curricular materials. Both teachers and students perceive as legitimate the expectation that teachers—by virtue of their office—are the final sources of authority on issues of content and debate. Thus, in some classes, what passes for inquiry is really little more than students trying to guess what is going on in the teacher's mind. Frequently, in these kinds of situations the teacher will engage in much manipulative behavior, often using social exchange and psychological affective inducements rather than normative ones—perhaps in an effort to be "indirect." But the fact remains that students and teachers continue to operate out of a structural framework which assumes that intellectual and social authority resides in an office. Sometimes even less satisfactory results may occur. Some teachers come to feel that there is a need to shift the authority from themselves to the students. Perhaps because teachers are unaware of the need to shift the basis of authority from a position base to a knowledge base or perhaps because in bureaucracies authority so "logically" resides in an office, the teacher may delegate some of his authority to the position of student. Thus, students and teachers adopt the attitude that, by virtue of delegation of authority (the new freedom), the student's opinion is now "equal" to the opinion of the teacher and all students' opinions are equal. Thus, bureaucratic authority has been made more diffuse, *but* the basis of authority remains position-related. The end result is that many students come away from their new "inquiry" classes with the attitude that one opinion is as good as another, and critics come away from these class discussions with the feeling they have witnessed an exchange of ignorance.

The curricular goals of many of the materials created during the 1960's are antithetical to the structure of bureaucratic-tight schools. Open inquiry cannot be taught in a repressive environment. Children cannot be coerced into thoughtfulness, any more than they can come to a better understanding of themselves and their own beliefs through a process of transferring their loyalties from their parents to a charismatic teacher. Even if the teacher is able to maintain some personal leadership, through the use of psychological affective and social exchange strategies, he is not likely to foster inquiry or reflection. Both psychological affective strategies and social exchange strategies insist on loyalty to person rather than loyalty to evidence and ideas. Intellectual autonomy is not the product of shifting loyalties from systems to people or from people to systems. Sincere seeking of reliable knowledge does not lead hither and yon, dependent on which position-related authority can generate enough power or influence to carry the day or the argument. Public verification is not the same thing as consensus. The authority of an opinion or belief does not hinge on the organizational position of its sponsor. The authority of ideas in the classroom is the authority of evidence and reason, not the authority of social power and influence.

At a less esoteric level, the ways schools are organized often make even the cursory and mechanical aspects of implementing new curricular materials and new curricular goals difficult—if not impossible. Some of the more calculative students, for example, may be more interested in learning those "facts" they need to pass the college boards than in systematically inquiring into the issues of concern to biologists or chemists.[4] In addition, some of the curricular materials that have as their goal "teaching the structure" of the disciplines may be appropriate in schools with students who are morally committed to the values of traditional academic education. But it is unlikely that students who are alienated from those values are likely to find more appeal in "inquiring" into biology than in being told didactically about biology. It may be, in fact, that in schools with significant alienated populations the progressive dictum of the child-centered curriculum, or a curriculum centered on the problems of the child, is the only viable solution. However, to accomplish this would require dramatic change in the structures of many schools. Unfortunately (assuming the analysis presented thus far is accurate), it is likely that schools with alienated students will drift toward bureaucracy, structural tightness, and product orientation. If this is the case, and an examination of inner-city schools suggests it probably is, much conscious effort will need to be given to reversing the "normal" course of events before new goals and materials can be successfully introduced.

POWER, INFLUENCE, AND ADAPTATION IN THE CLASSROOM

Inside the structure of the school, students and teachers live most of their school lives in classrooms. What they do there and how they do what they do determine what will be learned in school. It is now time to become even more microscopic and describe some of the dynamics of power, influence, and adaptation and how teachers and students enact their classroom roles. Cohen writes:

> It is most unwise to use a simple uni-directional causal model to characterize the classroom, for example, teachers affect students through what they say, how they question, how they explain, and through the use of curriculum materials. Studies of the classroom as a complex social system suggest that cause and effect can run in several directions. Students have effects on the teacher, who in turn affects the learning of the student. Students have effects on each other; the informal structure produces differential treatment of students by the teacher.[5]

Most of the empirical research on power, influence, and adaptation in the classroom has been based on sociometric data. Though these data tend to support the general line of reasoning presented here, they were not collected for the express purpose of testing hypotheses drawn from a theory of school organizations.[6] With the exception of the work of Adams and Biddle,[7] there is scant observational data directly relevant to the discussion at hand. What seems to be the case is that most who study classrooms are convinced that power, influence, and compliance structures are significant features of the classroom, that teachers are not the only sources of influence in the classroom; but precise behavioral descriptions of power, influence, and adaptation structures are difficult to locate, and systematic analysis of classroom power structures is almost totally lacking. Therefore, the best that can be done is describe what seems likely to be the situation, using available theoretical formulations to structure what empirical data there are, and remembering always Waller's caution about the dangers of going too far beyond common sense.

THE TEACHER AS ORGANIZATIONAL SPOKESMAN

The teacher's function as organizational spokesman and the behaviors that are related to that function have often been overlooked or subjected to biased (and negative) interpretation. The cult of personality that typifies so much educational thought apparently precludes many from accepting this function as legitimate. The fact is, however, that most of the teacher's day is likely to be taken up in performing organizationally prescribed functions. Frequently, the first activity the high school teacher will engage in each morning is the reading of the daily announcements from a script prepared by central office personnel. The next activities are likely to be taking the daily roll, collecting lunch money, and similar organizationally prescribed duties. Furthermore, teachers, particularly high school teachers, may be *required* to have a fixed number of test scores as a basis for the six weeks' average, a conventional number seeming to be one score per week. This means that the teacher will need to give from 5 to 20 percent of classroom time to testing students. This is compounded by the folkways of some student populations, which insist that reviews must always precede tests, and discussion of the test follow immediately after its administration.[8] Though no accurate data are available on how much time teachers spend administering tests, reviewing for tests, and discussing test results afterward, the figure would likely be astounding. In addition, in the capacity of organizational spokesman, the teacher is in a position of informing students about the stated school rules—even if the teacher finds the rules personally repugnant—assuring that he (the teacher), does not create a breach in the wall of colleagual consensus and solidarity that seems, in many schools, to characterize the relationships among teachers and students.[9]

In carrying out the functions of organizational spokesman, the teacher is likely to be required to rely on the normative power available from the system; but with alienative and calculative students, the effectiveness of normative strategies is always problematic. As many beginning teachers quickly learn, alienative and calculative students are sometimes less than responsive to the enthusiasm of beginning a new day or new school year, and are likely to be derisive when the building principal delivers his "Magic of September" speech in the first school assembly. It usually takes considerable moral involvement to participate fully in some of the rituals of school, and without such involvement, rituals are easy subjects of ridicule. When the moral symbols of the school's authority lose their compelling qualities, the teacher's function as organizational spokesman is difficult to maintain without coercion. Furthermore, the more alienated students are, the more the school is likely to require of the teacher in the way of organization representation (e.g., hall duty, patrolling restrooms, "guarding" cafeterias), and thus the more likely is the teacher to be forced to use coercive measures to uphold the authority of the school. And even though the teacher's use of coercion takes place *outside* the classroom, it is likely to have effects in the classroom. Eventually the teacher's out-of-class behavior may lead to a repressive atmosphere in the classroom.

THE TEACHER AS ENFORCER

From the preceding discussion it is probably clear that the teacher's functions as organizational spokesman and as enforcer are difficult to separate. Various observers of the school and teachers' behavior in schools have pointed to the teacher's role as disciplinarian, policeman, guardian of the public morals, and dominant authority as some of the more salient characteristics of the relationship between the teacher and the student.[10]   In the capacity of enforcer the teacher is called upon to uphold the rules of the organization, to take note of violations of those rules, and to assure they are conformed with in an acceptable manner.   In assuring conformity, the teacher has available to him the full range of organizationally available power.   In some situations, however, this power is not very great.   In study halls, for example, the teacher assigned to the role of monitor may find that the only way of enforcing the rules of silence, order, and propriety is to rely on coercive measures such as expulsion from the room, special seating arrangements, and detention.   For the most part, order in study halls is probably enforced by the willing compliance of positively involved students, and the overt coercion of the negatively involved.   Many schools, therefore, have taken up the practice of employing paraprofessional study hall monitors, who *ostensibly* relieve the trained teacher for more productive work.   Among the reasons for removing teachers from study halls is the recognition that the coercive measures teachers are required to use there may spill over into the classroom.   In the long run, the relationship between teachers and students cannot be typified by normative sanctions and positive involvement in the classroom, and coercive sanctions and alienation in other parts of the school.   Eventually one or the other pattern will come to dominate, and the unfortunate aspect is that coercion usually wins out—or so it seems.

Even within the classroom the teacher is often called on to be organizational enforcer, upholding rules that are not considered particularly germane to the setting.   For example, teachers may not be permitted to admit a student to the room who is tardy without first sending the student to the principal's office.   Frequently teachers are expected to enforce bans on gum chewing, flowing shirttails, feet on the desk, and so on.   Conflicts between *a* teacher and *a* student over these rules can often substantially disrupt a class.   Indeed, such conflicts may cause other students to reject the teacher's authority and encourage the teacher to move from reliance on normative and psychological affective strategies to reliance on coercive measures. Should this occur, the teacher will probably come to prize student retreatism as much as conformity, for at least confrontation and disruption are avoided.

THE TEACHER AS EVALUATOR

The evaluative quality of school life has already been noted, and little more need be said about the subject. What is important here is that the teacher, in spite of personal preference, training, or inclination, is unlikely to escape the expectation that he evaluates students, in terms of both their performance and their character. Teachers often attempt to escape the more onerous and personalistic aspects of this task by becoming increasingly bureaucratic (some say objective) in their decision making. By setting up standards beforehand and by giving so-called objective tests (multiple choice, true-false, and so on), teachers can create the fiction that "students earn the grades they get, the teacher does not give them." Other teachers try to escape the business of evaluating by giving all A's. All this practice accomplishes is to relocate the debilitating effects of grading from students who would have failed to those who "need" success.

Grading is not the only kind of evaluation that occurs in school. The faculty room is, as Boocock[11] points out, a place where teachers come to smoke, drink coffee, and gossip— primarily about students and administrators. The offhand, evaluative statements made by teachers in the teachers' lounge probably have more impact than the permanent data records. Furthermore, it is in the teachers' lounge that teachers come to learn whether their "objective" judgment of a student is accurate. Suppose, for example, that a beginning teacher gives his first test and finds that his students are all doing very well, but the more experienced teachers tell him his class is "below average." It will be the unusual beginning teacher who does not come to believe that his first test was too easy and that his standards were too low. This, perhaps, is one of the reasons beginning teachers are often advised by their teacher friends to remain silent about their evaluations of students and classes until they are more sure of themselves.

THE TEACHER AS ORGANIZATIONAL MEDIATOR

Blau writes: "To administer a social organization according to purely technical criteria of rationality is irrational, because it ignores the nonrational aspects of social conduct."[12] The emphasis of schools on rules, and of teachers on objectivity and rationality, often hides what Blau has called "bureaucracy's new face."[13] If students tried to perform according to the official rules, particularly in later school years, and if teachers tried to enforce all these rules, it is doubtful that the organizations could survive. Indeed, there are those who use rule obedience in an organization as a way of compelling changes in the official structure. Frequently, for example, a slowdown strike is nothing more than employees "going by the book." However, rule violation, in schools and elsewhere, is not a random, idiosyncratic phenomenon. Teachers must teach the "right thing to do" and also the *right way to do the "wrong" thing*. Systematic evasion is as much a part of the life of the school as it is in other social organizations.

The commonsense observation of teachers and students concerning the first few weeks of school as being a time of feeling out the situation probably is in part tied to the need for students and teachers to develop ways of symbolically communicating what "disapproved" behavior is *really not* disapproved, or is at least unlikely to be sanctioned. For example, few teachers will tolerate "cheating," but through cues, subtle hints, and knowing nods, students come to understand the fine line between cheating and cooperation with peers. One of the more important tasks the teacher has in mediating between the organization to the student is to communicate what is "really expected" in nonverbal ways. Students who are less socially aware or less sophisticated may find themselves at a disadvantage in picking up on what is really going on around them. Indeed, some students may find that teachers and students treat them as behavior problems precisely because they try to comply with the official rules.[14] For example, students who try to read an entire assignment instead of skimming may find themselves falling farther and farther behind. Students who only give answers that they are "sure of" on objective tests may find themselves penalized for not taking advantage of the laws of probability.

In performing the function of organizational mediator—and some teachers refuse to perform this function—teachers must rely heavily on psychological affective strategies and social exchange. Students must pick up the subtle nuances of meaning that can only be understood in the more intimate setting of the "ingroup," and those who are not so privileged may never really understand what is happening. Even those who are "in on the know" may be only vaguely aware of what is really taking place. Teachers, for example, are often shocked by objective data on their classroom performances which indicate that they are verbally communicating with very few students, or that they are talking considerably more than they think. Even more shocking to teachers is the fact that they sometimes permit certain students to dominate and control other students and to control the teacher as well.

THE TEACHER AS INTELLECTUAL GUIDE

The role of the teacher as intellectual guide has had considerable attention. Sometimes the teacher's functions in this capacity are referred to as mediator of learning, facilitator of student growth, gentle persuader, question formulator, and source of information. Regardless of the label, however, it is this function for which teachers are, officially at least, employed. It is to fulfill this function that teachers are submitted to courses in teaching methods, educational psychology, and curriculum planning. It is with the intention of promoting learning that lesson plans are developed, and that teachers develop their strategies of teaching. There are few who really doubt that this is the most important aspect of teaching. As Havighurst and Neugarten put it:

> The teacher's main role in relation to pupils, indeed the most significant of all his roles, is that of *mediator of learning*. In this role, he transmits knowledge and directs the learning process. In somewhat different terms, the main role of the teacher is to induce socially valued change in his pupils. This is at once the crux of the teaching profession and the most important criterion of the teacher's success.[15]

Most of the research on the teacher's role performance in the classroom has been directed toward understanding the teacher's function as intellectual or learning guide. How the role performance of the teacher affects student learning is the single most dominant research question dealt with by classroom analysts.

There is considerable evidence that the teacher's role performance, if it is to be effective and conducive to learning, must place heavy reliance on normative and psychological affective inducement strategies. Yet, the other functions of the teacher and the structure of the school often make these strategies difficult to bring to bear in the actual dynamics of the classroom. As Etzioni[16] rightly observes, the kind of relationship that is conducive to psychological affective strategies (Etzioni calls it social power) is horizontal. He suggests that superordinate-subordinate relationships usually do not develop the necessary bases from which social power can be generated. The typical teacher-student relationship is a superordinate-subordinate one, at least in bureaucratic schools, and sometimes in professionally oriented schools. Furthermore, in schools where the goals of instruction have little or no positive attraction to students, the teacher is hard put to use normative strategies. Contradictions and antagonisms between the structure of the school and the kinds of inducement strategies implied by contemporary teaching theories may explain why many teachers find existing theories of instruction irrelevant to their daily chores. In terms of most existing theories of teaching, the predominant role of the teacher is that of intellectual guide, and the basic strategies the teacher should use are normative and psychological affective. Yet, schools are frequently organized in ways which make it difficult to use successfully either psychological affective strategies or normative strategies. Indeed, the role of the teacher as intellectual guide is often overwhelmed by the kinds of relationships the teacher must develop to carry out his functions as organizational spokesman, evaluator, and enforcer.

STUDENT CLASSROOM PERFORMANCES

Amazingly little is known about the classroom performances and roles of students. The most sophisticated work on student roles and student influence, at least until recently, has been done under the direction or influence of those like Moreno,[17] who are interested in sociometry. In recent years there has been an increased interest in "classroom ecology," and some anthropological techniques have been applied to the study of the classroom.[18] Some researchers are beginning to take advantage of video tape as a research device, and, as Adams and Biddle[19] demonstrate, data from video tapes of classrooms combined with sensitivity to concepts from role theory and social psychology can provide provocative hypotheses about the role structure of the classroom. The fact remains, however, that in spite of some promising starts and provocative leads, most of the data on student classroom roles come largely from impressionistic sources: reports from untrained observers, novels, participant testimonials, and inferences from data collected for purposes other than the study of student role performance and classroom behavior (e.g., studies of teacher behavior).

Any effort to discuss systematically the classroom performance and roles of students must, therefore, go beyond the existing empirical data and move into the area of informed speculation. The centrality of student performance to an organizational theory of instruction provides a warrant for engaging in such speculation here. The primary discipline that must be imposed on such speculations is that they do not violate the available data and are consistent with what is known about social life.

STUDENT CONTROL OF TEACHERS

The centrality of the teacher in the life of the classroom and the research on classroom influence structures frequently distract attention from the reciprocal quality of the relationship between teachers and students. Even in superordinate-subordinate relations as extreme as those of slave and master, the subordinate may exercise some degree of control over the superordinate.[20] As the earlier discussion of students' boundary threats and the nature of social exchange strategies suggest, there are probably differences in the degree to which students are able to exert influence over their teachers.

Many observers have noted that some students get more of the teacher's time than do other students. Unfortunately, given the clinical view that dominates educational research, little attention has been given to the possibility that this giving of time has something to do with the nature of the student's position in the influence structure of the school or the classroom. Rather, most explanations of these differentiations are made in terms of the teacher's assessment of some psychological attribute of the student, such as ability, need for tutoring, or personal value. It is likely, however, that teachers respond to the influence of students as frequently as students respond to the influence of teachers. Furthermore, it seems likely that students develop strategies for dealing with teachers, and for inducing teachers to behave in ways that they, the students, see as desirable. Adams and Biddle suggest this possibility when they write: "Children obviously play games with teachers."[21] Students, like teachers, have access to power and influence, and it is naive to assume that students employ power and influence only in relationship to their peers. Indeed, in one recent experiment, students were taught to use behavior modification techniques on their teachers, and the results were surprisingly convincing.[22]

Among some of the more obvious kinds of controlling performances students may engage in are those of the supporting actor,[23] the strategic deviant, and the director. As a supporting actor, the student is aware of what the teacher wants and is willing and able to provide the information or performance the teacher might require. Frequently, teachers use supporting actors to discipline other students; that is, the teacher asks a question to which a student is unable to respond and then turns immediately to the supporting actor for the right answer. By playing the role of the supporting actor, some students are able to generate considerable social exchange influence with the teacher. The role of the supporting actor *may* place a student at a disadvantage with peers (e.g., the teacher's pet), but a socially sophisticated student may be able to use the influence he has with the teacher to generate reciprocal influence with peers. For example, a student whose supporting performances are valued by the teacher may be able to stall the teacher from giving an unwanted test by communicating to the teacher that he (the supporting student), too, is unprepared. From time to time, however, a socially unsophisticated student may become too obviously "aware" and cause embarrassment for himself, his classmates, and the teacher. The teacher's caution that "I always see the same hands" or that other people should have a chance may be a signal that the claim to the role of supporting actor is not honored. Peer sanctions of a too obvious supporting performance include such things as name-calling, chiding, and exclusion from desired group activities.

One of the more interesting student controls over teacher behavior is the performance of the strategic deviant. Given the perceptions of the typical classroom teacher, it is commonly assumed that the failure of students to respond to a teacher's inducements is an individual and idiosyncratic phenomenon. For example, if a teacher asks a question and a student is unable or unwilling to respond, it is usual to assume that the failure of response results from the student's not knowing the answer. If a student dozes off in class, it is usually assumed to be because the student is tired, bored, or personally wants to insult the teacher. These individually based factors may be the appropriate explanation for many individual failures to adapt to a teacher's inducement strategies. Probably more often than teachers and researchers now suspect, however, what appears to be an individual failure to respond to the teacher in an appropriate and expected manner is the result of the student's position in the social structure of the school and the classroom and the expectations that impinge on him as a result of his being in that position. It is in this latter situation that the behavior manifested by students is appropriately labeled "strategic deviance." Sometimes very able students find that the teacher's inducements are pushing them into a supporting actor role. If the student continues to respond to the teacher in the manner the teacher expects of him, he may find his position within the peer structures of the class compromised. Thus, the student may intentionally (though perhaps not consciously) indicate that he is not prepared or may intentionally do poorly on a test. By engaging in strategic deviancy, the student may be trying to redefine the relationship between himself and the teacher so that the teacher will have less control over him, and consequently the student will have more control. Another, more directly controlling form of strategic deviancy is the tendency of some students to "change the subject." Some students become quite adept at this procedure and gain support from peers for such activities.

That some students come to be expected—by their peers—to be able to change the course of classroom interaction seems clear. Furthermore, such expectations often take more dramatic turns than steering the teacher into a different subject. Sometimes, students will overtly reject the teacher's directives and normative inducements, and perhaps even offer counter inducements to the teacher. Though these situations may be treated as isolated discipline problems, they may be seen by students as a means of distracting the teacher's attention from an undesired course of action. For example, during study time some students may persistently place their heads on their desks, even though the teacher has issued a stern warning against the practice. It may be that the student is sleepy, or it may be that he is personally bored and has decided to stir up some activity. It may be also that the student sensed that he and his fellow students were bored with the inactivity and *in effect* caused the teacher to become more active. There is a chance, at least, that many students control teachers at precisely the moment the teacher seems to be asserting the greatest amount of authority. It is doubtful that any student who systematically violates rules like "no sleeping in class" is unaware that the teacher is likely to scold him. Unless the student is ill, or in grave need of personal attention (the latter is the common explanation for such behavior), it is likely that the student is performing a function for his peers—changing the course of action in the class by causing the teacher to respond in a predictable fashion.

Goffman[24] spends considerable time discussing the role and functions of directors in human interaction. No such elaborate treatment is intended here. Rather, the intention is to point to the fact that it is likely that one of the more significant, and often overlooked, student functions in the classroom is directing activity. On the surface it appears that the teacher is the director, and generally this is the case. But there are some students from whom the teacher will take cues about the quality of his own performance, or when it is time to move on to the next "act." For example, in research under way at the University of North Carolina,[25] it has been noted that when teachers ask questions like "Now, does everyone understand?" they usually look to the same one or two students for signals of understanding. If the signals are positive, the teacher will move ahead with the lesson; if they are negative, the teacher is likely to go back over the material that is proving difficult. But of more interest, perhaps, is that when these student-directors give cues that are at odds with other cues given off in the class, the teacher tends to move with the directors rather than with the majority of the class. Furthermore, teachers are seldom conscious of this behavior.

The role of director is not limited to directing teacher behavior. Some students are clearly more important to the peer influence structure than are others, and teachers are less sensitive to the nature of these structures than one might imagine. As a consequence, teachers may overlook some of the sources of student direction in the classroom, partly because teachers tend to focus their attention on those individuals with whom they are in interaction at any particular moment. Furthermore, the teacher assumes that he is, or should be, the center of attention of the other parties to the interaction. It is probably the case, however, that in numerous instances a student will be more interested in how his classmates received his performance than in how the teacher reacts to it. In effect, the student defines his peers as the audience, and the student sees himself and the teacher "on stage." The teacher, on the other hand, may assume that his role is that of audience. As a member of the audience, the teacher may fasten so intently on the performance of the student that he totally disregards the extent to which the student is responding to cues from other students—both as an audience and as directors.

In conclusion, it can be said that the degree to which teachers influence the flow of interaction in the classroom is considerable, but the fact that the teacher is such an obvious feature in the classroom distracts attention from equally vital centers of direction and control. Much contemporary educational theory suggests that student self-direction is good and teacher dominance is bad. Yet, the practice of teaching assumes that teachers should be in control at all times. Practice, in this case at least, has overwhelmed theory and this is nowhere so clear as in the relative wealth of data on patterns of teacher influence, and the relative dearth of data on patterns of student influence. It may be that students do not behave as do other human beings in other social settings, but it would be surprising if this were the case. Perhaps it would be useful if educational researchers became as interested in how students gain control as in how teachers maintain or lose control.

NOTES

1. Dennis Wrong, "The Over-Socialized Conception of Man in Modern Sociology," *American Sociological Review*, 26 (1961), 183–193.

2. As Bidwell notes, there exists little data or research that is explicitly directed toward questions of the dimensions here addressed. See Charles E. Bidwell, "The School as a Formal Organization," in *Handbook of Organizations*, ed. James G. Marsh (Chicago: Rand McNally & Company, 1965), p. 972.

3. Sociological Resources for the Social Studies, *Leadership in American Society: A Case Study of Black Leadership* (Boston: Allyn and Bacon, Inc., 1969), p. v.

4. In working with the implementation of SRSS materials in the public schools, I have observed that one of the more conservative forces in the school is the student body, particularly those students who are the A students. Frequently, they resist new curricular materials, perhaps because they find them disrupting to the system that has given them both success and comfort.

5. Elizabeth G. Cohen, "Sociology and the Classroom: Setting the Conditions for Student-Teacher Interaction," *Review of Educational Research*, Vol. 42, No. 4 (1972), 444.

6. For an excellent review of much of the relevant literature, see Jacob W. Getzels et al., "Socialization and Social Structure in the Classroom," in *Review of Child Development Research*, Vol. 2, ed. L. W. Hoffman and M. L. Hoffman (New York: Russell Sage Foundation, 1966).

7. Raymond S. Adams and Bruce J. Biddle, *Realities of Teaching: Explorations with Video Tape* (New York: Holt, Rinehart and Winston, Inc., 1970).

8. There are sound psychological reasons for providing immediate feedback on tests, and it would be inappropriate to suggest that the only reason the teachers review tests is pressure from students or administrators. Yet, one cannot help but be struck by the inordinate amount of time American schools give to testing.

9. See, for example, Howard S. Becker, "The Teacher in the Authority System of the Public School," *Journal of Educational Sociology*, 27 (Nov., 1953), 128–141.

10. The classic statement of this view is, of course, by Waller. Willard Waller, *The Sociology of Teaching* (New York: John Wiley & Sons, Inc., 1932, reprinted 1967).

11. Sarane S. Boocock, *An Introduction to the Sociology of Learning* (Boston: Houghton Mifflin Company, 1972), p. 182.

12. Peter M. Blau, *Bureaucracy in Modern Society* (New York: Random House, 1956), p. 58.

13. Ibid., p. 57.

14 Getzels et al., "Socialization and Social Structure," p. 226, reports findings that suggest that some children are labeled as emotionally ill for no other reason than that they are unaware of the social expectations of others.

15. Robert J. Havighurst and Bernice L. Neugarten, *Society and Education*, ed. 4 (Boston: Allyn and Bacon, Inc., 1975), p. 432.

16. Amitai Etzioni, *A Comparative Analysis of Complex Organizations: On Power, Involvement, and Their Correlates* (New York: The Free Press of Glencoe, Inc., 1961), p. 11.

17. J. J Moreno, *Who Shall Survive: A New Approach to the Problem of Human Interrelations* (Washington, D.C.: Nervous and Mental Disease Publishing Co., 1934).

18. See, for example, Louis M. Smith and William Geoffrey, *The Complexities of an Urban Classroom* (New York: Holt, Rinehart and Winston, Inc., 1968).

19. Adams and Biddle, *Realities of Teaching*.

20. A classic statement of this proposition is to be found in the work of Simmel. See Georg Simmel, *The Sociology of Georg Simmel*, translated, edited, and with an introduction by Kurt H. Wolff (Glencoe, Ill.: The Free Press of Glencoe, 1950).

21. Adams and Biddle, *Realities of Teaching*, p. 92.

22. Farnum Gray with Paul S. Grubard and Harry Rosenberg, "Little Brother Is Changing You," *Psychology Today*, Vol. 7, No. 10 (1974), 42–46.

23. The discussion here is much influenced by the thinking of Erving Goffman, *The Presentation of Self in Everyday Life* (Garden City, N.Y.: Doubleday & Co., Inc., 1959).

24. Ibid.

25. Phillip C. Schlechty and Norman E. Ellis, unpublished research.

9

Stability and Change in the Structure of Schools

Conflict is a major threat to schools. Conflict jeopardizes the predictable relationships that are essential if control is to be maximized. Schools are organized to maximize control. Therefore, when conflict or the potential for conflict arises, it creates a crisis for school organizations. The most common way schools react to such crises is to passively submit to the pressures that threaten conflict. The tendency of schools to deal with environmental tensions by passive adaptation has been noted by many writers.[1] Corwin, for example, writes:

> The school's relationship to students and parents is symmetrical. The school demands social adjustment from the child in matters of discipline and it expects economic support from the public, but in return it eagerly adjusts its own goals to the interest of students and the demands of its publics. In this sense, the public schools are an institutional compromise.[2]

But what does the school have to compromise? Programs, curricula, and teaching procedures? Perhaps. But more certainly, schools can compromise the ways they are organized. It is central to the life of the school that the organization be in a position to exercise positive control over students. When positive control is threatened, whether the threat comes from within the organization or from outside its boundaries, the structure of the school will be adjusted to maximize the organization's ability to control the behavior of students. Consideration of the typology presented in chapter 5 can shed some light on the nature and dynamics of the institutional compromises schools make in the effort to maintain control.

Each of the thirty-six schools represented in the matrix possesses unique characteristics, but some of these school types are similar to one another. For example, the type 3 school differs from the type 4 school only on one dimension, the dimension of structural tightness vs. looseness. (See Appendix.) On the other hand, some of these school types represent extremely different structures (e.g., type 1 and type 36). Whether differences are subtle or gross, their implications for control are, theoretically at least, significant. For example, schools in which students lean toward moral involvement could place heavy reliance on normative inducement strategies with considerable likelihood of successful control. Schools characterized by alienated student populations would find normative strategies generally unsatisfactory.

Students who are alienated will respond to control strategies differently than will students who are morally and calculatively involved in the system. It also seems reasonable that schools which define students as members would be likely to consider normative strategies and psychological affective strategies as legitimate. Schools that define students as products probably would not rely on normative inducements and would certainly be unlikely to use psychological affective strategies. Clearly, some of the schools suggested by the typology evidence considerable incongruence when one considers the kinds of inducement strategies likely to be employed and the kind of strategies likely to be successful.[3] For example, students who are alienated are not likely to respond to normative strategies, but schools that define students as members are likely to encourage the use of such strategies. In schools characterized as alienative-member, the organization's problems with control are likely to become severe largely because of the incongruence between the school's definition of the students' boundary position and the nature of the students' commitment to the school (see Appendix).

Similarly, bureaucratic structures are not conducive to structural looseness. Indeed, the long-run tendency of bureaucracy is to create tight structures. The needs for efficiency, centralized control, routinization of task, and standardization of record keeping almost force structural tightness. In organizations that are both bureaucratic and structurally loose, there is likely to be considerable tension between the lower-level units (e.g., classrooms) and units higher in the authority system. To maintain the loose structure, careful controls will need to be instituted, such as careful adherence to the norm of the closed classroom door, taboos on vertical communications about what is going on in class, and rigid codes for carrying on horizontal discussions of classroom operations. It is possible for schools that are both bureaucratic and structurally loose to exist, but such schools will probably develop very different relationships between and among teachers and administrators than will other types. Likewise, it is possible (though less likely) that schools could exist that define students as members, but where the students are alienated. One of the ways that schools attempt to accomplish this difficult feat is to maintain the academic portion of the program on a "membership" basis and exclude all alienated students from the college-bound curriculum. In fact, schools that have large populations of alienated students frequently become attuned to the idea of special programs for the gifted students.

Structural congruence and incongruence go far to explain much of what occurs in schools and in classrooms. As it is used here, the idea of congruence of structure has to do with relative degrees of compatibility between the components of mode of organization (bureaucratic-professional and tight-loose) as well as compatibility between student involvement and boundary definitions. That is, client-calculative, moral-member, and product-alienative are congruent types. Similarly, bureaucratic-tight and professional-loose are congruent types. Sometimes teachers react to classroom situations in ways that are inappropriate precisely because they fail to understand that what is occurring has its locus not in the classroom but in the school. Consider a situation suggested in the kind of school indicated by type 10. (See

Appendix for a description of the type 10 school.) This kind of school is quite volatile. Most of the students are alienated, yet the school persists in defining students as members. The school is dominated by bureaucratic employee expectations, yet the structure remains loose. Many different scenarios could be written about this particular type of school, but most likely is the oft-repeated situation of the "school in transition" (this is the euphemistic way of referring to a school that is undergoing a dramatic shift in the social composition of the student population it serves). Frequently, the school in transition has served a white middle class population, but because of shifts in housing patterns, redistricting, or court-ordered integration, students from poor black neighborhoods come to comprise a significant part of the population. As many of the critics of urban schools have pointed out, the nature of educational programs relevant to the needs of well-to-do white children may differ dramatically from the educational programs relevant to black children of poverty. As a consequence, teachers and programs that once inspired students to moral commitment to the goals of school become less compelling as the transition continues. In the initial stages of transition (unless, of course, the population shift is brought about dramatically) teachers and administrators are likely to adopt a clinical view of the situation. A few students will be isolated as potential sources of difficulty or singled out for special treatment.[4] As the few become many, the bureaucracy may respond by providing special sections of classes and special programs for these students. As the situation becomes even more pronounced, however, teachers will find that administrative solutions to their classroom control problems are more difficult to maintain. Teachers are likely to insist that more centralized control needs to be undertaken: a signal of a move from loose to tight structure. If the administration is unable or unwilling to respond to the teachers' demands for a structural solution, teachers may complain about lack of administrative support. The breakdown of discipline—when it is generalized—is usually laid at the principal's door. Unfortunately, teachers and adminis-

172

trators will focus on the students as the *cause* of the problem. The teachers may scapegoat the administration and blame the principal for weak discipline, and the principal will probably look to poverty and culture for his scapegoats. Few teachers or administrators will look to the system to discover the source of student dissatisfaction and alienation.

Slowly, however, the traditional member orientation will give way. Teachers will find that students do not respond to normative inducements (at least those normative inducements available in the system as it is). Tenured teachers may be rewarded by being assigned to teach advanced placement courses, thereby finding more students who conform with their prior definitions of student as member. Increasingly, though, teachers will be recruited who, by training or inclination, view the students as products. Behavior modification, behavioral objectives, and individualized instruction (all of which may be perfectly decent) will be turned to the ends of control. Increasingly, the school will adopt a human engineering approach. Increasingly, coercion will be applied in a routine manner. Over time, Bel Kaufman's *Up the Down Staircase*[5] becomes the reality of one more school.

THE THRUST TOWARD STABILITY

In the long run, schools move toward structural congruence in order to maintain control. Bureaucratic structures tend to be found in structurally tight schools; professional orientations tend to foster loose structures. Alienated students will come to be defined as products, for by defining them as products, the school is more free to apply coercion and to use remunerative strategies. The calculative students will come to be defined as clients, partly because their lack of moral commitment makes them a boundary threat if they are treated as members. Schools that reflect structural incongruence (e.g., moral-product schools, bureaucratic-loose structure schools) will probably experience some tensions.

Teachers will interpret these tensions in a clinical fashion, as will students and administrators. Discipline problems will be perceived as localized events—at least until the school reaches the critical point of a type 10 school—and teachers will be replaced if they do not manage the war on the local front. Over time, however, teachers and administrators will redefine the situation in a way that lends to structural congruence and thus will establish stability.

The direction in which the school organization will move in the quest for stability depends on a number of factors, the most important being the nature of the groups that are most directly submitted to the consequences of tensions within the structure, and the power of the groups that are motivated to impose new structural definitions. For example, in the professional-structurally tight setting it is probable that teachers will feel that their professional behavior is being compromised by the tightness of the structure. They may seek to have the structure loosened up, at first individually and then collectively. The teachers' actions may be something as simple as gaining the right to control textbook adoption or something as profound as negotiating the basis of teacher evaluation. The actions taken to bring about change may be as gentle as a humorous but telling comment to the principal or as militant as a long and vicious strike. Whether the teachers (or other groups) will be able to impose new definitions on the situation is more than a matter of communication and goodwill. Frequently, for example, building principals find that they cannot loosen the structure even when they want to, for the tightness of the structure has its origins in the district building.

The question of direction and thrust will be determined largely by the extent to which the contending and competing groups can develop sufficient power and influence to induce others to follow their lead. Sometimes groups that have never before worked together form alliances or coalitions for the purpose of imposing a new definition on a resisting organization. For example, in crisis-oriented schools (e.g., type 10) teachers and parents may join in an alliance to force the administration to

174

accept new definitions of the students' positions or change the nature of control over classrooms. From time to time teachers and students may ally to force more structural looseness and greater student membership. Sometimes young teachers and students will ally themselves for the purposes of redefining the students' position. Usually, however, the power and authority of the school will be on the side of those who are moving the school, or seem to be moving the school, toward structural congruence, for it is the congruent situation that maximizes control in schools and leads to maximum stability.

In the typology presented in chapter 5, the schools that tend toward maximum stability are types 1, 4, 17, 20, 33, and 36. (See Appendix for a description of each type.) Each of these types is maximally congruent in mode of organization and in student position and student commitment. Some of the other types are relatively stable also (e.g., types 2 and 3). Thus, while the six highly stable types represent a *target* cell, that is, a cell toward which schools tend to move, some of the less congruent but relatively stable configurations probably represent more accurately the structure of most schools. It seems reasonable to hypothesize, therefore, that schools will be thrust by their internal dynamics toward one of these stable configurations. The institutional compromises that are made represent the price paid to arrive at or maintain one of these stable or relatively stable positions.

THE DRIFT TOWARD INCONGRUENT STRUCTURES

If the thrust of school organizations is toward stability and congruent structures, the drift of social life in schools and in communities they serve is toward incongruence and disruption. Schools are usually in a state of uneasy equilibrium with their environments. Even in the most labile of schools (e.g., type 1) there are always some students who reject the prevailing commitments, and some teachers who chafe against the prevailing expectations. If the school is typified as professional, there are some teachers who find the claim of professionalism more than they can bear[6] and prefer the safety of a tight bureaucracy. Even if the majority of students are morally committed, there are always some on the fringes of classrooms and schools who are alienated.

So long as the parents of the alienated students are not also the politically or socially powerful, their minority status in the school makes the alienated students relatively easy to control. An expulsion here, a special education class there, even remunerative rewards may be employed. The teachers who chafe against the looseness of structure and the lack of bureaucratic certainty will constitute a threat only if they begin to articulate their concerns to parents in a way that conveys that the administration is laissez faire and without standards. Furthermore, in a moment of crisis (e.g., a psychopathic student attacks a teacher) dissatisfied teachers have the potential of unleashing a torrent of horror stories that are apt to cause a significant crisis of control.

In the larger community the world goes on. In many ways the school is, as Waller describes it, a separate society.[7] But it is a society imbedded in the larger culture and the community. The drift of events in this larger world eventually makes its way into the school. As Corwin writes:

> It is quite possible that many present educational practices and philosophies are direct responses to public pressures (often conflicting ones) rather than the result of reflections on the place of education in American society. Whatever its philosophical and theoretical merits, the study hall, for example, has provided the school with a major defense against two types of public criticism; one that students do not work hard enough, and the other that they have too much homework.[8]

One cannot help but wonder how much of the current fascination with middle schools is an effort to deal with some of the control problems that are thought to result from racial integration. Age grading and subject matter specialization may have at least as much basis in the control needs of schools as in the psychology of children or the structure of disciplined knowledge.

Schools cannot control the course of events in the outside world, but they are compelled to adapt to them. Sometimes the ways in which they adapt create structural dislocations which lead to further internal tendencies toward disruption. For example, some schools have gone to the open classroom as a means of meeting the demand that individual differences be accommodated, and have thereby broken down many of the traditional supports of adult authority available to teachers in traditional classrooms. These events in turn create a thrust toward re-establishing stability. In the course of these events, schools tend to become increasingly rigid. They develop structures that seem likely to make it possible to be minimally responsive to the outside world and at the same time to maintain stability and control within. Perhaps it is the thrust toward stability and the drift toward incongruence that lead many schools to become increasingly bureaucratic and tight in structure, to define students as clients, and to encourage calculative involvement.

THE OPTIMUM SOLUTION TO THE PROBLEM OF CONTROL

The word optimum represents a value choice. The discussion that follows is not, however, a description of a preferred state of educational affairs. Rather, the intent is to illustrate how it is that those who run schools come to view bureaucracy, passive student involvement, rigid structures, and depersonalized relationships between teachers and students to be the best of all possible worlds. Critics of public education may be correct in their description of the mindlessness of schools and those who run them, but they are generally not very clear as to why this mindlessness develops and what it is a response to.

The school type represented in cell 4 of the typology is commonly used as a basis for theoretical discussions of schools and teachers. Those who teach teachers usually assume a considerable amount of structural looseness in the schools. Seldom are teachers in training told about the organizational constraints on their behavior. Rather, they are encouraged to make individual decisions and to be creative and imaginative. Sometimes it is not very clear whether the arguments about professionalism and teaching are statements of preference (i.e., teaching should be a profession) or statements of fact (i.e., teaching is a profession). In any case, most discussions of teaching operate from the assumption that the *proper* role expectations for teachers are those expectations characterized as professional.

The idea that the student is, or should be, a member of the school organization has considerable support in prevailing philosophies of education and the rhetoric of school reform. At least since the days of Dewey, thinking about schools has been dominated by a view of the school which includes the idea that students are members of the school community.

Most educational theories, particularly the tutorial models that dominate educational thought, are predicated on the assumption of positive student commitment to the goals of the school. One of the consequences of this assumption is the marked preference for intrinsic motivation that typifies so much modern educational thought. Somehow, the image of Mark Hopkins on one end of a log and a student on the other is a difficult one to discard. The personal quality of significant learning encounters has a way of being translated into a reverence for those relationships that seem to be present when learning occurs. Thus it is that educational theory assumes that students and teachers must come to develop significant personal relationships—rapport, meaningful communications, and so on—if significant learning is to occur.

In brief, the assumption of the type 4 school and of most education theory is that teachers are morally involved, students are morally involved, and each is likely to develop primary ties with the other. Although the type 4 school is possible, the facts of public school life are somewhat different from the image of the type 4 school.[9] Public schools operate under compulsory attendance laws. Furthermore, many schools experience considerable population mobility. Thus, students from many different backgrounds, with many different expectations and diverse school experiences, come together in a single building. These conditions are not conducive to the development of strong moral commitments to a particular school, its programs, symbols, and rituals.

Through careful planning of programs, a judicious use of coercive and remunerative strategies, and a willingness to compromise goals, schools are sometimes able to minimize alienation, though urban schools are seldom able to generate significant moral involvement. In most schools, teachers are satisfied if students are generally compliant and willing to meet minimum performance criteria.[10] It seems almost too much to expect that many students will be strongly committed to the school. Given the situation of most schools, mild alienation and mild positive involvement (calculative involvement) is the best possible world—or so it seems to many educators. To generate positive involvement of a moral variety would, in many situations, call for more dramatic shifts in the goals and programs of schools than the community would support or teachers would tolerate. Calculative involvement is an institutional compromise that maximizes control and minimizes change in traditional patterns of schooling.

Philosophically, it may be desirable to treat students as members, but in the typical school, students represent one of the most significant threats to the boundaries of the school and the classroom.[11] Their loyalties to the classroom and to the school are always suspect and under tension.[12] "Outsider" peer groups may call on students to provide assistance in making school or classroom boundaries more permeable. The precarious world of the classroom teacher makes teachers particularly reluctant to share membership privileges with students. Students who are treated as members may come into possession of information that can be used to invade the boundaries of schools and classrooms. This may be particularly crucial in situations where parents are influential or politically aware (e.g., middle class suburbs). The organization must count on the loyalty of its members to maintain its boundaries. It is especially important that those who occupy boundary positions be loyal, since the loyalties of boundary role persons are always suspect. Students as boundary role members are especially subject to suspicion, for they suffer the additional disadvantage of a child-adult relationship. Thus, the tendency of schools and teachers is to define students as clients. Students may be defined as members when it is absolutely safe to do so, and defined then as products if need be, but the best of all possible solutions—or so some seem to think—is to view the student as a client. As a client, the student is outside the organization, but he remains in a position of dignity. The goal of the organization is to meet the needs of the client, to serve him and his community. The fact that compulsory attendance laws sometimes coerce students into the role of unwilling client is a factor that must be dealt with, but it is not insurmountable. Athletic teams, for instance, are often used to generate in alienated clients sufficient positive attraction to the school that they become calculatively involved. That the relationship is a passive or symbiotic one seems clear, but that many schools value the convenience of such a relationship is apparent to those who reflect on life in schools.[13]

Given the problems of size, economy, and the public demand for efficiency, the tendency of the school toward bureaucracy is almost irresistible.[14] From the point of view of administrators and school boards, the problems of schools are often viewed as problems of management and corporate decision making. The recent drive toward accountability is only the most recent evidence of the degree to which the bureaucratic ethos permeates the thinking of those who run schools. The factor of geographic mobility is in itself an inducement to bureaucratization. Highly mobile populations almost demand standardized programs that can be transferred from building to building and system to system. Furthermore, without casting undue criticism at teachers, it seems clear that many who are attracted to teaching are not by training or inclination the kinds of individuals who thrive on the indeterminate situations inherent in nonbureaucratic organizational structures (e.g., colleagual governance). Many teachers come to teaching precisely for the security it offers, and that security is best expressed in the bureaucratic form, with its emphasis on tenure, rewards for longevity, authority by virtue of position, and so on. Bureaucracy is further reinforced by the temporary nature of the commitment to teaching that typifies many of those who enter the teaching ranks.

Though professionalism may be the goal of many, the tendency of the school toward bureaucratization is unmistakable. It is likely that this may cause considerable discomfort for teachers and administrators who value the idea of professionalism, but in the long run, the tendency of the school is to impose bureaucratic employee expectations on all who are on the payroll, from custodians to building principals. That bureaucratic employees may possess a high level of technical competence and be thoroughly skilled in their assigned tasks is an assumption of bureaucracy. Practice, however, is the assumed source of competence in a bureaucracy, and authority comes from a position held. For the professional, on the other hand, competence has its basis in specialized knowledge, and authority resides in demonstrated competence. Indeed, those who argue for competency-based teacher education are correct in their assertion that to make teaching a profession it is necessary to assure the professional competence of the practitioners. Unfortunately, inspection of competency-based programs suggests that most of these programs are relatively sophisticated techniques to provide early practice and socialization for the rising bureaucrat. The demands of school systems often take precedence over the demands of clients, even in teacher education programs designed to "produce" competent professionals. Indeed, many teacher education programs pride themselves on the fact that school administrators value their "products" because they *adjust quickly* to the local conditions. It is sometimes forgotten that *"the situation that is most satisfying to teachers and administrators does not necessarily provide the best education for the child."*[15]

Perhaps the most compelling reason that teachers and administrators prefer a bureaucratic mode of organization has to do with ability of bureaucracies to maintain boundaries, or at least to optimize boundary maintenance abilities. By careful regulation of staff and line positions, control of vertical communication can be maintained, thus providing a gatekeeper function at the bounds of each organizational unit. By designating particular officers as community contact persons, the diffuse nature of the boundaries can be tightened and strengthened. It is much safer to have one officer (e.g., a guidance counselor) responsible for dealing with potentially threatening external relations than to give authority for such contacts to each and every teacher. The loyalty of one functionary is much easier to assure than the loyalty of all participants. Given the drift toward disruption that is present in school environments, bureaucratic forms come to be valued not only for this efficiency, but also because they optimize control. Professionalism may be desired, but it is often sacrificed on the altar of control.

In the early elementary grades, loose structures tend to reinforce teacher control. Thus it is common that schools which are otherwise bureaucratic and tight tend to reflect structural looseness in the early years. In schools where discipline problems are intensive in early school years (e.g., schools in poor rural areas or inner-city schools) value may be given to structural tightness even in primary school. Structural tightness provides some degree of organizational control and limits the possibility that idiosyncratic factors will disrupt the system.[16] For reasons already suggested, teachers often prefer structural tightness, as do administrators. Furthermore, students find tightness of structure reassuring, as they know where to go and what is expected.

In sum, the client, calculative, bureaucratic, structurally tight school (see type 17 in Appendix) reflects in practice what the type 4 school represents in theory—a form of "practical utopia"—and many of the "better" upper middle class suburban schools approach this type very closely. Students are calculatively involved, as are their parents.[17] The desire for a good educational program is quite real, but the motives are mixed. Frequently, the worth of such programs is judged by the percentage of graduates who gain admission to the college of their choice. Teachers see students as clients, and the teachers are generally technically competent. Indeed, teachers may style themselves professionals, much in the manner that engineers and baseball players consider themselves professionals. The services they provide to students may be superb, but these services are often prescribed by the syllabus, the program of instruction, and a rigorously monitored testing program. Special services and high degrees of specialization typify such schools. Guidance counselors and school psychologists usually abound. Departmental boundaries and job specifications are carefully drawn and jealously maintained. The guidance counselor advises, the school psychologist diagnoses, and the teacher of advanced placement American history studiously avoids discussions about the non-western world or government in Russia. These are subjects to be taken up by another teacher at another time. The few students who do not fit into this system are usually well provided for; for instance, a carefully planned woodwork and metal shop may be available. Alienated students may find themselves located at a far end of the building—all in the interest of decreasing the impact of machine noise on the school. Predictability, regularity, and high standards are the order of the day and of the year. Creativity is encouraged, but only in its proper place: the art class, the drama club, or the creative writing class. Schooling is serious business, for success in school confirms one's passport to the world of the future. From time to time teachers in these schools lament the fact that students are so callous and work only for grades, but academic success continues to be the highest award teachers can imagine. Indeed, teachers may compete with one another to demonstrate that they have high academic standards, usually evidenced by their students' performance on departmental tests and perhaps later in college.

SUMMARY

It is in the nature of schools that they move toward stability. Though communities will tolerate—in crisis situations—considerable brutalization of other people's children, they will not tolerate such behavior for too long, or with their own offspring. Eventually, excessive brutalization and the extensive use of coercion will be called into account. Schools cannot, and most teachers will not, continue the routine application of coercion to children. Eventually, conflict and crisis will result. Therefore, schools attempt to establish organizational modes that are conducive to the use of coercion when it is needed, but that also make remunerative, normative, and psychological affective strategies available. Indeed, even social exchange strategies can come to have a legitimate place in some schools.[18] The school that is most conducive to these ends is the type 17 school. Unfortunately (or perhaps fortunately), where student alienation is extreme, this type of school is difficult to establish and to maintain. Extremely alienated students tend to reinforce each other, thus creating more alienation. Alienation leads to the use of coercion, and coercion produces more alienation. As a consequence, the "better schools" that deal with alienated students often find the best of all possible worlds in the type 33 school. This type of school differs from the type 17 school only in that students are identified as products (see Appendix). As products, the scientific, regularized application of overt external control measures can be made legitimate. One need not be opposed to operant conditioning and similar undertakings to recognize that these programs are less dependent on the assumption of intrinsic motivation than is the case in many other instructional approaches. In the alienated school, intrinsic motivation cannot be assumed. If the goals cannot be changed enough to reduce alienation (and some feel they cannot be), then it is argued the solution is to systematically and "scientifically" develop extrinsic rewards and punishments that induce students to behave in ways that are assumed to lead to learning. Though many find themselves uncomfortable with this conclusion, given the nature of schools and the sterility of modern theories of instruction, it is understandable that even decent men and women find treating people as things a preferable option to not treating them at all.

NOTES

1. Willard Waller, *The Sociology of Teaching* (New York: John Wiley & Sons, Inc., 1932, reprinted 1967). Waller was one of the earlier observers to note the schools' tendency toward passive adaptation.

2. Ronald G. Corwin, *A Sociology of Education: Emerging Patterns of Class, Status, and Power in the Public Schools*, p. 392, © 1965. Reprinted by permission of Prentice-Hall, Inc., Englewood Cliffs, New Jersey.

3. The idea of congruent types is suggested by Amitai Etzioni, *A Comparative Analysis of Complex Organizations* (New York: The Free Press of Glencoe, Inc., 1961). The present discussion differs from Etzioni's framework but has been considerably influenced by his formulations.

4. Initially, this special "treatment" may be nothing more than expulsion, routine detention, or other punitive measures. But as the number of these discipline problems increases, more institutionally acceptable means will need to be devised. Paddling a few children per week may be accepted, expelling even more may be tolerated, but there comes a point at which coercion becomes too widespread and more "humane" means of control must be developed. Enter special education and behavior modification.

5. Bel Kaufman, *Up the Down Staircase* (Englewood Cliffs, N.J.: Prentice-Hall, Inc., 1964).

6. See, for example, Gerald H. Moeller, "Bureaucracy and Teachers' Sense of Power," *Administrators Notebook*, 11 (Nov., 1962).

7. Waller, *The Sociology of Teaching*.

8. Corwin, *A Sociology of Education: Emerging Patterns of Class, Status, and Power in the Public Schools*, © 1965. Reprinted by permission of Prentice-Hall, Inc., Englewood Cliffs, New Jersey.

9. It is likely that some of the laboratory schools and experimental schools inspired by the progressive education movement were similar in structure to the type 4 school.

10. See Charles E. Silberman, *Crisis in the Classroom: The Remaking of American Education* (New York: Random House, 1970).

11. Waller does much with the proposition of antagonisms between students, teachers, and schools. Waller, *The Sociology of Teaching*.

12. Robert L. Kahn et al., *Organizational Stress: Studies in Role Conflict and Ambiguity* (New York: John Wiley & Sons, Inc., 1966).

13. See, for example, Silberman, *Crisis in the Classroom*, and Philip W. Jackson, *Life in Classrooms* (New York: Holt, Rinehart and Winston, Inc., 1968).

14. Corwin, *A Sociology of Education*, pp. 35–54.

15. Ibid., p. 389.

16. Schools that are structurally loose, particularly high schools, provide the opportunity for charismatic teachers to generate considerable personal influence with students, which could be turned to ends that threaten the boundaries of the organization.

17. For an autobiographical account of life in such a school, see Charles G. Rouscoulp, *Chalkdust on My Shoulder* (Columbus, Ohio: Charles Merrill, 1969).

18. The reader may want to review these strategies as they are presented in chapter 7.

10

Conflict and Structural Congruence in Schools

There is little in the language or training of teachers and administrators to suggest awareness of the interrelationships among the social structure of the school and the behavior of teachers and students in classrooms. In the process of becoming a teacher or administrator, however, it is necessary to develop some insights into the social processes of schooling, for without such insight survival in schools is impossible. As Waller puts it:

> let no one be deceived, the important things that happen in schools result from the interaction of personalities. Children and teachers are not disembodied intelligences, not instructing machines and learning machines, but whole human beings tied together in a complex maze of social interconnections. The school is a social world because human beings live in it.[1]

Waller's observation that experience provides the teacher with rough empirical insights into the social nature of schools, particularly the classroom, is probably correct. Yet, as Jackson has found, the social insights of teachers are generally not at a level of sophistication that can be articulated.[2] The teacher's social insight is intuitive. When teachers and administrators begin to talk about the nonclassroom social life of the school (e.g., peer groups and faculty groups), it becomes clear that a truncated view of the social network of schools dominates their thinking. Teachers are vaguely aware that the school is somewhere out there, but basically they perceive it as a threat to the autonomy of the classroom and an imposition on their freedom of action.[3] Administrators are aware, as are some teachers, that the community affects the school, but few can describe the relationship between the school and the community in other than particularistic terms (e.g., the names of school board members). Teachers and administrators are aware of the possibility of conflict with the community. Seldom, however, are conflicts in schools (teacher-student conflicts, teacher-teacher conflicts, and teacher-administrator conflicts) thought to be connected with larger social structures in schools or in communities. Conflict in the school is interpreted—as is almost everything else in school life— in personalistic, individual, and clinical terms. When tensions arise between individuals, groups, or factions within schools, the tendency is to locate the cause of conflict within the structure of the personality of individuals, or within the immediate surroundings in which the conflict is manifest (e.g., in the classroom). Those who live in schools usually think of school-related conflict in ways which conform with C. Wright Mills's conception of private troubles. Mills defines personal troubles as follows:

> *Troubles* occur within the character of the individual and within the range of his immediate relations with others; they have to do with his self and with those limited areas of social life of which he is directly and personally aware. Accordingly, the statement and resolution of troubles properly lie within the individual as a biographical entity, and within the scope of his immediate milieu. . . .[4]

Certainly, much that occurs in the classroom is located in the interactions peculiar to the classroom and the personalities of the participants, but this is not always so. Unfortunately, a preference for personalistic explanations of the sources and cause of conflict sometimes makes school conflicts an especially intensive psychological experience for the participants. When the source of conflict is personal—and sometimes it is—it may be that emotional intensity is a necessary factor in resolving the issue. But when the conflict has its locus and origins beyond the particular personalities and interactions of the disputants, intensifying the interpersonal aspects of the issue does little to relieve the tension. Furthermore, such intensity may indeed do harm to the disputants. Conflict that is located outside those areas of social action over which the disputants have control can never be resolved by the *direct* actions of the disputants. At best, individuals may work out accommodations that will make it possible to survive the tension. At worst, the disputants will destroy each other and not affect the source of the tension that leads to the self-destructive behavior. For example, it frequently happens that a particular student will have talents and abilities which are needed in a number of different settings in the school, but which cannot be employed simultaneously in more than one setting. Football coaches and basketball coaches often find they have need of the same students at the same time. Band directors often need access to students for their marching band programs at the same time the football coach needs them on the playing field. Usually teachers work these matters out in ways that do minimum damage to children or to programs. From time to time, however, these structurally based conflicts come to be viewed in personalistic terms. Students are accused of being "disloyal," coaches are accused of being opposed to "esthetic" values, and band directors are accused of being opposed to manly sports. The fact that there is no way the student can meet all of the structural requirements that might impinge on him may be lost sight of. From the student's point of view, the conflict might seem very much of a personal trouble, as it may for the competing teachers. But the locus of the problem is not with the teachers or the students. The *tension* cannot be resolved at that level. The band director may resign himself to the fact that he will lose many of his better band members during football season, but that does not make the loss any less real. In the interest of harmony, the basketball coach may play his first game without the services of his star forward, but that does not make the team loss any less real.

Some structural conflicts, such as the foregoing illustrations, are so obviously *not* located in the personality or character of the interfering groups that only the callous or petty would make children suffer the pain resulting from competition for structural advantage. Other conflicts, with their bases as much in the structure of relationships as was the foregoing illustration, are not so clear-cut. Frequently, therefore, educators react as if they were dealing with personal troubles when they should be dealing with issues at the level of structure. In defining issues, Mills writes:

> Issues have to do with matters that transcend these local environments of the individual and the range of his inner life. They have to do with the organization of many such milieux into the institutions of an historical society as a whole, with the ways in which various milieux overlap and interpenetrate to form the larger structure of social and historical life.[5]

Some of the more devastating intraschool conflicts have their origin in the structure of the school, yet are responded to in interpersonal terms. It is, indeed, the failure to recognize the structural origins of conflicts, and the tendency to treat conflict clinically, that so often makes conflict in school so serious. Minor organizational problems are sometimes exaggerated until they have catastrophic effects on individuals. Students may be expelled from school because of structural tensions; teachers may be fired because they cannot accommodate to some of these tensions, and bitterness and rivalry between and among teachers and administrators may be intensified as a result of structurally based antagonisms. Yet it is seldom that attention is given to the structural nature and origins of school-related conflict. Rather, they are explained as resulting from personal and philosophic differences between and among the participants. Seldom, however, do such personalistic and philosophic explanations resolve the real issues.

If the issue is indeed structural rather than personal, dealing with the problem on a personal level can at best bring only temporary relief to the situation. Some of the combatants may resign, officially or psychologically, and thus provide the illusion that the matter is resolved. But over time, tensions in the structure will manifest themselves again and once more claim their toll in the lives of teachers and students. Until the structural source is recognized and managed, resolution of such tensions is both illusory and transitory.

CLASSROOMS AND SCHOOLS: TENSIONS OF BOUNDARIES

As Bidwell[6] accurately points out, there is a tendency for school systems to reflect structural looseness. This is probably at the high school level as well as at the elementary school level, though there is reason to believe high schools are typically more tight in structure than are early elementary schools. Yet, the relationships between the school and the classroom and between school buildings and district level units are sources of considerable tension and conflict. Jackson found, for example, that one theme running through his interviews with teachers was a concern about autonomy. Jackson writes:

> Our interviewees mentioned two main threats to the teacher's autonomy, or at least two hypothetical conditions, which, if either materialized, would arouse complaint: one concerned the possibility of an inflexible curriculum; the other concerned the possible invasion of the classroom by administrative superiors bent on evaluation. . . .[7]

The autonomy of the classroom is under constant threat. The more bureaucratized a system becomes, the more likely is the threat to become a source of conflict. For example, with increased emphasis on teacher accountability, principals are coming to be required by the central office and board policy to "invade the teacher's classroom bent on evaluation." The reaction of the teachers' unions and professional associations to teacher accountability is in no small measure related to the potential for conflict implicit in such invasions. Indeed, building principals and supervisors sometimes find that their evaluative functions make them unwelcome strangers in the classroom. Even when their appearance is for the announced purpose of providing assistance and support to the teacher, teachers frequently distrust the presence of superordinates.

In order to fulfill the organizational requirement of evaluation, and at the same time maintain some degree of receptivity to their visits in the classroom, building principals and supervisors frequently adopt the practice of announcing prior to entering the classroom the days and times of their visits. In this way the teacher and students can be prepared to present their best team performance. Consequently, principals and supervisors seldom see the real life of the classroom; they see the classroom as the teacher thinks the supervisor would like it to be.[8]

In many schools the central supervisory staffs cannot gain access to classrooms without the prior permission of the building principal. Furthermore, building principals and teachers frequently work together to establish and maintain building level autonomy.[9] Thus, it is not only the boundaries of the classroom that are carefully guarded, but also the boundaries of the school. Threats to the boundaries of schools and classrooms create considerable tensions between and among participants in the life of schools. The relationship between teachers and students cannot be fully understood without attention to boundary maintenance behavior. Similarly, boundary behavior must be understood if one is to understand the relationship between teachers and principals, teachers and colleagues, and building principals and central office personnel. In a sense, both the teacher and the building principal serve in the capacity of boundary role person for two separate, *and sometimes competing,* social systems.[10] To the extent that a teacher's classroom comes to possess system-like qualities, the teacher is a part of that subsystem. Indeed, the teacher is a critical link between the classroom subsystem and the administrative structure of the school. At the same time the teacher is on the outer edge of the administrative structure of the school and thus represents the school to the classroom. Thus, housed in the office of teacher is the Januslike expectation that he represents the school to the classroom and the classroom to the school. Similarly, the building principal is expected to face inward toward the school and represent the district administration, and face out from the school to represent his building clientele. The nature of administrative role conflict in such situations has been well documented,[11] but there is little research on the kinds of boundary role conflicts that impinge on teachers. Yet the tensions must be considerable, for there is good reason to speculate that many teachers leave teaching precisely because they cannot manage the tensions involved.[12]

The threat to classroom boundaries makes the position of students within classrooms much more powerful than is commonly realized. As indicated in an earlier discussion, the ability of students to report on the teacher's classroom performance can generate considerable social exchange influence for students. Furthermore, there is reason to believe that teachers who are aware of a student's family's relative standing in the power structure of a community tend to give rewards based on these ascriptive qualities.[13] In part, this behavior may be attributed to the status aspirations of the teachers, but it may also be an unarticulated strategy to maintain the loyalty of those students who are in a position to make the boundaries of the classroom permeable.

Even within the school there seems to be a tendency to give rewards to those who seem to have influence with administrators and other teachers. There is, to be sure, a certain tautological quality to the line of reasoning implied here. Based upon the data available, however, it seems reasonable to infer that at least some of those who get rewards from teachers gain them primarily because they are perceived to be influential with other teachers and school administrators, rather than influence's being a result of achievement. Among the reasons that influential students are given rewards must be the fact that they may pose significant threats to the boundaries of classrooms.

At the building level, it is common for principals to carefully monitor and control teacher and staff communications with outsiders. Based on the behavior of some building principals, one could reasonably infer that central office personnel constitute more of a boundary threat than do parents or students. Teachers are often free to communicate with parents without prior clearance with the principal. In many schools, however, teacher attempts to communicate "downtown" without first going through the principal's office would be a serious breach of expectations. In part, this may be attributable to the staff and line mentality that typifies bureaucracies, but some part of the explanation for such behavior must reside in behavioral accommodations to boundary tensions.

Some teachers, by virtue of their tasks and duties, pose more of a threat to the boundaries of the school building than do others. Thus, it often becomes necessary for the principal to go to unusual lengths to assure the loyalty of some faculty members (much like the relationship of teachers and children from influential families). One of the complaints often heard from teachers is that coaches receive favored treatment from the principal's office.[14] The usual explanation for this behavior is that the principal is a former coach and thus feels an affinity to coaches. The behavior can also be explained with the assertion that community pressure for excellence on the playing field makes it necessary for the principal to support the coaching staff. Both of these explanations probably have merit in particular situations, but there is the possibility of a more structural explanation. Coaches, unlike most of their teacher colleagues, routinely come into contact with many of the more influential members of the community. The athletic program is highly visible in most communities, as are coaches. The newspaper editor may not know who teaches advanced calculus, but he will undoubtedly know the name of the coach. In addition, the coach is in a position to do favors for influential community members (special seating, sports news tips, and so on). Thus, he is in a position to generate considerable social exchange influence outside the school. Negative comments about the school and its programs from a successful coach are likely to be heard in places of influence and are likely to be taken seriously. Negative comments from the Latin teacher may stir up a fuss among colleagues and start a few rumors in the community, but usually a crisis of this sort is easily contained by an allusion to the eccentricities of the teacher and some other personalistic counterattack. The coach is a more formidable boundary threat, for community influentials know the coach personally. It behooves principals and superintendents, therefore, to develop different relationships with those who occupy coaching positions than with other teachers. That the special relationships may result in interpersonal conflicts on faculties is beyond doubt, but that the relationships have their origins in the banality of administrators or the ancestry of those who coach is subject to question.

STUDENT-TEACHER CONFLICTS: SOME NONCLASSROOM SOURCES

The relationship between teachers and students is always an uneasy one. It is not generally admitted, but there is a built-in antagonism between the world of the teacher and the world of the child. As a number of observers have noted, the teacher does represent adult authority.[15] Furthermore, the direction that adults would have children go and the ways in which children are likely to move without the active intervention of adults are not always the same.[16] That adult authority can be humane and decent is not at question; it can be, just as it can be vicious and capricious. But even humane and decent authority has about it a controlling function that will meet with some degree of resistance from all but the most compliant students. Children are not fully socialized human beings and one function of the school is socialization. Though some find it ideologically repugnant, the fact remains that many of the things teachers do to the young are done because the conditions of society demand that it be so. As Durkheim notes:

> education, far from having as its unique or principal object the individual and his interests, is above all the means by which society perpetually recreates the conditions of its very existence.[17]

Clearly, such a view runs directly counter to much prevailing educational thought, but it does square with the facts of school life. Furthermore, because much educational thought is less than precise—or honest—about the relationship between the child and socializing agencies like the school, many of the conflicts between the child and adult authority are perhaps more brutalizing than would be the case if the nature and origins of these conflicts were properly understood. The misbehavior of children in school is as often a result of *the fact that they are children* as of some inherent character flaw in a particular child.

In the early years of school many of the conflicts that students have with school are located in the relationship between the teacher and the individual student. Indeed, folk wisdom concerning the importance of the first grade teacher may have considerable basis in the social realities of school. Whether a child will come to develop an accommodating and cooperative relationship with school may be determined by the way the child relates to his teacher or teachers in the early years of schooling, and the ways his teachers relate to him. Over time, students develop associations with other students, and these associations form the structure of the peer group life of schools. Some students will associate themselves with group structures that accommodate the goals and purposes of schools, while others may find their loyalties lie with groups that are antagonistic to the ends of the school. As Coleman[18] has made clear, by the time students reach high school they have developed distinct status systems and distinct patterns of prestige and privilege. Indeed, these patterns are so distinct that Coleman and many others have dared to posit the existence of a separate "adolescent society."[19]

Whether or not one accepts the proposition of an adolescent society, it is clear that students' peer relationships have much to do with how students relate to teachers, and how students behave in school. Coleman, at least, seems convinced that there is a tendency toward conflict between the norms and values of the adolescent society and those of the larger school system. At the same time, Coleman and others view the existence of student groups as a potential resource in the educative process. Coleman, for example, suggests:

> [A] possible strategy is . . . to take the adolescent society as given, and then *use* it to further the ends of adolescent education. Rather than bringing the father back to play with his sons, this strategy would recognize that society has changed, and attempt to improve those institutions designed to educate the adolescent toward adulthood.[20]

Some observers overlook the possibility that a monolithic view of *the* adolescent society may distort the realities of schools and classrooms, nearly as much as failing to recognize the importance of peer relationships in the first place. Boocock writes:

> students, even within the same school, may be increasingly divided into two separate "subsocieties"—one consisting of those who are reasonably compliant to the expectations of the learning system and who will move on through ever higher levels of education; the other consisting of active rebels, who disrupt the smooth functioning of the system and who are viewed in every negative way by school personnel, and of passive withdrawers, who simply mark time in the school until they are old enough to drop out.[21]

In fact, the situation is probably even more complex than Boocock pictures it. The reactions of the school to student groups may force those who have negative orientations to behave as a single unit, but it is likely that negative students are as much in conflict and competition with one another as they are in conflict with the school. The involvement of positive students is also probably qualitatively and quantitatively different, depending upon the peer groups to which they have allegiance. To categorize students into two groups—those who are with the school and those who are against it—misses many of the subtle nuances of conflict and compliance that need to be understood if insight into the nature of school and classroom life is to advance.

Student groups that actively support the programs of the school and the prestige structure of faculties are more likely to reap positive rewards from teachers than are those students and groups of students who passively submit to the expectations of the school. Though passive submission is valued in schools, active support is more highly valued. Students who seek positions on the student council and participate in school-sponsored clubs usually have more esteem with teachers than do those students who do *nothing* more than maintain a high standard of academic performance. Certainly academic performance is valued, but one need only examine high school yearbooks and read recommendations teachers and guidance counselors write for college admission officers to understand that teachers, as well as students, place considerable value on active participation in extracurricular activities. The labels grind, and bookworm is as much a part of the vocabulary of teachers as it is the vocabulary of students. Sometimes, in fact, teachers will advise outstanding students to become more involved in nonacademic matters—ostensibly for the students' mental health and in order to develop leadership abilities commensurate with academic attainments.

Few classroom teachers were themselves outstanding scholars.[22] Most were students who gained their success as students from a combination of passable scholarship and generally cooperative behavior. In fact, some school systems shy away from beginning teachers with outstanding academic records, ostensibly on the grounds that brilliant students are often more interested in ideas than in students. It may be considered unkind to say so, but education gets more than its share of those college graduates who were *not* on the dean's list.[23] Students who are creative, relatively independent of peer groups, and generally unwilling to uncritically accept teacher direction may find themselves in conflict with the teacher, precisely because they *do not* go along with peer pressure toward conformity. Conflict between teachers and these independent students is sometimes explained in terms of the students' lack of responsibility, their disrespect for authority, and their tendency toward narcissistic behavior. Teachers may also find themselves in conflict with their colleagues if they take on the role of ombudsman for such students.

The relationship of these matters to student conflict with teachers seems clear. Students who are in support of the school are more likely to come under increasing amounts of school-based power and influence. Though such students will gain influence in the school, and with teachers, they will also need to accept more influence and direction from teachers and the school. On the other hand, students who are not in support of the school will be less available to school-based and teacher-based power and influence. One cannot kick a student off the basketball team if the student does not try out for the team in the first place. Students who do not aspire to seek office on the student council are not likely to be motivated to achieve good grades by the provision that only those who have a B or better average will be permitted to serve. A reasonable inference from the data available is that schools provide activities for those students who support the expectations of the school, but those students who fail to provide active support for these expectations must make do on their own.[24] Furthermore, when a student participates in school-sponsored activities, the scope and pervasiveness of the school *vis à vis* the student's social behavior increase dramatically.

One of the consequences of these conditions is that schools are frequently unable, structurally and in fact, to control the behavior of dissident student groups. Schools often exclude vital segments of the student leadership structure from the internal boundaries of the school. The reasons for doing so often seem obvious to school officials, but the effects are not always so clearly understood. Leaders of dissident student groups are often singled out, by teachers and administrators, as the *cause* of control problems, and dealt with clinically and punitively (e.g., by expulsion). If, however, these individuals are in fact leaders of dissident student groups, coercive treatment by teachers and the school may become a mark of status and in effect the basis of prestige among peers. Schools that define most students as members, but treat those students who are alienated as products, may find that they are actually further alienating both the individual students involved and those students who look to the alienated students for leadership.

FACTION AND GROUP

There is little empirical research related to faculty peer group relationships.[25] It is not at all clear, for example, the extent to which the peer group, work group, and interest group structure of faculties is a significant factor in the lives of teachers. Some observers suggest that the structural looseness and fragmented work structures tend to minimize colleagual interaction and control.[26] Teaching is a peculiar occupation. It is doubtful that any other professionals, and few middle-level management personnel, do as much of their vital work outside the view or inspection of peers. It is not only that teachers prepare their performance outside the view of their peers (surgeons and attorneys do also), but it is also that teachers seldom give their performance before any audience other than students. Waller's speculative analysis of what teaching does to teachers, though dated and perhaps jaded, is predicated on an observation that is central to understanding the relationships between and among teachers, as well as relationships between the teacher and the community. *If the teacher is to teach effectively, the teacher must, temporarily at least, relinquish some of his claims to adult status.*[27] The nature of the teacher's work cuts him off from most adult contact (except contact with other teachers) and even contacts with parents are seldom contacts of two adults joined in a co-equal interaction. The special interest of the parent in his child and the teacher's more general interest in all the children in his class make the relationship one of insider to outsider. Conversations between parents and teachers are always strained through the sieve of the interests and problems of the child involved.

Waller suggests that it is possible for a teacher to maintain his adult standing, but to do so "he must interpose between himself and his students an immense distance, and then the teacher-pupil relationship becomes one of dominance and subordination in its strictest form."[28] The alternative is to sacrifice a certain amount of one's adulthood for the purpose of increasing teaching effectiveness. "The teacher must talk to boys of the things in which boys are interested. He must understand adolescent roles, and live vividly roles of his own not wholly incompatible with the roles of adolescence."[29] There is a third alternative. The teacher may develop sufficient insight to relate to the world of the child at the level of the child, and the world of the adult at the level of the adult. As Waller warns, however, "This insight . . . is rare, and it could lead to the complete isolation, in feeling, of the individual from society."[30]

What impact these factors have on factions and groups in school is presently a matter of speculation, but several possibilities seem reasonable. First, there is some evidence (in the folklore of teachers, impressionistic literature, the reports of students, and so on) that older, more experienced teachers tend to be more stern, more aloof from students, and to maintain "relationships of dominance and subordination in the strictest form."[31] These individuals may constitute a significant faculty grouping, correlated with age and experience, but not *caused* by age and experience. In effect, this group comprises those individuals who have chosen to maintain their adult roles, *at almost any cost*. These teachers will view any but the more docile adolescent and children's groups with suspicion and dismay, for the possibility of conflict is ever present. Furthermore, teachers who do not share with them the expectation that teachers should always "behave as adults" and "maintain social distance" and likely to be subject to out-group suspicion and hostility.

Second, it is probably true that younger teachers find the necessary adaptation to student identification roles less constraining, for younger teachers are closer (in terms of age) to these adolescent and childlike roles. That young teachers may find themselves banded together as a group and antagonistic toward older teachers seems almost inevitable in these circumstances. The relationship between age and these groupings is not, however, a causal one. There are older teachers who will maintain a student-oriented stance, sometimes to the dismay of their age peers. Furthermore, there are young teachers who opt for the more adult-oriented role, thus quickly aligning themselves with their older colleagues.

There remains, however, the third group—those teachers with sufficient insight to play at roles in both worlds. Generally these teachers have the trust and respect of the younger teachers, the older teachers, and most of the students. Somehow they seem to manage the task of maintaining their adulthood while making themselves compatible with the world of the child. It is easy to make this teacher a "hero," but his lot may be even more depressing than the lot of the perpetual child, or the stern adult. For, if Waller is correct, such a role performance tends to produce so much anxiety and tension that alienation may result. Initially, this anxiety and tension may be dealt with in a flurry of organizing activities. It is likely that such individuals become active in professional associations, teachers unions, and so on. It is likely that some of these individuals will be attracted to administration, in the hope of reconciling the competing claims of the world of children and the world of adults. Sometimes these individuals may join together and form very exciting little enclaves in a school or school district. Often, however, the results are more pathetic. Over the years, the insightful teacher may become more and more alienated from his colleagues, his students, and the school. He may revert to bitter cynicism, and while his stories of past agonies and defeats may titillate young

activist teachers, it is painfully obvious that his fervor for reform
is lost. His position in the school and the community may be
sufficiently secure that he can serve as organizational conscience
and gadfly, but the possibility of his ever becoming positively
involved or committed to the organization is remote.

Age and orientation toward adults and students are not the
only sources of conflict between and among factions and groups
in school. Sometimes, the divisions are related to subject matter
taught or grade level taught (e.g., the vocational versus the
academic programs, the elementary teachers versus the secondary
teachers). Furthermore, the ways schools are organized tend
both to create the conflicts and to isolate them. Whatever antagonisms exist between elementary and secondary teachers, for
example, are often offset by the barriers of building separation.
Separation reinforces in-group, out-group perceptions, but since
the groups are sufficiently isolated from each other, they seldom
come into direct interference or open conflict. Even within the
same school, competing groups become isolated both by formal
arrangements and by informal agreements. In some schools it
is commonly understood that certain "faculty only" areas are
reserved for the more adult-oriented teachers. Sometimes the
area is called the *nonsmokers' lounge,* sometimes the teachers'
workroom. Other areas of the school, perhaps a second *work
area,* perhaps a furnace room, become the gathering places for
the student-oriented, or those who "tell dirty stories," the resident
cynics, or whatever grouping is characteristic of the school. The
interaction that takes place in these areas reinforces groups and
builds alliances. Beginning teachers are often advised by their
experienced teacher friends, therefore, "Don't smile before
Thanksgiving, and don't commit yourself to any faculty member
before Christmas."

Factionalism and group conflict between and among teachers
are further exacerbated by the growing tide of teacher militancy.
In most schools there will be a group or faction of teachers who
are seen as "anti-administration" and another group who are
seen as "pro-administration." Increasingly, these pro- and anti-
forces are becoming formalized into organizations and associa-

tions. Professional negotiation is a formal recognition of what many teachers and administrators have known for years; there is considerable tension within the apparently tranquil school building. Although the ideology is that all are working for the "good of the child," the fact remains that there are very different perspectives on how that good is best served. In a society of organizations, it is not surprising that these informal factions and groups are taking on more formal and powerful shapes and characteristics.

REFERENCE GROUPS

Social scientists have long recognized that human beings orient their actions toward groups they consider to be important to them. One of the more powerful concepts used to account for this orientation of behavior is that of reference groups. Merton writes:

> reference groups . . . are not mere artifacts of the author's arbitrary scheme of classification. Instead, they appear to be frames of reference held in common by a proportion of individuals within a social category sufficiently large to give rise to definitions of the situation characteristic of that category. And these frames of reference are common because they are patterned by the social structure.[32]

Within the school setting at least three different frames of reference impinge on the relationships between teachers, students, and schools. These frames of reference meet the conditions of reference groups, which are as follows: (a) they are sufficiently regular to indicate patterns; (b) they are influential on the nature of the group structures of schools; and (c) they are clearly related to the structure of schools. The orientations that reflect these conditions are (1) local-cosmopolitan, (2) professional-bureaucratic, and (3) university–public school.[33]

Local and cosmopolitan orientations have been widely discussed in the literature of sociology and social psychology.[34] In addition, a number of scholars have made direct applications of these ideas to the study of schools.[35]   Since there is already literature available to the reader, the concepts will be dealt with briefly here.   For present purposes it is sufficient to note that the basic distinction between a local and a cosmopolitan orientation is that the cosmopolitan individual has an orientation to the world outside the local scene, whereas the local takes most of his direction and orientation from his immediate social milieu. Cosmopolitan orientations probably reinforce professional orientations and university orientations, but it is conceivable that one could be cosmopolitan in orientation and neither professionally nor university oriented.   In order to make this point clear, it is necessary to describe more fully these latter orientations.

By professional orientation is meant an acceptance of professional expectations as having a preferred status, and superior values to bureaucratic employee expectations.[36]   The professionally oriented individual will reconcile conflicts between bureaucratic and professional expectations by honoring the demands of professional expectations.   Conversely, when there is conflict between bureaucratic demands and the demands of profession (e.g., loyalty to client or superiors), the bureaucratically oriented individual will comply with bureaucratic expectations.

By public school orientation is meant a view that holds public school teaching as a calling in its own right.   University orientation denotes a view that holds teaching as a lower-status professorial post.   Some teachers, for example, seem to be oriented to elementary and high school teaching as a entity distinct from the university structure and separate from the status system of the university or higher education.   Other teachers, however, seem to view their task as lower-level college teaching. Members of this latter group frequently view university values as criteria for judging the worth of their own performance and the performance of their colleagues.   It is this latter group who are here labeled "university oriented."

Many conflicts in public schools over standards, curricula, and programs can be best understood in terms of faculty groups centered on the orientations suggested above.   Teachers who are university oriented will be likely to oppose subject matter consolidation (e.g., they will oppose social studies and support history, sociology, and economics). The university-oriented teacher will probably uphold the sanctity of the scholarly disciplines, emphasize the worth of high-quality academic programs, and view efforts at coordination as a threat to academic freedom.

The public school–oriented teachers will be more likely to insist that curriculum interest give way to the problems of children, as opposed to the problems of the disciplines. In seeking alliances and support outside the public school, public school–oriented groups will be likely to turn to faculty members in departments of education and schools of education, whereas university-oriented teachers will look to members of academic departments for guidance. Indeed, many of the conflicts between educationists and academicians that occur at the college level may be relocated in high schools and fought out in the already fragmented world of the public school. The resulting inconsistencies and curricular contradictions would, in themselves, be worthy of a major study.[37]

Local teachers will be more likely to place emphasis on such matters as citizenship, leadership ability, and willingness to cooperate. The local teacher is likely to value students who are morally committed to the school and the school program. On the other hand, cosmopolitan teachers are likely to band together to keep "irrelevancies" out of grading. They may agree with their local colleagues that moral student involvement is desirable, but they are less likely to feel a student should be penalized for failing to demonstrate such commitment. Cosmopolitan teachers will be willing to settle for calculative involvement so long as student performance meets their expectations.

Teachers who are professionally oriented are likely to join together (formally and informally) to maintain or establish structural looseness. They are likely to find themselves at odds with the administration and some of their colleagues on questions of record keeping, grouping, the use of punishment, and the routinization of administrative procedures dealing with student "behavior problems." For example, it is doubtful that professionally oriented teachers would support a standardized policy of merits and demerits, although bureaucratically oriented teachers might find considerable attraction in the notion.

It is clear that some of these orientations would be more supportive of the structures of some types of school than of other types, and in the long run, schools probably recruit and retain individuals who are oriented in ways which support the structures that typify the school. In the short run, however, antagonisms between orientations and structure may be quite intense.

One very interesting possibility is that in school districts exhibiting considerable structural looseness at the building level (e.g., the building is relatively free of district direction), centralized employment practices can, by accident or design, create conflict in a school building, particularly when the faculty turnover rate is high. For example, in a structure typified as bureaucratic, a central personnel decision to hire professionally oriented teachers would certainly create tensions.

SELF AND SOCIAL STRUCTURE

That teachers, administrators, and students find life in schools constraining seems beyond question. Life in all organizations is constrained by the requirements of collective group action, although the constraints of school are, perhaps, more intensive than those in some other agencies. It is likely that people in schools feel organizational constraints more directly, for the expressed purpose of education is to liberate men and women from the bondage of ignorance and habit. Ideas of democracy, freedom, rationality, and reason dominate much of the *discussion* that takes place in schools. Thus, the contradictions between the irrational, constraining, and nondemocratic aspects of organizational life may have an especially significant impact on those who live in schools. Perhaps as a result of these contradictions schools frequently develop elaborate fictions to account for the differences between what is taught in school and how schools, as organizations, behave.[38] Through these fictions, most represssive aspects of school can be rationalized in terms of the welfare of the majority. For example, "A few students should not be allowed to disrupt the activities of the many." "Most students really want to learn; the majority of students want structure and order." And as with all fictions, these school fictions have a way of becoming self-fulfilling. Given the emphasis on routine and order that typifies schools, students and teachers come to value it. Teachers and students come to view benevolent paternalism and democracy as synonymous. Students come to expect that each day's lesson will have a beginning, a middle, and an end. Students come to expect closure on ideas, and teachers are uncomfortable if each day's lesson does not reach some objective. Ambiguity, uncertainty, and openness come to be devalued. School is seen as purposeful. Everyone, especially teachers, should have a purpose. Answers may be couched in the language of rationality and democracy, but they must have a ring of finality and closure. Thus, teachers quickly learn to state with moral certainty what their "lesson plan" is and where it will lead.[39] Students, too, learn that their activity must be purposeful and have meaning. Each moment of the student's day is seen as time to be filled, with study, with choir, with gym, and with classes. One must always be "doing something." Contemplation, accompanied by a vacant stare, is daydreaming. Rummaging around in the world of ideas is often called meaningless and pointless discussion. Lesson plans must be elaborate and clearly point somewhere. Furthermore, the teacher must indicate how he will get where he wants to go. Otherwise, how— some will ask—would the teacher know if he were off the subject? Having an exciting lesson is desired, but if students are excited each day, both students and teachers begin to wonder if there is anything serious or important going on. Too much excitement will make colleagues and administrators suspicious. Indeed, one dominant fiction of school is that important knowledge can be gained only through tedious and boresome work.

Discipline, instead of meaning intensive and efficient pursuit of goals, becomes sticking to the subject and the lesson plan. If students or teachers get off the subject or away from the lesson plan, they are likely to feel that they are sinning, at least a bit.

It is probably not a coincidence that many high school texts have thirty or more chapters, for that is the approximate number of weeks in the school year. Teachers who skip chapters or start in the middle of the book are often viewed as innovators, and students often find such irregularity highly disconcerting. As one observes teachers at work, it seems that textbooks are viewed like novels. Textbooks apparently should be read from beginning to end. Somehow the *plot* will be given away if one reads a text from end to beginning. If one must miss some part of the book, it is usually thought better to miss the end than the beginning, for the beginning of a text is thought to be more basic.

Such fictions, and the list could go on, protect both teachers and students from facing many of the contradictions in their school lives, and thus make school more tolerable. From time to time, however, some students and some teachers may ask why they *must* do what they do. This question may signal the beginning of innovation. It may also signal the beginning of the systematic destruction of human beings. Teachers who begin to doubt the fictions of the school are potential threats to the system. If they are young, their doubts may be attributed to naïveté and immaturity. However, if they are older and more experienced teachers, they constitute a significant threat to the status quo. Sometimes the system handles threats by experienced teachers by co-opting the teacher. For example, an experienced and imaginative teacher may be promoted to a supervisory position, ostensibly so that he may inspire others. The effect may be, however, that the burden of administrative work and the requirements of the new role will remove a vital grass roots source of change.

Students who are innovative may suffer a less noble fate than the co-opted teacher. Some will simply be ignored, or viewed as arrogant. Others will be encouraged to pursue their interests, but in areas of the school where creativity is tolerated— art, music, drama, and perhaps metal shop. In the "basic" program of the school, it is infrequent that eccentric personal qualities, in either students or teachers, will be valued, and sometimes such qualities are not tolerated. It is, therefore, small wonder that some of the more creative teachers and students are often found in the fringes of schools, in drama, art, music, and sometimes even homemaking and industrial arts.[40] In these fringe areas teachers are not really expected to teach anything *too* important and students are not expected to learn all that much. The students in which the school has a vested interest will, however, expend their energies in courses that are more substantial than these fringe programs.

SUMMARY

What teaching does to teachers and what schools do to children is a subject that is little understood. The tendency to confuse ideology with analysis often clouds the issues. Supporters of the status quo in schools argue that education does liberate, teachers do respect individual differences and human dignity. These arguments are, apparently, based on the assumption that because it should be so, it can be so if men but will it.

Critics of the status quo lament the brutal qualities of the school, and point to how schools destroy human beings, squelch the human spirit, and generally work evil on human kind. These critics often attribute the perceived evil to pernicious systems and to callous or stupid men. It is probably true that some school structures promote viciousness and that some teachers and administrators are brutalizing tyrants. But one does not overcome the tyranny of systems by arguing that it is possible to create systems that in no way limit freedom. One of the costs man must pay for civil society is that he become a part of the whole and give up some of his egocentric whims. In schools, designed as they are to move human beings from the family to the larger world, it is necessary to infringe on the freedom of the yet-unsocialized child. At the same time, however, one must remember that future humanity is created through socialization. What makes schools dehumanizing, perhaps, is the moral certainty of those who run them and the failure of critics and reformers to understand that the issue cannot be stated so simply as man versus society. The aim of democratic socialization is maximum human freedom in society. Dignified societies dignify men. School reform will advance, and school structures liberate, only when those who run schools and who teach develop a more adequate appreciation of the social nature of their task. Until that time, in conflicts between self and social structure, self will likely be sacrificed in the interest of order and control. Schools that are truly human would be more willing to accept and deal honestly with the coercive nature of socialization.

Because socialization is constraining, educators often feel compelled to deny their essential functions through myth and fictions. Yet it is these myths and fictions that conceal, even from the well-meaning, all manner of barbarisms committed in the name of freedom.

NOTES

1. Willard Waller, *The Sociology of Teaching* (New York: John Wiley & Sons, Inc., 1932, reprinted 1967), p. 11. Reprinted by permission of the publisher.

2. Philip Jackson, *Life in Classrooms* (New York: Holt, Rinehart and Winston, Inc., 1968), pp. 143–149.

3. Ibid., pp. 129–133.

4. C. Wright Mills, *The Sociological Imagination* (New York: Oxford University Press, 1959), Evergreen edition, 1961, p. 8.

5. Ibid.

6. Charles E. Bidwell, "The School as a Formal Organization," in *Handbook of Organizations*, ed. James E. March (Chicago: Rand McNally & Company, 1965), pp. 975–977.

7. From *Life in Classrooms* by Phillip W. Jackson. Copyright © 1968 by Holt, Rinehart and Winston, Inc. Reprinted by permission of Holt, Rinehart and Winston, Publishers.

8. Though there is little research that bears directly on the issue, researchers are well aware of the potential impact of observers on the behavioral settings they are attempting to study. It seems difficult to believe that principals and supervisors can ever become so nonthreatening that they do not change the nature of interaction in classrooms, perhaps even more than other outside observers. Perhaps observers would be better advised to study classroom interaction as what Goffman has called a "team performance." To the extent that the classroom is a social system and teachers are a part of that system, it seems clear that the perceived threats from the outside—whether these perceptions are the teachers' or the students'—would induce a different pattern of interaction than that which might be present if the threat were removed. See Erving Goffman, *The Presentation of Self in Everyday Life* (Garden City, N.Y.: Doubleday & Co., Inc., 1959).

9. Bidwell, "The School as a Formal Organization," p. 976.

10. J. Stacy Adams, "The Structure and Dynamics of Behavior in Organization Boundary Roles," manuscript in press, UNC, 1974. This paper contains an elaborate discussion of boundary role behavior and is useful in consideration of the role of teachers and administrators, although it is not specifically addressed to school-related issues.

11. See, for example, Jacob W. Getzels, James M. Lipham, and Ronald F. Campbell, *Educational Administration as a Social Process: Theory, Research, Practice* (New York: Harper & Row, Publishers, Inc., 1968).

12. See, for example, Hal Lenke, "Surviving, More or Less," *Peabody Journal of Education*, 49 (1972), 126–137.

13. C. Wayne Gordon, *The Social System of the High School: A Study in the Sociology of Adolescence* (Glencoe, Ill.: The Free Press of Glencoe, 1957) p. 41.

14. Sometimes the complaint extends to favored treatment by the district office also. A particular sore point in some schools is the tendency to give coaches a lighter teaching load than their colleagues, yet pay them extra for their coaching duties.

15. See, for example, Waller, *The Sociology of Teaching*.

16. That socialization is necessarily restrictive to individual impulse does not mean that the process must be brutal or repressive. On the other hand, there is a tendency among some educators to

underplay or deny the necessarily constraining role of socialization and argue that any action on the part of the school that directs or acts against the whims of children is inherently undemocratic. Similarly, those who seem to prefer repressive systems overplay the coercive aspects of socialization. What is needed is less ideology and bias, and more careful analysis of the socializing roles of schools. As an illustration of such an analysis, see Robert S. Dreeben, *On What Is Learned in School* (Reading, Mass.: Addison-Wesley Publishing Company, 1968).

17. Emile Durkheim, *Education and Sociology*, trans. Sherwood D. Fox (Glencoe, Ill.: The Free Press of Glencoe, 1956), p. 123.

18. James S. Coleman, *The Adolescent Society: The Social Life of the Teenager and Its Impact on Education* (New York: Free Press, 1961).

19. Though the nature and impact of adolescent subcultures is a subject of some controversy among social scientists, most seem to agree that adolescents do develop significant substructures. See Sarane S. Boocock, *An Introduction to the Sociology of Learning* (Boston: Houghton Mifflin Company, 1972), particularly chapter 11.

20. Coleman, *The Adolescent Society*, p. 313.

21. Sarane S. Boocock, *Introduction to the Sociology of Learning*.

22. See, for example, William H. Whyte, Jr., *The Organization Man* (New York: Doubleday-Anchor, 1956), pp. 86–110, or James D. Koerner, *The Mis-education of American Teachers* (Baltimore: Penguin Books, 1963).

23. Ibid., p. 91.

24. See, for example, Roger Barker et al., *Big School—Small School: Studies of the Effects of High School Size upon the Behavior and Experiences of Students* (University of Kansas: Midwest Psychological Field Station, 1962).

25. See Boocock, *Introduction to the Sociology of Learning*, chapter 9.

26. Charles E. Bidwell, "The Sociology of Education," in *Encyclopedia of Educational Research*, ed. 4, ed. R. Ebel (New York: Macmillan Publishing Co., Inc., 1969), pp. 1241–1254.

27. Waller, *The Sociology of Teaching*, p. 59.

28. Ibid.

29. Ibid., p. 60.

30. Ibid.

31. Ronald G. Corwin, *A Sociology of Education: Emerging Patterns of Class, Status, and Power in the Public Schools* (New York:

Appleton-Century-Crofts, Inc., 1965). Chapter 10, "Interpersonal Relations in Education," contains many illustrations of this point. The illustrations come from interviews conducted by Corwin.

32. Robert K. Merton, *Social Theory and Social Structure*, 1968 enlarged edition, p. 298. Copyright © 1957, 1968 by The Free Press. Reprinted by permission of Macmillan Publishing Co., Inc.

33. As will be seen shortly, there is considerable overlap between and among these orientations. For purposes of analysis it might be well to collapse the categories, but for the purposes of description it seems well to keep them separate.

34. See, for example, Merton, *Social Theory and Social Structure*, chapter 7.

35. Robert E. Jewett, "An Educational Theory Model: Theory of Local and Cosmopolitan Influentials," in Elizabeth Steiner Maccia, George S. Maccia, and Robert E. Jewett, *Construction of Educational Theory Models* (Cooperative Research Project No. 1632, Columbus, Ohio: Ohio State University Research Foundation, 1963), pp. 282–297.

36. See chapter 5 for a distinction between bureaucratic and professional expectations.

37. Those who have worked with national curriculum projects and with various funding agencies are certainly aware that the power struggles between academic departments and professional educators go well beyond the boundaries of the campus. Frequently, schools will hire consultants from the same university, one from a department of education and one from an academic department, only to find these experts giving them mutually exclusive advice, particularly on matters of curriculum design.

38. For an excellent treatment of the idea of fictions in social life see Robin M. Williams, Jr., *American Society: A Sociological Interpretation,* ed. 2, rev. (New York: Alfred A. Knopf, 1960), pp. 391–395.

39. One need not be in favor of disorganization and chaos to recognize that certainty of outcomes places considerable limitation on intellectual pursuits. If the purpose of school is to encourage the young to think well and critically, it is difficult to see how this can be accomplished in an atmosphere of dogmatism and moral certainty.

40. This is, of course, a judgment that would be difficult to support with empirical evidence, although it could not be refuted with such evidence. The basis of the judgment is long experience with teachers and schools.

11

Structural Fit, Curriculum, and Instruction

The fact that school organizations affect curriculum and instruction has not escaped the attention of educators. A number of plans have been devised to make schools more responsive to curricular demands and alternative patterns of instruction. Perhaps the best known of these is the so-called Trump Plan.[1] Among the more significant dimensions of this plan is the emphasis on flexibility of time schedules and class size. In this way it is possible to vary the length of time given to any one activity, as well as the number of participants in any one setting. Theoretically this variance could extend from fifteen minutes (or less) to a full day on the time dimension, and instruction in large classes of one hundred or more to individual study and tutorials. The Trump Plan also carries with it implications for school plant, scheduling, and staffing. As L. Craig Wilson[2] points out, however, the Trump Plan gives very little attention to substantive issues of curriculum and instruction. Rather, it is an attempt to develop an administrative solution to the constraints of rigid time schedules and standardized class sizes.

Others in the area of curriculum and instruction seem sensitive to the interconnections between school organization and instruction, for example, Wilson[3] and Goodlad.[4] All are handicapped, however, by the fact that at present there exists no adequate formulation of those organizational properties that are likely to be related to curriculum and instruction. Thus, specialists in curriculum and instruction are compelled to center on some of the more obvious features like time schedules, promotion policies, staffing arrangements, class size, and resource allocation. They, like the sociologists of learning mentioned earlier in this book, assure that such obviously constraining features must be differences that make a difference in student learning. Yet, the research on the effects of variable staffing patterns (e.g., team teaching), modular scheduling, and nongraded schools is not particularly convincing. Based on the research available, one could make nearly as good a case that such differences make no difference, as that they are significant factors in the teaching-learning situation. There may be many reasons for these mixed results, including poor research design, inadequate implementation of programs, and technical errors. There is reason to believe, however, that much of the inconclusive and mixed quality of research on variations of administrative features of schools results from conceptual difficulties inherent in current thinking about school organizations. Among other things, there is a tendency to equate administrative arrangements (schedules, class size, and promotion policies) with social structure and to assume that by manipulating administrative arrangements one is directly restructuring the social milieu of the school or the classroom. It may or may not be the case that altering administrative arrangements will alter the social structure of the school. For example, team teaching can be fully implemented without touching the essential relationships among teachers or between teachers and students. If teachers are able to develop patterns of interaction that resemble those they had when teaching in their self-contained classrooms (and this often happens), the only thing that team teaching accomplishes is to make the teacher who once taught independently *alone* teach independently *together* with one or more colleagues.

INDIVIDUALIZED INSTRUCTION:
AN ILLUSTRATION OF STRUCTURAL FIT

One way to illustrate the relationship between the social structure of the school and curriculum and instruction is to consider the situation of individualized instruction. Although the idea of individualized instruction is not a new one (Socrates had some views on the subject), in recent years there has been an upsurge of interest in implementing individualized programs in schools. Some of these programs have been well received and have met with approval. Other efforts at individualization have met with resistance from teachers, students, and parents. The evidence on the learning effects is scant and of mixed quality. Overall, it seems that research on individualized programs reflects the same patterns as research on most other innovations in education: no significant differences overall, although studies vary. Some studies claim to demonstrate the superiority of individualized procedures; others are not so positive.

Aside from intuition and ideology there is really no reason to prefer individualized instruction over any other instructional format. However, the success or failure of individualized instruction is not likely to be dealt with in terms of the ability of such programs to produce measurable differences in achievement scores. Research on individualized instruction *has* been based on assessments of achievement scores, but when teachers and administrators speak of individualization "working" or "not working," it is unlikely that they are referring to student achievement. It is more than likely that they refer to the ability of their school system to accommodate the new instructional program. To say that individualized instruction works—given the present state of research on school effects—is probably to say that a school or schools can accommodate the program with minor tensions or conflict. To say that a program of individualized instruction failed to work is most likely to mean that the organization dislocations created by the program were not accommodated in or by the school system.

If the definition of success is "meeting with acceptance," one of the more sensible questions about individualized instruction is: "Why does individualized instruction succeed in some schools but not in others?" There are, of course, numerous possible answers to this question, but some of the more obvious are: (1) the schools into which programs of individualized instructional programs are introduced are fundamentally different; (2) the means by which the programs are implemented are somehow different; (3) the individualized programs are different; (4) some schools are more discerning; and (5) some combination of the above.

On the surface it would seem that bureaucratic, structurally tight school organizations would be less conducive to the successful implementation of individualized instruction than would professional, structurally loose school organizations. One explanation for variance in the success of individualized programs is that the programs were introduced into different school structures, some being bureaucratic-tight, others being pofessional-loose.

This may, indeed, account for some of the variance. It is probably not a coincidence that individualized programs are generally more favorably received in elementary schools than in secondary schools. Elementary schools seem typically more loose in structure (if not more professional) than are high schools. But the bureaucratic-professional, tight-loose arrangement is only one possibility. Another, and more probable, line of explanation for the success or failure of individualized instruction is that the programs of individualization are basically different. This being the case, when different programs are introduced into equivalent structures (e.g., bureaucratic-loose), some of these programs receive structural support while others create tensions or are not supported by the structure. In support of this latter proposition, consider the following. Patterns of individualized instruction fall into two broad categories. The first category includes programs designed to individualize the means of instruction, but which hold the end or goals constant for all students, at least for all students in a designated category.

The second pattern of individualization (some prefer personalization)[5] is to assume variance in both the goals of instruction and the means of instruction. In this latter situation, the total curriculum is designed around the individual child.

The differences between these two views are substantial and particularly significant in regard to required structural support. Individualized instruction that accepts desired learning outcomes (goals) as a given or constant feature but assumes variations in the means of achieving the goal could tolerate considerable emphasis on task efficiency and routinization of procedure. Structural looseness would be a desirable circumstance, in that variations of means, particularly at the classroom level, would be necessary. Bureaucratization, however, would tend to support the required emphasis on minimum performance levels, uniformity of outcome, and efficiency of practice.

Like those who would individualize the means of achieving standardized goals, proponents of the second orientation toward individualization (personalization) would seem also to require structural looseness—and for much the same reasons. Bureaucratization, however, would be anathema to a program that individualized both goals and procedures, for the necessary routinization insisted on by bureaucratic procedures would create tensions at almost every level. Individualizing both goals and procedures insists on the uniqueness of the client's problems, and establishes goals in terms of those problems. Stress would be placed on flexibility, research, and change, as opposed to efficiency of task achievement. The orientation would be toward the achievement of the goals determined appropriate to the situation rather than on producing a uniform outcome of some predetermined quality.[6]

Partly as a result of inadequate understanding of the relationship between the social structure of schools and patterns of curriculum and instruction, the battles between those who hold one or the other orientation toward individualized instruction are often more productive of hyperbole than insight. The scant research that has been done on the effects of individualized instruction has been undertaken on the basis of assumptions that can do little but confuse the issue even further. And, perhaps more important, when one or the other of the programs of individualization proves successful (i.e., the teachers, administrators, and community seem to accept it), few are in a position to suggest why the situation developed as it did. Conversely, when one or the other of the procedures is tried out and rejected, there is little understanding of the basis of the failure. The usual explanations of both success and failure are cast in terms of the training the teachers received (adequate or inadequate), the degree to which the community was informed and involved, the extent to which required material resources were made available, and the receptivity of teachers to innovation and change.[7] However, a more adequate basis of explanation is possible. It may be that, through luck and happenstance, the social structure of the school was either accommodating of the change or nonsupportive of the change.

To date there are few data available upon which to base a judgment of the extent to which various programs of individualization have met success, even if one defines success as nothing more than teacher and community acceptance and continuance of the undertaking. Some schools have tried various programs of individualization and have given up on the effort. Other schools have become increasingly committed to patterns of individualized instruction, even to the point of investing funds in school buildings designed expressly for the purpose of encouraging even further individualization. A review of the available literature leads to the speculation that programs of individualization that have held the "outcomes" as relatively constant and have individualized the means are more widespread than those which would individualize both means and ends. Furthermore, those programs of individualization that have been abandoned have usually been discarded on the basis that "students did not learn as much as before" or that discipline problems have become "too severe."[8] Thus, it seems likely that the most marked failures are among those programs that attempt to individualize both means and ends. Why is this the case? The most obvious answer is that the one type of individualization is somehow better than the other. Perhaps students learn more (though there is no convincing empirical evidence that this is so), or perhaps teachers and students feel that students learn more under the one program than under the other. Perhaps, indeed, the individualization of both means and ends is one of those things that "is fine in theory but it won't work in practice." A more likely explanation may be that those who would individualize instruction seldom distinguish between bureaucracy and structural looseness. Consequently, organizational reform is likely to be at the level of structural tightness and structural looseness rather than at the level of behavioral expectations. Many who would individualize instruction seem to assume that if enough materials are present in the classroom, the teachers are well trained, and classroom autonomy is maintained, individualization is almost certain to work out. It is not that simple, however. So long as bureaucratic structures are retained, there is litle chance that individualization of both means and ends can be implemented in schools. Indeed, if such programs are successfully implemented in bureaucratic schools, tensions will be created at the level of behavior expectations. Should this occur, the bureaucratic expectations would need to be altered, or the innovation would become subject to hostile organizational response.

Programs which try to individualize both means and ends are more likely to fail than those which individualize only means, precisely because the former require a much more significant structural shift in the mode of school organization than do the latter. Schools, particularly elementary schools, are most likely to be structurally loose bureaucracies. Thus, programs designed to individualize means but hold goals constant cause minimum tension. Success or failure largely depends on the technical competence of the teachers and the availability of resources. On the other hand, the individualization of *ends and means* requires more than technical competence and material resources. It requires, at least in most instances, that the expectation structure of the school organization be shifted to accommodate the new program. One cannot, for example, apply measures of central tendency (e.g., average class achievement in reading) to programs that may have the goal of teaching one child to read and another child to gain information through other techniques. It may be that in the long run all children should learn to read, but in programs that individualize both means and ends of instruction there is no possible way of stating with precision the exact time, place, or level at which this skill will be developed. Instead of efficiency in teaching reading, the goal would be to assure that each child—eventually—learned those skills and developed those understandings that were determined to be essential to his particular situation. It is difficult to imagine how mass education, in complex school organizations, could individualize instruction to the extreme that some suggest should be possible, but it is clear that those who advocate such extreme positions are seldom aware of the organizational conditions in which and upon which they must act. Whether or not extreme individualization is practical and realistic, it is clear that practical and realistic efforts at implementing such programs cannot occur so long as the only dimension of school organizations reformers see as relevant is the tightness or looseness of the structure. Indeed, it could be argued that individualization of instruction (i.e., personalized instruction) can be implemented only if the structure is tight and the expectations are professional. In this way the student would become the center of both the decisions of the teacher and those of the organization.

CLASSROOM ENVIRONMENTS AND THE STRUCTURE OF SCHOOLS

Emphasis on structural looseness and clinical explanations has led to the mistaken notion that the establishment and maintenance of classroom environments is basically a function of teacher behavior and student response to that behavior. This is true only in some types of schools. For example, in a school characterized by loose structure, professional expectations, student members, and positive student commitment (e.g., the type 4 school), it is probably true that who the teacher is and what the teacher does are the basic determinants of the environment of the classroom. On the other hand, in a school that is bureaucratic, structurally tight, with an alienated student body whose members are defined as products (e.g., type 33), the impact of the teacher on the classroom environment is minimal. So long as the teacher in this latter situation accepts the official expectations of the school as legitimate (and structural tightness suggests that teacher behavior would be carefully monitored), there is little chance that the teacher will be in a position to deal directly with students. The only leadership the teacher will be able—legitimately—to exercise in the classroom is leadership of an institutional variety. Personal leadership is compromised, if not totally suppressed, by the existence of bureaucracy and structural tightness. The fact that students are defined as products and are alienated suggests that the teacher's classroom inducement strategies will be limited to coercive strategies (including that strange form of coercion in which the lack of punishment becomes a positive reward). Frequently, schools like the type 33 school will develop systematic plans for making some remunerative strategies, such as work-study programs, legitimate and available to teachers, but the school's capabilities along these lines are often severely limited by its location in the community.

Schools like the type 33 have a tendency to encourage teachers to develop refined and "humane" techniques of coercion. Other kinds of strategies will need to be developed—simply to survive in the classroom—unless, however, the teacher is willing to become increasingly repressive and coercive. It is likely that over the long haul this type of school will recruit or retain teachers who find themselves comfortable with such measures. And it is here that what Blau calls "bureaucracy's new face"[9] becomes so clear in the classroom. Teachers, to be at all effective personally with students, must have access to strategies other than coercive and remunerative ones. Personal leadership in the classroom cannot rely on punishment and the manipulation of material rewards. Normative inducements, which tend to be supportive of the personal authority of the teacher, are not likely to be available to the teacher, since the student body is alienated and not likely to respond to such inducements. The alienated student is not likely to be overly concerned if the teacher tells him he is doing poorly, and may respond quite unpredictably to overt signs from the teacher of moral approval for his actions.[10] The nature of structurally tight bureaucracies is that psychological affective strategies are largely unavailable, at least so long as the teacher maintains his role as institutional leader, which, to repeat an important point, bureaucratic-tight organizations almost compel the teacher to maintain. Thus, the teacher is almost compelled to establish and maintain a repressive classroom environment *or* the teacher must be willing to take actions that compromise his role as institutional leader. In a structurally tight organization such compromises involve considerable personal risk, for the teacher's behavior—if brought to official attention—will be treated as an overt attack on bureaucratic authority. Without such attacks on bureaucratic authority, however, the teacher cannot have any personal impact on the environment of the classroom. Thus, some teachers systematically set about developing special relationships with students and employ various social exchange strategies (e.g., bureaucratic scapegoating and strategic leniency), all of these in order to develop a modicum of personal loyalty and commitment from students. In this way, at least, the teacher is able to exercise some personal control over events in the classroom. But, in accomplishing this end, the teacher also increases the power of students who may be defined as members or clients of the school organization. For example, in some schools of the type described (i.e., type 33) teachers may adopt the practice of permitting students a great deal of latitude about what and how they will study, up to the point that the departmental test is about to be administered. Then the teacher will insist that all students work together and cram in order to maintain a sufficiently high class average, so the teacher can "prove" that what he is doing is appropriate. If students should fail to achieve a sufficiently high class average, it is likely that the next grading period will reflect a more rigid class structure. If, however, students perform up to minimum expectations, the students are in a position to request continuation of the more flexible policy. This circumstance is not the major threat to the teacher and the teacher's position, but by permitting latitude and variation in performance, the teacher has *in effect* condoned and encouraged officially disapproved student behavior. Should a student—particularly one who is defined as a member—fail an examination or do poorly, trouble for the teacher could result. A report to another teacher or the building principal that the reason for the poor student performances was the teacher's lack of discipline or low standards will likely lead to closer supervision of the teacher. Closer supervision, in turn, diminishes further the teacher's opportunities to deviate from the bureaucratic rules. If the situation becomes sufficiently grave, the teacher may be relieved of his duties, transferred perhaps, or it will be recommended that the teacher's contract not be renewed.

In the short run, individual teachers can have some impact on classroom atmosphere in situations like the one here described (the type 33 school), but in the long run, teachers as a group will make very little difference in the classroom. From time to time an individual teacher may muster the courage to go against the system, develop considerable social exchange and psychological affective influence with students, and be, for a little while, a difference that makes a difference to a few students. Eventually, however, the teacher's deviant behavior will be officially recognized and he will undergo severe sanctions. Even if an individual teacher becomes a master of evasion and creates a fortresslike boundary around his classroom (and sometimes this happens), his behavior is likely to be explained and institutionalized in much the way that some primitive tribes handle physical deformities and mental illness. He will be set apart as someone special, always to be counted on to do weird things but not to be taken as a model or even taken seriously. In the end, he too shall pass. Furthermore, the tendency of this kind of teacher toward extreme alienation seems clear and the psychological cost must be great indeed.

It seems, therefore, that there are likely to be school organizations in which the behavior of the teacher in the classroom will be so homogenized and institutionalized that differences between and among teachers will make little difference in the classroom environment. In other situations (e.g., type 4), differences among teachers will make considerable difference, for it is up to teachers to decide which strategies to employ, which goals to pursue, and what kind of relationship to develop with students.

SCHOOL STRUCTURES: INDUCEMENT
AND ADAPTATION

From the preceding discussion, the reader has probably inferred that some kinds of school structures are conducive to the use of some forms of inducement and adaptation, while other structures support other kinds of inducement and adaptation. Furthermore, the extent to which inducement strategies will be effective is in part related to the structures of the schools in which they are applied. The purpose here is to give more precision to this observation.

Bureaucratic schools tend, almost by definition, to be punishment centered. This does not mean, however, that coercion is necessarily the only or chief mode of inducement available or effective in bureaucratic arrangements. Students who are morally involved in the organization may develop loyalty to bureaucratic superiors such as teachers and administrators. When this is the case, the normative symbols that uphold the bureaucratic structure (e.g., seniority, promotion, public acknowledgment of task efficiency) become as compelling to students as to other bureaucrats. Senior skip day is a bureaucratic privilege given those who have seniority (no pun intended).

Moving up through the grades becomes morally important and compelling to students, as is the publication of the honor role.

In schools where students are defined as members, the tendency will be to emphasize and rely on normative strategies of inducement. The extent to which this will be effective will depend on the type of student involvement that is present. Conformity could be expected in situations in which the students were morally involved or even if they were only mildly positive in their orientation toward school. Mild negative orientations would lead to more diffuse adaptive responses. Some students might conform with the expectations implicit in the normative inducement; others would overtly resist. Perhaps more likely responses to normative inducements in mildly negative situations would be ritual performance, or retreatism. In alienative situations, students would be likely to resist normative inducements, except in those situations where the routine application of coercion would be likely to follow such resistance (e.g., type 33, bureaucratic, structurally tight, product schools). In this case retreatism would be the most likely student response.

Psychological affective strategies are possible in most types of schools, although they are less likely to emerge or be effective in bureaucratic settings. Furthermore, bureaucracy coupled with structural tightness will probably have a tendency to decrease the utility of psychological affective strategies. Structural looseness and professionl expectations enhance the opportunity to develop the kinds of relationships upon which the effectiveness of these strategies depends, although professional environments do not *cause* such relationships to occur.

Like psychological affective strategies, social exchange strategies are likely to develop in any type of school or classroom. Both psychological affective and social exchange strategies are the result of more personalistic features than are the more organizationally based factors of coercion, remuneration, and normative inducements. Bureaucracy has a tendency to increase the use of social exchange in that it decreases the amount of interpersonal relationships possible and increases the reliance on institutionally approved means of inducement. Thus, in bureaucratic schools, social exchange strategies become the sieve through which the personality of the teacher is strained in the effort to come into personal contact with students.[11]

Psychological affective strategies are largely idiosyncratic phenomena and not likely to be used outside early elementary school, although in structurally loose schools, teachers may show marked variance in the degree to which they use these techniques. Furthermore, personality-related variances will probably be significant in the use of social exchange strategies, for the congruence of structure and social exchange strategies is more qualitative than quantitative. In tight structures, teachers will be more likely to use social exchange strategies that emanate from their authority in the hierarchy, but in loose settings, the exchanges are more likely to be based on personalistic and particularistic phenomena, such as a student's ability to defend or invade the boundaries of the classroom.

Because of the nature of inducement and adaptation, the patterns will tend to conform to the structure of the school of which they are a part. School structure tends to move toward congruence, and so do patterns of inducement and adaptation. Alienated students tend to be found in environments that use coercive strategies as a primary source of inducement. Normative strategies are likely to dominate in schools that define students as members. Calculative students are likely to respond to remunerative strategies.[12] The inability of the school to generate much in the way of remunerative power means that schools with a calculative student body will be likely to supplement remunerative strategies with either normative or coercive ones, depending on the positive or negative tendencies of the students' calculative involvement.

Retreatism and ritualism are more likely to occur and to be accepted modes of adaptation when the setting is bureaucratic than when it is professional. The more client-centered aspects of the professional orientation make retreatism more likely to be detected and dealt with than would be the case in a more impersonal bureaucratic setting. Ritualism is more likely to be distinguished from conformity in the professional setting, since the goals of the student become as much a part of the data as are the overt behaviors of the student. In the bureaucratic setting, on the other hand, behavior is the primary data of concern.

Rebellion is likely to occur in any setting, but when rebellion becomes structured and takes on a nonidiosyncratic quality, it is more likely to occur in settings that are structurally incongruent. Some congruent systems, for example, are sufficiently repressive that they can eradicate all but the most determined rebels. Thus, potential rebels, when put in congruent settings, probably retreat or engage in ritualistic behavior.

To summarize, it seems that the social structure of the school is likely to make certain kinds of inducement strategies more salient in the school and in the classroom. Furthermore, the kinds of adaptive measures possible and legitimate in these different settings will be, at least in part, shaped by the larger structure of the school. Assuming that this is the case, it is clear that there are a number of implications for theories of instruction, most of which are at present only vaguely understood.

CURRICULUM CHANGE AS ORGANIZATIONAL CHANGE

Those who work in the area of curriculum and instruction disagree about many things, but there are a few points of general agreement. (1) The first step in curriculum development, at the school level, is selecting and specifying goals. (2) The second step is the development of a plan to achieve these goals. (3) The third step is developing a plan for implementing the curriculum indicated. (4) The final step in curriculum development is evaluation and revision. This list could be lengthened or shortened, but the message would be the same: goals, plans, implementation, and evaluation. Two aspects of this process are of concern here—the selection of goals and the nature of implementation. In a later chapter detailed attention will be given to both of these matters, but of immediate concern is the proposition that the selection of goals (a) indicates what structural changes will need to be made if implementation is to be successful and (b) determines whether the indicated curricular change is indeed an organizational change or simply a substantive reordering within a given structure.

Most educational "innovations" are little more than a reshuffling of some of the more obvious and easily managed features of school organizations. For example, some would suggest that the introduction of Asian studies into the junior high school course of studies (perhaps in lieu of world history) would constitute an innovation. Accepting this definition of curricular innovation or change, it is clear that some types of curricular change do not necessarily require a realignment of the existing structure of the school. As indicated in the discussion of individualized instruction, however, some kinds of change in curricular or instructional patterns do require organizational realignments, at least if they are to be implemented successfully. In order to determine whether or not structural realignments are to be required, the curriculum innovator needs to have two kinds of data at hand: (1) an accurate description of the structural characteristics of the school system with which he is working and (2) the explicit and implicit goals of the program or change he desires to implement. Curricular goals carry with them implications for the nature of the relationships that will need to exist among teachers, students, and schools if the goals are to be successfully pursued.

Clearly, for schools to accomplish many of the goals they publicly proclaim (e.g., critical thought, developing in students the ability to lead, democratic attitudes, personal autonomy, and a respect for the dignity and worth of the individual), it would be necessary for many schools to dramatically alter their present structures. It is likely, in fact, that one of the reasons so many theoretically sound educational reforms fail "in practice" is that educators do not recognize the kinds of structural changes that are needed if the reform is to be fully implemented, or, if they do recognize them, they are unwilling or unable to make the necessary shifts in the structure. Thus, many innovations are doomed to failure even before they are tried. Curricular change, if it is to be more than a reshuffling of existing priorities, is organizational change. Without organizational change, changes in curriculum are more likely illusory than real.[13]

SUMMARY

One of the basic hypotheses of this book is that when administrative or curricular innovations are introduced that are compatible with the existing social structures of the schools, they are likely to have some measurable effects. If, however, administrative or curricular innovations are introduced that are not compatible with the existing social arrangements in the school or classroom, one of three results seems likely. (1) The innovation will be modified to fit existing patterns of behavior and thus not affect student learning. This, for example, is what has apparently happened with many efforts to introduce integrated language arts–social studies programs. Teachers simply took larger blocks of time and rescheduled their activities to conform to the traditional breakdown of history, geography, grammar, and literature. In many cases, the only "innovation" combined language arts–social studies programs produce is that in grading social studies papers, teachers are a bit more sensitive to spelling, grammar, and punctuation. (2) A second possible result of introducing innovation into incompatible structures is that the innovation will meet resistance and will eventually be abandoned because it is thought to be "inappropriate to the local situation." Indeed, unless there is a conscious effort to change that structure, this conclusion may appear to be the only logical one. Apparently this is what is happening with some efforts at adapting the British infant school to the American school system. (3) A final consequence of lack of structural support for innovation could be that the tensions created by the innovation will cause the social structure of the school or classroom to shift in ways that will accommodate the change. This, of course, is the desirable circumstance, assuming it is intended that administrative or curricular changes will have a measurable impact, but unfortunately it is not what usually happens. Indeed, because most educators have an inadequate view of the social structure of the school, they are apt to view the tensions or conflicts resulting from an innovation as evidence that the change will not work in their school. The result is that innovations are adopted and abandoned for reasons that have little to do with their potential *benefit to children. Rather, they are adopted and abandoned on the basis of their fit with the existing structure of the school.*

NOTES

1. J. Lloyd Trump and Dorsey Baynham, *Focus on Change: Guide to Better Schools* (Chicago: Rand McNally & Company, 1961).

2. L. Craig Wilson, *The Open Access Curriculum* (Boston: Allyn and Bacon, Inc., 1971), pp. 9–10.

3. Ibid.

4. John I. Goodlad, *School, Curriculum, and the Individual* (Waltham, Mass.: Blaisdell Publishing Co., 1966).

5. The distinction between individualized and personalized instruction was first brought to the author's attention by Professor Jack Blackburn.

6. The parallels between the nature of bureaucratic employee expectations and professional expectations and the requirements of the two programs of individualization are not mere contrivances to make a point. The researcher is invited to inspect various programs of individualization—including the so-called open classroom and nongraded primary—and determine the extent to which they vary in terms of relative emphasis on, or compatibility with, professional and bureaucratic orientations. The variance will be considerable, and in most schools, those programs that emphasize bureaucratization of ends will most likely succeed.

7. A thoughtful and well-documented case study of the failure of an innovation aimed at greater individualization can be found in

Neal Gross, Joseph B. Giacquinta, and Marilyn Bernstein, *Implementing Organizational Innovations: A Sociological Analysis of Planned Educational Change* (New York: Basic Books, 1971).

8. Ibid.

9. Peter M. Blau, *Bureaucracy in Modern Society* (New York: Random House, 1956), p. 57.

10. Frequently teachers unwittingly punish students when they intend to reward them. For example, teachers sometimes publicly acknowledge excellent work on the part of a student. In some settings such public recognition causes students considerable embarrassment among their peers and may result in the "rewarded" student feeling he/she has been punished for doing well.

11. See Willard Waller, *The Sociology of Teaching* (New York: John Wiley & Sons, Inc., 1932, reprinted 1967), p. 189, for a similar argument.

12. The reasoning here is directly parallel to the arguments presented by Etzioni in his discussion of congruent types. See Amitai Etzioni, *A Comparative Analysis of Complex Organizations: On Power, Involvement, and Their Correlates.* Copyright © 1961 by The Free Press of Glencoe, Inc., pp. 12–14.

13. One of the better analyses of the illusion of change in schools is presented by Seymour B. Sarason, *The Culture of the School and the Problem of Change* (Boston: Allyn and Bacon, Inc., 1971).

12

Teacher Characteristics

Researchers in education are becoming disenchanted with conventional studies of the relationship between teacher personality and teacher effectiveness. Increasingly there is a tendency toward the study of the relationship between patterns of teacher behavior in the classroom and teacher effectiveness.[1] There is much in the move toward more behaviorally oriented studies that is deserving of encouragement. Yet, the fact remains that thousands of years of folk wisdom and the intuition of wise observers hold that the personal attributes of the teacher are at least as important as the precise behavior patterns of the teacher. Knowledge with such a long and deeply imbedded tradition should not be discarded lightly. There surely must be some basis for the conventional knowledge that the individual teacher is an important variable in the learning of students. Just as surely, there must be a basis for the assumption that the personality of the teacher is linked to whatever impact a teacher has in the classroom. Why, then, have researchers been unable to produce evidence that this is so? Perhaps the answer can be found in the assumptions underlying most research directed toward the understanding of teacher personality variables.

Katz and Kahn write: "It is usual for psychologists to treat the characteristics of adult personality as relatively fixed, having been formed during earlier years of life and by earlier experiences."[2] Educational researchers tend to share the view of psychologists, particularly in the study of teacher personality and teacher characteristics. As Getzels and Jackson note:

> Investigators seem for the most part content to take their subjects where they can find them, implying that a teacher is a teacher whether his school is in the country or in the city, in Mississippi or in California, in an upper-class suburb or in a lower-class slum.[3]

If the structure of schools makes a difference in the personality of teachers, it then follows that research on teacher personality and characteristics which fails to account for structural variables between and among schools would be difficult to interpret, if not misleading. For example, certain types of schools may attract and reward teachers with particular kinds of personality characteristics, whereas other types of schools attract and reward teachers with other kinds of characteristics. If this is the case, the compounding effects on most research related to teacher personality must be considerable. Consider, for instance, one of the more common designs for studying the relationship between teacher personality and teacher effectiveness. Often a researcher will locate his population of effective teachers by asking colleagues, students, or administrators to nominate them. If the study is a comparative one, the researcher may also locate ineffective teachers in the same way. Whatever systematic effects the structure of the school has on the evaluations and perceptions of participants will clearly be built into such a sample. Thus, if the researcher limits his study to the faculty of one school building, he is likely to discover some systematic relationship between personality characteristics and teacher effectiveness. However, given the tendency of educational researchers to focus on individual human beings as their unit of analysis, it is unlikely that the population will be drawn from a single school. Rather, in the quest for a "random" sample, teachers from many schools will likely be included in the study. If, by chance, all of the teachers in the sample teach in schools with similar structural properties, systematic correlations will result, but if (as is more likely) the schools from which the teachers are drawn differ in their structural properties, it is then likely that the differences in teacher personality will appear unrelated to teaching effectiveness. Put simply, some kinds of personalities may be effective in some schools, others in other schools. To disregard the structure of schools is to hide the significance of individual variation.

In order to overcome the compounding effects of structural variables, researchers must become more sensitive to the existence and importance of these variables. Given this sensitivity and a relatively adequate description of salient structural characteristics of schools, it may be possible to gain new insight into the relationship between individual characteristics and the teaching-learning process. It is in the hope of pointing to some directions in which such insight might lie that the present chapter is written.

AN APPROACH TO THE STUDY OF TEACHER CHARACTERISTICS

The idea that organizations affect the personal character of those who hold positions in them is widely accepted among social scientists. Controversy exists regarding the nature of these effects, but few social scientists would argue that there is no linkage between personality and organizational structure. This linkage is, however, based more on deductions from theory than on empirical observation. Katz and Kahn write:

> The empirical evidence for the effects of role experience and behavior on personality is thin, perhaps because it has not been often sought. The truth of the folk saying "you become what you do" has yet to be put to systematic test. . . .[4]

Given the sparsity of solid empirical evidence, even in the more general literature, a scholar who would attempt to examine the relationship between the personality of teachers and the structure of schools is confronted with a major difficulty. If the analysis is to be convincing it must be more than personal impressions. Yet, beyond some rather solid theoretical propositions and a smattering of empirical research, there is not much data upon which to build a concept of the relationship between teacher personality and school organizations.

When confronted with this kind of situation, the scientist can make one of two choices: drop the inquiry until sufficient evidence is accumulated from which a better-grounded analysis can be presented or develop a methodology that permits as much rigor and discipline as is possible under the circumstances. Because the relationship between teacher characteristics and the structure of schools is central to an organizational theory of instruction, it would be unthinkable, particularly in the context of this book, to drop the inquiry. Therefore, it becomes necessary to adopt and develop a methodology that will provide as much rigor and discipline as possible.

When confronted with similar situations, social scientists have often resorted to the construction of ideal types. (Indeed, the construction of ideal types has been an implicit procedure throughout this book). When a researcher attempts to construct ideal types of individuals, however, he must be certain his audience clearly recognizes what he is about, for it is easy to confuse ideal types with stereotypes. Furthermore, if the researcher avoids stereotypes, it is likely that the concept of the ideal type will become confused with the concept of ideal in the sense of the perfect or the desirable. *Ideal types are neither stereotypes nor conceptions of the desired state of affairs.* "The ideal type," as Martindale puts it:

> is a strategy in empirical explanation. It is framed in terms of the scientific knowledge available to the researcher at the time of his study and in terms of the empirical situations he is trying to understand.[5]

In line with the inquiry suggested here, there is a need to put forward some explanations concerning the relationship between the structural properties of schools and the behavioral and personal characteristics of teachers. Present limitations in empirical research make precise formulations of that relationship impossible, at least in the immediate future. However, using the ideal-type framework makes it possible to gain some insight into the relationship, as well as to suggest the general directions in which empirical research will need to move if more precise statements are to be forthcoming. Of particular interest here is the relationship between different structural features (as indicated by the mode of organization and the position and commitments of students) and the characteristics of teachers.

Idiosyncratic differences between and among teachers create considerable variety in classroom performance. At the same time, the structural properties of schools work to emphasize certain kinds of performances and thus implicitly give impetus to the emergence of particular types of teacher attitudes, beliefs, and values. In order to gain insight into the process by which the structure of schools affects teacher personality and behavior, it is necessary to construct an ideal typology of teachers that is logically and empirically related to variances in the structure of schools.

BUREAUCRATIC TYPES

In the typology of schools presented in chapter 5 there are eighteen bureaucratically oriented schools. Assuming that students of school organization are correct in their assessment, it is probable that the vast majority of American public schools are represented by these eighteen types, for it appears that the predominant expectations in schools are those typified as bureaucratic. Thus, both theoretically and empirically bureaucratic types of organizations are important to the understanding of teaching in America.

In general, bureaucratic organizations have been much more carefully studied than have other organizational types.

Perhaps this is because of the predominance of bureaucratic organizations in American society, or perhaps it is a result of the influence of Weber's classic formulations of the problems and issues related to bureaucratic structures. In any case, a discussion of the impact of bureaucratic organizations on the personality of participants in the organization can proceed over relatively well-trodden—if not well-charted—ground.

Robert K. Merton[6] has advanced the notion of the bureaucratic personality. It is Merton's view, and the view of many others, that external control of members is not effective in the long run. Therefore, participants in the life of bureaucracies must internalize many of the expectations of the organization, which results in the emergence of the "bureaucratic personality." Merton writes:

> If the bureaucracy is to operate successfully, it must attain a high degree of reliability of behavior, an unusual degree of conformity with prescribed patterns of action. . . . Discipline can be effective only if the ideal patterns are buttressed by strong sentiments which entail devotion to one's duties, a keen sense of the limitation of one's authority and competence, and methodical performance of routine activities. The efficacy of social structure depends ultimately upon infusing group participants with appropriate attitudes and sentiments. . . .[7]

The significance of the bureaucratic personality is a subject about which there is considerable controversy. Some researchers suggest that the emergence of the bureaucratic personality is limited to individuals who occupy middle-level management positions.[8] Others have suggested that the forces at work within any complex organization are so conflicting that no single personality type is likely to emerge as dominant.[9] In spite of the controversy and criticism, however, there remains much in the concept of the bureaucratic personality that is provocative and useful. The concept is particularly useful in an effort to develop insight into the relationship between the structure of schools and the characteristics of teachers. Three varieties of bureaucratic personality will be taken up here: the moral leader, the technician, and the manager.

The Moral Leader

One variant of the bureaucratic personality that may emerge in the public school is the moral leader type of teacher. In many ways the teacher as moral leader conforms to the traditional stereotypes of the teacher—rigid, unimaginative, loyal to superiors, timid, and committed to routine. At the same time, however, the teacher as moral leader sees himself in a position of moral superiority as well as authority over children. One gets to be a teacher because one has special qualities that are above and beyond the worldly requirements of the community. Age and seniority are signs of wisdom as well as a basis of tenure. The teacher as moral leader sees virtue in doing things as the routine of the system insists that they be done and accepts the obligation of infusing students with loyalty to the ends the system defines as good.

The teacher type here characterized as a moral leader would be most likely found in the type 1 school (bureaucratic, tight, moral, member)[10] but would also appear in most of the other bureaucratic-type schools. Though schools that are professional and loose may recruit some teachers with characteristics like those of the moral leader, teachers with moral leader characteristics would be likely to be uncomfortable in other than bureaucratic settings. Indeed, it seems likely that individuals who are characteristically like the moral leader would be dissatisfied in professionally oriented schools and would respond almost pathologically in professional, structurally loose settings. Conversely, teachers whose values or beliefs would make them uncomfortable with behaving as moral leaders would find that systems like the type 1 school would create real conflicts for them. The type 1 school places considerable stress on personal moral involvement. The moral leader teacher has incorporated within his own personality the expectations of the system and the system's definitions of propriety, decency, and honor. In the short run a teacher may maintain a cynical performance as a moral leader, but in the long run it seems likely that, through internalization, the personality would come to authenticate the performance. Indeed, because the performance of the moral leader is so emotionally compelling, failure to internalize the performance could result in psychological deterioration.

The Technician

Another type of bureaucratic personality is the technician. Unlike the moral leader, the technician need not develop strong sentiments about the propriety of his task. Rather, the technician emphasizes the dispassionate, the objective, and the hard nosed. The technician can find personal satisfaction in a job well done—well done being measured by approval of bureaucratic authority. Whereas moral leader characteristics are likely to emerge in bureaucratically organized elementary schools, technician characteristics are more likely to be manifest in the high school setting.[11] The technician is likely to place considerable emphasis on the limits of authority and responsibility. The technician values the feeling of closure and certainty. Given a task with which he is familiar or in which he is "trained," the technician proceeds with efficiency and dispatch. Placed in indeterminate and problematic situations, the technican manages poorly.

In contrast to the moral leader, the bureaucratic technician is unwilling to take responsibility for the actions of others. Furthermore, he will accept responsibility for his own actions only insofar as they are within the areas he defines as his span of authority and competence. The technician may, however, speak in the language of professionals and use the jargon of the trade. The technician-type teacher, though clearly a bureaucratic personality, may identify himself as a professional and insist that what he wants and needs is autonomy. The autonomy he wants, however, is carefully limited to those areas in which he has been trained to work as a specialist. He is likely to feel uncomfortable and dissatisfied if he is required to exercise judgment in other areas. For instance, the school psychologist who, as a faculty member, is asked his opinion on the worth of ancient history, may refuse to comment on the basis that his area is not curriculum and instruction.

The teacher-technician would be most likely to emerge in bureaucratic schools that are client oriented and serve a calculative student body. The reason for this seems clear. The impersonality with which the technician approaches his task would not be as highly valued in the moral-member setting. Furthermore, though the technican would be able to function in the product-alienative setting, he would be unlikely to opt for such an arrangement, if for no other reason than that alienative settings are probably less predictable than calculative or morally involved ones.

One interesting possibility in regard to the teacher-technician is that there may be an affinity between this type and certain kinds of professional organizations. The language the technician is likely to employ and his insistence on technical competence and specialization may attract him to structurally tight professional organizations. In the more structurally loose professional organizations, however, the technican would probably find more autonomy of action than he is likely to find satisfying. Furthermore, as the rigidity with which the technican approaches his task becomes apparent, it is likely that the performance of the technician will be devalued in professional organizations.

The Manager

The teacher-manager is the final bureaucratic type to be considered here. The teacher as moral leader finds pride and satisfaction in being identified with a "good school and good students." The technician finds satisfaction in accomplishing specified tasks with efficiency and dispatch. The manager finds his source of satisfaction in manipulating people and in the application of rules. The manager-type teacher is likely to value structural looseness and for this reason may be mistakenly perceived as valuing autonomy. The manager type does want autonomy in deciding which rules to apply, but not the creation of rules. The manager, like the moral leader and the technician, accepts the validity of the system. He values his position in the system and recognizes the authority of his superordinates. For the manager, control and manipulation are synonymous. He prides himself on being able to inspire recalcitrant students to do as he wills them to do, and he may develop elaborate techniques and strategies for getting them to do so. But like the other bureaucratic types, he relies heavily on organizationally pre-scribed strategies, and most of the functions he fulfills are organizational in nature (e.g., the function of organizational spokesman). The manager type may attempt to use social ex-change strategies in his manipulation of others. These strategies will probably cause him personal discomfort and uneasiness, however, for like all bureaucratic personalities, he has internal-ized loyality to the system and the prescribed procedures.

The manager-type teacher may be attracted to some kinds of professionally oriented schools, but he will not flourish in these schools. Precisely because the manager values the manipulation of others, he may value symbols that give moral worth to his manipulative strategies. Thus, the manager type may speak of individualization of instruction, helping relationships, facilitating student growth, democratic decision making, and classroom democracy.[12] But under the façade of openness is a person who strives for control and predictability, and who has a need to send students home with "the right answer." For the manager type, the right answer is always in the book, the syllabus, or the statement of objectives.

PROFESSIONAL TYPES

Unlike the literature of bureaucratic organizations, the literature on professional organizations is not very suggestive regarding kinds of relationships that might exist between structure and per-sonality. Indeed, most of the literature on the relationship be-tween professionals and organizations has focused on the role con-flicts implicit in the contradictions between bureaucratic and professional expectations. By inference, though, it is possible to gain some insight into the general characteristics of the types of individuals that are likely to flourish in professional types of organizations. Among those characteristics would be personal autonomy, tolerance for ambiguity, experimentalism, person-centered as opposed to system-centered evaluations, risk-taking ability, acceptance of peer criticism, and the ability to think divergently. Frequently, critics of education—and organizational life in general—use the personal characteristics that seem to typify the professional personality as a foil against which to cast into a negative light the characteristics of the bureaucrat. Given the ideological preferences of most students of education, it is difficult to avoid this gambit. It is not, however, the intention here to describe good guys and bad guys. What is intended is to indicate the character requirements of professional organizations. In doing so, it may become clear that one of the reasons there are so few schools that reflect professional modes of organization is that the kinds of educational systems that presently exist—including those which prepare teachers—are not likely to produce individuals with the kinds of personal characteristics that would flourish in or be supportive of professional organizations.[13] Furthermore, those few individuals who do come through the present educational organizations and maintain or develop the characteristics typically needed in professionally oriented schools are unlikely to go into teaching, if for no other reason than that other professions provide more prestige and greater financial remuneration for them.

The Facilitator

Among teacher educators, words like *facilitator* carry highly charged meanings. Given the clinical orientation of most teachers, and the impact of the guidance and mental health movements on teacher education, many teacher educators place considerable value[14] on the indirect teaching techniques suggested by words like facilitation, helping relationship, and nondirective guidance.

Both the research and the ideology of teacher education give preference to the teacher type suggested by terms like democratic, open, warm, permissive, and tolerant. Teacher characteristics that are seen as authoritarian, closed, dogmatic, intolerant, and lacking in warmth are devalued. What most teacher educators seem to want is to develop teachers who are of the facilitator type, but what most schools require are managers, technicians, and moral leaders. Thus, there is a built-in conflict between the real world of schools and the theoretical world of teacher education. At least there is an ideological conflict. *Unfortunately,* the conflict is probably less real than the rhetoric of practitioners and teacher educators might lead one to believe. Teacher education programs sometimes purport to be in the business of developing facilitator-type teachers; it is likely that all but the most unusual of these programs are in fact bent on producing managers. The language of the manager and the facilitator often overlaps. (Perhaps it is this fact that makes some of the group therapy techniques so attractive to managers of large corporations as well as school executives.) The facilitator-type teacher will not be likely to find support in the typical bureaucratic arrangement of most public schools. Furthermore, those few teacher education programs that are successful in recruiting teachers with facilitator-type characteristics will probably enjoy little prestige in most public schools.[15] Facilitator-type teachers are, in fact, dysfunctional in bureaucratic schools. The lack of willingness to submit to bureaucratic moral imperatives makes the facilitator-type teacher an unpredictable quantity in bureaucratic systems. Bureaucracies require predictability. In the short run, the facilitator teacher seems destined to a life of misery in the typical public school. The type of school that is most likely to encourage the emergence of characteristics suggested by the facilitator is the type 4 school (professional, loose, member, moral), but as already indicated, this type of school is seldom found outside of the laboratory school on the college campus. It seems likely, therefore, that teachers who have facilitator-like qualities will follow one of three career patterns: (1) leave teaching in dissatisfaction and disgust; (2) move toward the college campus, either in the laboratory school or into teacher education; or (3) develop the characteristics of the bureaucratic manager.

The Craftsman

A second professional type teacher is the craftsman. Unlike the facilitator, the craftsman is less likely to find all of his satisfaction in people-oriented undertakings. Though the craftsman type values people as a part of his enterprise, he also takes pride in his own work and the results thereof. One might expect the craftsman to be a bit less altruistic and more self-centered than the facilitator, although this would not necessarily be the case. It is clear, however, that the craftsman would find it easier than would the facilitator to separate out the nature of his craft from the people to whom the craft is addressed. In this regard at least, the craftsman is similar to the bureaucratic technician. Unlike the technican, however, the craftsman has a need for wide latitude for action, and he finds systemic constraints frustrating. The craftsman follows tested rules and principles, but he is willing to take risks and establish new precedents. The craftsman, unlike the technician, does not need the approval of superiors for a job well done. Rather, he values the approval of other craftsmen and the response of clients. The craftsman may evidence certain relatively unbending characteristics and show considerable intolerance for work he considers slovenly. In this regard, then, he manifests some of the characteristics of the moral leader, as well as some of the characteristics of the technician.

The craftsman-type teacher is most likely to flourish in the professional, structurally loose, client, calculative situation. The craftsman is, however, the most versatile of all the teacher types. He is likely to survive and flourish in almost any type of school *other* than the structurally tight. The structurally tight school is anathema to the craftsman, for he cannot develop sufficient latitude of action, and his personality is likely to chafe against overt authority. In the bureaucratic-structurally loose schools the craftsman may be a source of difficulty and frustration. The craftsman may himself be frustrated, but he can survive. The craftsman type is strikingly like Waller's insightful teacher, and like the insightful teacher, the craftsman may become aliented from himself, his tools, and his products.

The Scientist

Perhaps the most prestigious of the professional types is the scientist. The scientist is most likely to emerge in the product-oriented school, although the type can flourish in most of the professional-type schools. It seems probable that the scientist-type teacher would be most frequently attracted to positions in school psychology, special education, and similar programs, for it is in these areas that one is most likely to find scientific principles applied to instruction.

Among the more salient characteristics of the scientist is commitment to experimentalism, rigorous analysis, and sophisticated measurement. The manipulation of experimental situations may make the scientist appear to be much like the manager. The manager, however, is more concerned with controlling situations as an end in itself, whereas the scientist controls situations for the purpose of experimentation. Like the technician, the scientist is interested in precision, but the scientist is also interested in exploring new areas; in brief, the scientist is more adventuresome than is the technician.

The background and training of the scientist are likely to have a firm basis in psychology, though the scientist type may operate from substantive bases in other of the behavioral sciences. The scientist-teacher is certain, however, to operate from some theoretical base, or at least perceive himself as doing so. The scientist-teacher is likely to show a preference for quantifiable propositions and a certain disdain for subjects that lack precision. Therefore, it would be unusual that the scientist-teacher would be found teaching subjects like literature or history. Furthermore, when the scientist-teacher does teach some of the more humanistic subjects, there is a strong possibility that he will give emphasis to teaching procedures that have overtones of behaviorism. For example, he may emphasize criterion-referenced instruction, or programmed learning.

SUMMARY

Just as it is unlikely that there is a pure type school, it is unlikely that one would find any of the six teacher types existing in pure form. Yet, each teacher type is an empirical possibility. Furthermore, it is likely that some of the characteristics indicated by these types would be more likely to be found in schools which have structures that reward and support the behaviors suggested by the characteristics. For example, the scientist-teacher would be most likely to be found in the type 36 school (see Appendix), for in that school the system would need and reward individuals with the kinds of characteristics indicated by the scientist.

The fact that some of the teacher types are empirically difficult to distinguish (e.g., there is a considerable overlap between the manager and the scientist) suggests the possibility that in the real world of schools researchers would find that individual teachers manifest combinations of characteristics. Furthermore, particular combinations of characteristics may be systematically present in conjunction with particular school structures. Should this be the case, it might serve as a basis for predicting interpersonal and intrapersonal conflict in schools, as well as conflicts between particular types of individuals and particular types of schools.

NOTES

1. As pointed out in chapter 2, however, conventional studies of teacher personality and characteristics continue to be a predominant area of inquiry. Though there is a change in the direction of educational research, the change is not dramatic.

2. Daniel E. Katz and Robert L. Kahn, *The Social Psychology of Organizations* (New York: John Wiley & Sons, Inc., 1966), p. 195.

3. J. W. Getzels and P. W. Jackson, "The Teacher's Personality and Characteristics," in *Handbook of Research on Teaching*, ed. N. L. Gage (Chicago: Rand McNally & Company, 1963), p. 575.

4. Katz and Kahn, *Social Psychology of Organizations*, p. 195.

5. Don A. Martindale, *The Nature and Types of Sociological Theory* (Boston: Houghton Mifflin Company, 1960), p. 382.

6. Robert K. Merton, *Social Theory and Social Structure*, enlarged edition (New York: The Free Press, 1968).

7. Ibid., pp. 252–253.

8. Roy G. Francis and Robert C. Stone, *Service and Procedure in Bureaucracy: A Case Study* (Minneapolis: University of Minnesota Press, 1956), pp. 160–161.

9. See, for example, Ronald G. Corwin, *A Sociology of Education: Emerging Patterns of Class, Status, and Power in the Public Schools* (New York: Appleton-Century-Crofts, 1965), pp. 254–257.

10. See Appendix for a description of the type 1 school. The fact that this school is likely to be in rural areas and generally stable communities probably reinforces the position of the moral leader–type teacher.

11. Among the reasons for the greater incidence of technician characteristics in high schools is that elementary teachers are less likely to specialize than are secondary teachers. Furthermore, the relationship between elementary teachers in the self-contained classroom and secondary teachers in more compartmentalized classes would seem likely to encourage the emergence of technicians at the secondary level and moral leaders at the elementary school level.

12. There is a fine line between manipulation and facilitating personal growth, as anyone familiar with some of the group dynamics approaches to executive training must surely recognize. It is probably the case that the manager-type teacher will develop an affinity for either group dynamics approaches or for behavior modification. Group dynamics can be used to conceal manipulation; behavior modification makes manipulation legitimate.

13. An interesting study would be to contrast the organizational style of departments and schools of education with other academic departments. Given the fact "trained administrators" seem so frequently to emerge in positions of authority in schools of educa-

tion, it seems reasonable to speculate that these organizations would be more likely to be bureaucratized than other departments. Should this be so, it would be small wonder that so few professionally oriented teachers are available. It is difficult to create a professional orientation using bureaucratic means.

14. This value can be positive or negative. There are many in teacher education who find the impact of the guidance and mental health movements a source of distress. Additionally, there are many who find the impact insignificant and strive to increase its influence.

15. Though direct evidence is lacking, it seems likely that one of the reasons for the failure of some teacher corps projects is the fact that the projects recruited teachers who possessed facilitator-like characteristics and placed them in bureaucratic schools. This speculation is based on conversations with individuals who directed or participated in teacher corps programs.

13

The Future

The intent of this book has been to present the broad outlines of an organizational theory of instruction. In the first four chapters some of the more critical issues confronting modern educational researchers were described. Particular attention was given to issues of concern to researchers who are especially interested in the relationship between teaching and learning. In addition, some of the reasons for the continuing distance between educational theory and classroom practice were indicated.

Chapters five through nine presented a series of propositions about schools and teaching. For the most part these propositions were based on ideas derived from organizational theory. Most of the evidence to support these propositions was drawn from the literature of sociology and education. Chapters ten through twelve served to illustrate the kinds of answers an organizational perspective might provide to a number of the perennial questions asked by educational researchers—questions like "Why does individualized instruction seem to work in some schools but not in others?" The Appendix has been designed to provide the reader with a more detailed account of the kinds of "informed speculations" one might develop concerning the impact of variation in organizational structures on the behavior of participants in the life of schools.

The line of argument pursued in the preceding chapters is relatively straightforward. Based on the assumption that schools are complex social organizations, an effort has been made to identify and describe some of the more salient characteristics of school organizations that impact on the behavior of teachers and students. The primary tenet upon which this book is based is that teaching is, above all else, a social act. Furthermore, teaching is a social act with a clear intent: to induce students to behave in ways that are assumed to lead to learning. Though the importance of psychological factors is not denied, an effort has been made to demonstrate that a social science perspective can bring into focus many features of school life that are overlooked when a strictly psychological perspective is used to study the realities of school life. For example, to study teacher style without giving attention to those organizational features that shape and mold teacher performance is likely to provide a distorted image of the power and significance of the individual teacher. Such distortions can easily lead to frustration, both for researchers and for practitioners. So long as it is assumed that individually based differences among teachers are the prime determinants of school learning, little progress can be made in understanding the nature of school life, since that life is shaped by the structural and organizational characteristics of schools.

This book should serve to encourage students of education to give further consideration to the ways in which social science perspectives might be applied to the realities of schools. As has been indicated throughout this book, educational research clearly stands in need of an alternative perspective, and there are indications that alternatives of the type discussed would be welcomed by educators.

For example, in the past four years both the *Review of Educational Research*[1] and the *American Educational Research Journal*[2] have contained editorial commentary that explicitly recognizes the need for alternative approaches to educational studies. The editors of the *AERJ*, certainly one of the more prestigious research journals in education, explicitly acknowledged that the *AERJ* had been rather exclusively interested in:

methodological studies in experimental design, measurement, evaluation, and statistics, or largely psychological studies of

verbal learning, short-term retention, and educational technology
. . . while the examination of other subjects or those of different
research persuasions *unfortunately* seemed to lie outside of the
domain of concern of the *AERJ*.[3]

Though a preponderance of the articles published in journals
like the *RER* and the *AERJ* continue to be based in psychology
or concerned somehow with the measurement of mental processes, there has been a noticeable increase in the appearance of
social science–oriented articles and research reports.

Furthermore, the recent upsurge in observational studies,
especially studies of classrooms,[4] has caused educational researchers to become interested in the methodologies and research
procedures employed by social scientists, especially the methodologies of anthropologists and sociologists. Whether this interest
in social science methodology will extend to social theory is a
matter yet to be determined. To date it would appear that most
educational researchers—especially those who study classrooms—are not especially interested in social explanations for
their findings, though some are.[5]

Unfortunately, there is little in the tradition or the training
of teachers or educational researchers that is likely to encourage
professional educators to consider the practical significance of
social science perspectives as a source of guidance in shaping
teaching theory and educational policy. Though there are many
reasons why the social sciences have not had a significant impact
on educational theory (some of these reasons were dealt with in
considerable detail in the first three chapters of this book),
among the most significant sources of difficulty is the present
condition of the field of study called "social foundations of education." It is in the field of social foundations that most professional educators come into contact with what little social science
they do encounter, and it is in the reorientation of the field of
foundational studies that the hope of a productive future for an
organizationally based theory of instruction lines. The remainder
of this chapter, therefore, is committed to examining the present
status of foundational studies in education and to developing
suggestions about ways in which this field of study might be

reoriented. Such reorientation should provide a systematic ac-
cumulation of empirical knowledge upon which an organizational theory of instruction could be built. Hopefully, as data
are collected using the methods of the social sciences, educational
researchers will discover that social theory *as well as* the research methods of the social sciences are useful for gaining
insight into the realities of classroom life.

FOUNDATIONAL STUDIES:
A NEED FOR DIRECTION

For most teachers and administrators, social theory applied to
education is represented by what they remember about some
vague and nondescript course called "social and cultural
foundations of education." (Sometimes other equally descriptive appellations are given these courses.) Though some graduate
schools of education do have recognizable social science departments, in most teacher education institutions any social science
theory that finds its way into the thinking of teachers (and most
future educational researchers) must first be strained through the
sieve of foundational studies. One need only review some of the
more widely used introductory foundations texts to understand
how fine this sieve really is, and how quickly it can turn promising intellectual fare into bland gruel.

Many introductory foundations texts are nothing more than
books of readings. Sometimes these readings seem to have been
carefully selected; at other times this is not so. In some popular
texts a wide range of writers address themselves to selected
subjects and organize their efforts according to "discipline" areas,
such as social foundations, historical foundations, or philosophic
foundations. Though many of the individual readings may be
theoretically quite sophisticated, and some may even have clear
practical implications, it is difficult to believe that a beginning
education student, or even a more advanced one, would find
much in these pages to convince him that the social sciences
have anything to do with theories of instruction.

After the book of readings arranged around discipline areas, the next most popular format for the introductory foundations text is the discussion of topics thought to be of interest to educators, such as organization and administration and pre-elementary education. Because of the diversity of the topics typically covered in such texts, the result is a superficial treatment of many very important and complex issues. Indeed, because this type book usually covers such a wide range of topics, these texts are probably less theoretically sophisticated than are those that give brief surveys of the disciplines.

Sometimes an inspired instructor can work with even the most abominable materials to produce an experience in which students come away excited and wanting to pursue the inquiry even further. Unfortunately, there is a dearth of such teachers in nearly every field. Furthermore, as with most introductory courses, there is a tendency to assign beginning foundations courses to professors who need the course to fill out their "load" or to uninspired graduate students who are nearly as confused about the study of education as are the students in the course.

Thus it is that many teachers and prospective educational researchers come away from their first exposure to social theory as applied to education with a feeling of frustration and hopelessness. They are frustrated because they cannot understand what they were supposed to have learned from what they studied, and they feel hopeless because they find little in educational theory that has real worth to them in the world they anticipate entering. The unfortunate consequence is that most teachers, looking back on their experiences with foundational studies, find it difficult to believe that social theory is any more relevant to their task than is psychologically based theory. Indeed, psychologically based theory, for all its problems, may appear more relevant, for it does seem to address some issues of direct concern to teachers, such as motivation and assessment.

Perhaps even more damaging to the future of education is the unpleasant probability that some promising future researchers are repelled from giving serious consideration to the potential of social theory in educational studies by their initial experiences in foundational studies. It is unfortunate, for example, that many graduate students never *directly* encounter the works of such seminal thinkers as Waller, Durkheim, and Dewey. Indeed, if they see other than secondhand accounts of the work of such men, it is often late in their course of study and usually quite by accident. Social scientists in schools of education must face up to the fact that not only does the culture of educational research impel students toward a psychological perspective, but also initial experiences with social theory applied to education too often repel students from the social sciences.

In the past the appeal of psychological studies in education, as well as psychologically based theories of instruction, was a positive one. Future educational researchers were attracted to this perspective because they saw in it the promise of systematic theories of instruction and the hope of improving the quality of schooling afforded the young. Increasingly, educational researchers have come to see that these traditional perspectives on teaching and learning are fruitless avenues of inquiry for those concerned with instructional theory. This has left a serious void in the study of education.

Unfortunately, foundational studies, unfocused as they are, have not rushed in to fill this gap. Rather, what has occurred is an increasing reliance on a shallow type of empiricism—atheoretical in its base and nontheoretical in its promise. Though the recent move toward intensive classroom observation and case studies of college, university, and school life is a commendable step in a desirable direction, such observations, uninstructed by systematic theory, are no more likely to yield a knowledge base for a professional approach to education than are studies of the personality profiles of teachers and students. Until educational researchers in general, and social researchers in particular, are more clear on the range of their questions and the theories and methodologies appropriate to their work than is now the case, there is little likelihood that social science will be more productive of a useful knowledge base for instructional theory than has been psychology.

For example, one of the most persistent problems in most contemporary observational studies of classroom behavior is the tendency of researchers to confuse studies of milieux with studies of structure.[6] Few studies of classrooms properly locate the classroom studied within the larger structural framework of the school in which it exists, and even fewer attempt to isolate those structural variables within schools that might be shaping the behavior of teachers and students in classrooms. Rather, most studies proceed from the assumption that the causal mechanisms for classroom behavior are properly located within the particular milieu of the classroom, and more specifically within the peculiar behavior patterns of teachers and students in those classrooms.

Another difficulty is the tendency to confuse the methodology of social science with social theory, or the failure to make explicit the theoretical propositions upon which particular methodological decisions are based. For example, Good, Biddle, and Brophy argue, quite correctly, that one of the major weaknesses of teacher effectiveness studies is the lack of a teaching theory in most of these studies. They write:

> Much of this effort [the effort to study teacher effectiveness] may be characterized as "dust bowl empiricism." Studies have been conducted on a wondrous array of teacher characteristics including, among others, teachers' eye color, voice quality, clothing style, musical ability, and even strength of grip! Why anyone would expect any of these to relate to teacher effectiveness is a mystery.[7]

After making this observation they go on to insist that the basis for generalizability of findings should be the type of research setting in which the research is done. They write:

> Research on teaching should be conducted in the settings to which the investigator wishes to generalize his results. If first grade reading groups are of interest, the research should take place in the first grade classroom during reading lessons.[8]

The recommendation that studies of teaching take place in naturalistic settings is one with which most social scientists would have considerable sympathy, for with the exception of some social psychological research with small groups, most social research takes place in naturalistic environments. But, it is doubtful that many social scientists would agree that age and task are necessarily the most significant variables to consider when one is describing the setting in which the research is being done, even if the research is limited to schools. Yet Good et al. clearly assume that age (e.g., first graders) and task (e.g., reading) are likely to have a significant effect on how teachers and students behave in classrooms. This is a proposition of no minor significance to one interested in an organizational theory of instruction.

Whether this assumption is warranted is not at issue. Rather, the concern is that to assume that social variables like age and task are likely to affect teacher or student behavior and design studies based on this assumption makes it difficult—if not impossible—to determine the extent to which such assumptions *are* warranted.

Apparently, the tradition in educational research which insists that the only variables of relevance to a theory of teaching are those relating to the behavior of individuals is a difficult one to abandon, even by those who are sensitive to the issues involved.[9] The idea that teacher and student behavior are probably related to the structure of schools and classrooms is clearly accepted by Good et al. However, they seem to fail to accept the notion that an adequate theory of instruction requires that researchers study how these structural components relate to behavior. Rather, they assume structural or contextual effects are likely to be present and must therefore be controlled by design if one is to study those variables that are *truly* appropriate to theories of teaching, that is, the behavior of teachers and students in classrooms.

If social scientists in education, or social scientists who study education, permit themselves the comfortable illusion that the movement toward classroom observations and case studies of schools means that the questions educational researchers are now asking differ from those asked twenty years ago, it is unlikely that social theory will ever be as instructive to educational researchers as it might be. To date, the most dramatic change in the study of teaching has been a methodological one. The questions asked remain essentially the same as they were twenty years ago when learning theory was the only basis for studies of teaching. What is needed now is a theoretical reorientation that will make it possible to raise new questions, questions for which the data of observational studies in classrooms will have direct relevance. Giving shape and form to this orientation should be the task of foundational studies in education. In the process of giving this shape there should emerge, within the field, a new sense of direction and feeling of intellectual excitement that could attract both practitioners and future researchers to the undertaking.

FOUNDATIONAL STUDIES:
A TECHNOLOGICAL PERSPECTIVE

For most Americans the word technology carries with it connotations of hardware, computers, and mechanical gadgets. As social scientists have come to use the term, however, its meaning is both simple and profound. Perhaps the most straightforward definition of the term is provided by Dreeben.

> Technology pertains to the means of getting a job done, whatever the means and job happen to be. Hence, we should not equate technology with hardware, nor exclude hardware from the definition of technology, for the latter is a very general concept.[10]

At least four aspects of schools can be identified in terms of their technological elements:

1. Instructional processes and programs, where questions of technology concern methods of presenting curricular materials, developing classroom activities, coordinating the activities of various classrooms

into larger instructional units (e.g., coordinating the activities of teams of teachers), and so on.

2. Motivation—the means by which schools engage participants in instructional activities and establish favorable sentiments toward school and the schooling process.

3. Social control—managing the assemblage of pupils and teachers, maintaining order, and creating a climate conducive to learning.

4. Changing social arrangements within the classroom, within the school, and among the school and other school-related agencies.[11]

A substantial case can be made that foundational studies in education, properly conceived, would be concerned with (a) the creation of knowledge related to understanding educational technology and (b) the dissemination of knowledge about educational technologies to practitioners and to those concerned with the formation of educational policy. The study of educational technology is a potential common bond among the diverse elements that compose the typical foundations faculty within teacher education institutions.

Among faculties of schools of education those in social foundations are the most likely, by training and inclination, to be competent to study educational technology. For example, the means by which schools develop positive sentiments among teachers, or the means by which schools produce negative sentiments, is more likely to be fruitfully studied by one trained in sociology—especially the sociology of occupations—than by a specialist in instructional methods or learning theory.[12] Similarly, the relationship between means and ends (e.g., what are the ethical and moral considerations involved in the application of behavior modification techniques with minority children?) are more likely to be of central concern to educational philosophers than to specialists in mental measurement.

A second reason for making the study of educational technology central to educational foundations has to do with the too infrequently acknowledged differences between the role of the social scientist in a teacher education institution and the role of the social scientist in a social science department of a liberal arts college. There are many things about education that a social scientist might study that do not involve educational technology as either an independent or a dependent variable. It is doubtful, however, that a social scientist in a professional school of education should concern himself with these matters. It might be better if he left such inquiries to his colleagues who have a primary allegiance to advancing the knowledge in a discipline. The commitment of the social scientist in a school of education must be to understand educational processes. Though the one commitment does not exclude the other, it does shape the emphasis of one's studies.

There is probably no good reason for a social scientist to affiliate himself with a school of education other than that he assumes that he can contribute something of use to those in the profession of education. The social scientist who joins the faculty of a school of education and continues to do only those things he might have done in a social science department probably does neither himself nor education any particular good. Clearly, there are certain status risks for the social scientist affiliated with a school of education,[13] and just as clearly schools of education do not have unlimited resources to expend on supporting faculty that could as well be located elsewhere. If the social scientist does not do something different from that which he might have done in the social science department, the status risks and role ambivalence seem a considerable price to pay, and professional schools would be foolish to expend their resources so unwisely.

By centering foundational studies on educational technology, both social scientists and professional educators have some assurance that the talents of social scientists in schools of education will be turned to inquiries—no matter how esoteric—that have potential payoff in the real world of schools. Furthermore, such a focus provides a clear mission for the social scientist in education and may serve to clarify his status and role in teacher education agencies.

A third reason for orienting foundational studies toward investigations of educational technology is that by centering attention on the technological aspects of education, one is almost forced to wed theory to practice. Indeed, one is theorizing about the existing practices of education. That some in foundational studies may need to consider whether existing practice should be as it is cannot be denied. But equally important is the development of a data base from which existing practice can be described and a theoretical framework into which these descriptions might be placed. Only when educators—especially those in the area of foundations—recognize that theory is not a set of preachments about what should be done in the classroom, but a set of interrelated explanations of what is done and to what effect, will an instructional theory be possible.

Fourth, by concentrating on educational technology as the subject of study, foundations faculties will be encouraged to look beyond the behavior or attributes of individuals for dependent as well as independent variables. The relationship between structure and technology would be a primary focus of study. It seems likely, furthermore, that until technology and structure become variables of concern in educational research, an organizationally based theory of instruction will not be clearly established. It is the relationship between technology and structure that constitutes the fundamental inquiry of an organizational theory of instruction.[14]

Perhaps the most compelling reason for making educational technology a primary point of concern in foundational studies is that it centers the researchers' attention on the fact that research in education, if it is to be useful, must be concerned with questions of fundamental causation. There has grown up in the social sciences a strong resistance to seeking basic causes, but educational researchers are, by the nature of their calling, forced to seek causal mechanisms.

By splitting the object of study into multiple factors it is possible to cast doubt on the notion of primary causes. By making the number of factors infinite it is possible to make the issue of causation seem too complex to be managed.

Yet, those who teach, those who manage schools, and those who shape educational policies necessarily operate from the assumption that what they do has effects and that what they do could cause some response in their environment. Therefore, social research in education—especially that done under the auspices of professional schools of education—must seek out those causes that may shape action in classrooms, schools, or wherever educational decisions are made and implemented.[15]

If the reorientation suggested here should occur, there are a number of likely consequences for those who teach and do research in the area of foundational studies. Unlike the present situation, in which research in foundations is unfocused and without clear direction, foundations faculties would have a clearer notion of where energies should be expended. Studies that were not somehow related to educational technology (either as cause or effect), though perhaps of interest to academic scholars, would no longer consume the energies of researchers in education.

Second, though foundational studies would remain firmly tied to the social science disciplines for support and sustenance, the nature of that support and sustenance would be clearly specified. Thus the jurisdiction of foundational studies, as a research area in its own right, would be established. It seems likely that orienting foundational studies toward inquiries into the nature of educational technology would force considerably more attention to the theories and methodologies of the social science disciplines than is now the case. Similarly, it would also divert attention from the study of specific topics within these disciplines (e.g., social problems) or matters of momentary concern and debate within the disciplines, unless, of course, the debate dealt with theory or methodology.

A final consequence of the reorientation here suggested is that graduate training programs for foundation specialists could be more sharply focused. The type of investigation suggested here requires that educational researchers be well grounded in the theory and methodology of one or more of the social science disciplines. By centering attention on methodology and theory, doctoral students could avoid the topical smorgasbord that so often typifies the course of study of those few education graduate students who do look to the social sciences for a substantive base.

CONCLUDING REMARKS

Nowadays it is popular to debunk the utility and efficacy of school reform. Though much of this debunking is based more on personal preference and ideological commitments than on substantive data, there are those who maintain there is evidence to prove that schools are failures and that the cause of school reform is a fruitless one to pursue. And as Good and colleagues point out, these criticisms have not gone unheeded. Indeed:

> Well intentioned schoolmen and school board members have used such reports as reasons for radical shifts in their programs. State legislators have used these same studies as reasons for cutting support for schools or for instituting programs of radical "reform." Citizens in general have cited them in arguing the advisability of ceasing programs that might heretofore have been thought to improve the educational effort.[16]

Unfortunately, many Americans are coming to believe that school reform has failed because the schools cannot be reformed. Some defenders of schools attempt to counter such charges by attacking the research used to demonstrate the failure of school reform. From the point of view presented in this book one can accept the idea that school reform has failed—perhaps even as badly as some of the radical critics suggest—and yet retain faith in the viability of schools and the promise of school reform. From the point of view presented here it is possible to suggest that the reason school reform has failed lies not in the fact that schools are not reformable but in the fact that reformers too often start from faulty premises, premises that insist that personalistic variables are more important in schools than are structural ones. Perhaps it would be better to assume that the affairs of men are as much shaped by the institutions men build as by other men, and that reform of institutions involves structural as well as personal changes. To try to change the behavior of individual school participants can lead to little more than personal frustration and the failure of reform. It is reasonable to believe that schools can be reformed, if we but understand the level at which reform is needed. Knowledge of the structural sources of classroom behavior will provide a clearer view of where needed reform might be instituted.

NOTES

1. *The Review of Educational Research*, Vol. 42, No. 4 (Fall, 1972).
2. *American Educational Research Journal*, "Message from the Editors," Vol. 10, No. 3 (Summer, 1973), 173.
3. Ibid. (italics added)
4. Recently (1974) a book appeared that systematically reviewed many of these studies. As the authors correctly note, theirs is probably the first text published that is explicitly concerned with the study of teaching. As they also note, ". . . we are more certain of a few findings about teaching than we are of theories that might explain them." See: Michael J. Dunkin and Bruce J. Biddle, *The Study of Teaching* (New York: Holt, Rinehart and Winston, Inc., 1974).
5. Throughout this book reference has been made to the works of various individuals who have attempted to apply social theory to the study of classrooms. Some, like Phillip Jackson, Thomas Good, and Jere Brophy seem to intuitively understand that social theory might be helpful in their explanations, though they are often not precise in their applications of these theories. Others, like Elizabeth Cohen and Bruce Biddle, make more systematic use of theory derived from the social sciences.
6. C. Wright Mills presents a useful discussion of the difference between milieux and structure in his book *The Sociological Imagination* (New York: Oxford University Press, 1961), pp. 67–71.
7. Thomas L. Good, Bruce J. Biddle, and Jere E. Brophy, *Teachers Make a Difference* (New York: Holt, Rinehart and Winston, Inc., 1975), p. 14.
8. Ibid., p. 37.
9. In fairness to Good et al., other aspects of their presentation do suggest that they are aware that structural variables are quite different from behavioral variables. Biddle most obviously understands the difference between structural and personalistic variables, for many of his other publications are explicitly concerned with aspects of this distinction. See, for example, Bruce J. Biddle

and Edwin J. Thomas, *Role Theory: Concepts and Research* (New York: John Wiley & Sons, Inc., 1966). Unfortunately, much of the volume entitled *Teachers Make a Difference* is not as careful about this distinction as one might hope would be the case.

10. Robert S. Dreeben, *The Nature of Teaching: Schools and the Work of Teachers* (Glenview, Ill.: Scott, Foresman and Company, 1970), p. 83.

11. Ibid., p. 87. These four aspects of school closely parallel Dreeben, though I have expanded his meaning considerably by casting the discussion in terms of the broader context of schooling (rather than simply teaching). For example, Dreeben discusses motivation largely in terms of students, but I see questions of teacher motivation related to the technology of schooling as much as is the question of student motivation. Indeed, it seems likely that in the real world of schools the motivation of teachers and students is probably so interdependent that it is meaningless to separate them for other analytic purposes.

12. For a useful illustration of a study of this particular question see Elizabeth G. Cohen, "Open Space Schools: The Opportunity to Become Ambitious," *Sociology Of Education*, Vol. 46 (Spring, 1973), 143–161.

13. The degree to which these status risks are real, and the degree to which they are deserved, is not the question here. The point is that many social scientists, both those in schools of education and those in academic departments, perceive the problem to exist, and act accordingly. For a more elaborate discussion of this and related issues see Donald Hansen, "The Uncomfortable Relation of Sociology and Education," in *On Education: Sociological Perspectives*, ed. Donald Hansen and Joel Gerstl (New York: John Wiley & Sons, Inc., 1967).

14. See, for example, Joan Woodward, *Industrial Organization* (London: Oxford University Press, 1965), and Edward Harvey, "Technology and the Structure of Organizations," *American Sociological Review*, 33 (April, 1968), 247–249.

15. Mills presents a useful discussion of the issues related to the study of social causes in his book *The Sociological Imagination*.

16. Good et al., *Teachers Make a Difference*, p. 12.

Appendix

The purpose of this appendix is to provide the reader with a more detailed description of each of the schools represented by the typology of schools in chapter 5. To make the presentation more understandable and to facilitate comparisons between and among school types, a common format has been developed for the description of each school type. Each of the thirty-six school types will be described in terms of the following features: probable location (e.g., rural, suburban, and inner-city); probable size; grade level of student body; typical relationships between teachers and students; intra-faculty relationships; and teacher and administrator relationships.

These descriptions are necessarily speculative. Any of the thirty-six schools represented in the typology could, for example, be located in rural, urban, or suburban areas. Therefore, to suggest that a particular type of school is likely to be found in rural areas does not exclude the possibility of an empirical illustration of the type being found in an urban center. It does, however, seem reasonable to speculate that different types of community structures would be apt to support or encourage the development of schools with particular structural features. As a safeguard against unfounded speculation, each description will be followed by a brief rationale related to the judgments implicit in the description itself. In this way, the reader will be in a better position to evaluate the relative merits of the arguments presented here.

The reader will note that no precise definition of terms such as small, moderate, rural, and urban has been provided. To offer operational definitions for relative concepts such as small and large suggests much more certainty and closure than any of the descriptions should portray. Commonsense definitions will be sufficient to provide the clarity needed, and by relying on commonsense definitions, the danger of suggesting that speculations are certainties is at least guarded against.

SCHOOL TYPE 1
Bureaucratic—Tight—Member—Moral

Probable Location:
Rural communities, small towns, well-established residential suburbs of middle-sized cities.

Probable Size:
As compared with urban schools, small, although some consolidated rural high schools may be relatively large.

Probable Grade Level:
K–12; most likely to be found in secondary schools, i.e., grades 7–12.

Teacher-Student Relationships:
Teacher-student relationships are typified by teacher's placing heavy reliance on normative strategies of inducement and students' responding to these strategies in a conforming manner. Student rebellion will likely be treated as a violation of community morality (e.g., codes of good citizenship). Those students who do not respond to normative strategies are likely to be treated in a coercive manner, with expulsion and corporal punishment among the more frequently employed coercive measures.

Intra-Faculty Relationships:
Considerable emphasis will be given to evidence of loyalty to administration. Experienced teachers will identify with administrative superiors, and will subject new teachers to careful scrutiny regarding their support of prevailing rules and norms. Factionalism will be more *sub rosa* than overt. Frequently, factions will develop around pro- and anti-administration issues, but for the most part these issues will not be clearly articulated. Usually, indeed, these issues will be viewed as interpersonal quarrels between older and younger teachers or between immature and mature teachers.

Administrator-Faculty Relationships:

Perhaps best typified as benevolent paternalism. The emphasis on bureaucratic rules, student moral involvement, student membership, and structural tightness reinforces the position of the administrator as something of a tribal elder in a community agency, that is, the school. Teachers are seen as adult representatives of the community. The administrator, in dealing with teachers, will place heavy reliance on normative symbols like maturity, dedication, commitment, the interest of the community, and "shared responsibility" with parents.

Rationale:

Given the nature of student moral involvement, school type 1 would likely be serving a relatively stable and homogeneous population. Although the rural community is not as stable or homogeneous as is sometimes believed, there is probably more homogeneity in the small town than in the urban center.

Though size does not cause diversity, the greater the size of an organization, the more likely is it to be populated by divergent groups. Moral involvement suggests relative homogeneity of commitment and values and thus the likelihood of a relatively small school.

Although student age is not as clearly indicated by the structure of the type 1 school as are other factors, it seems likely that junior high schools and senior high schools would be more frequently represented in this category than would early elementary schools. Early elementary schools, even small schools, seem to be typified by considerable structural looseness at the classroom level.

The basis for the description of faculty-student-administrator relations seems almost self-evident, but a couple of comments may add some clarity. The type 1 school is bureaucratic, and thus somewhat impersonal, yet the view of the student as member and the moral involvement of the students suggest considerable integration between the values of the school and the values of the local community. Thus, there is heavy reliance on normative inducements. The tendency to move to coercion—particularly

273

expulsion—when rejection or rebellion occurs is reinforced by two factors: (1) the punitive nature of bureaucratic administration and (2) the perception that the bureaucratic rules of the schools represent, also, the moral code of the larger community.

SCHOOL TYPE 2

Bureaucratic—Loose—Member—Moral

Probable Location:
Same as type 1.

Probable Size:
Same as type 1.

Probable Grade Level:
Most likely 4–6, though some high schools and some primary schools will reflect these structural characteristics.

Teacher-Student Relationships:
Same as type 1.

Intra-Faculty Relationships:
Generally the same as type 1, except that direct communication between teachers regarding classroom performance is somewhat less likely to occur.

Administrator-Faculty Relationships:
Similar to type 1, but with considerably more tension related to monitoring and evaluating teacher classroom performance.

Rationale:
The arguments presented in regard to the type 1 school hold, in general, for the type 2 school also. Given the subject matter

differentiation and the specialization of supervisory functions at the secondary level, however, structural tightness is more likely to accompany bureaucracy in secondary schools than is the case at the elementary level. On the other hand, the relatively un-socialized (to the norms of schools) quality of children in early elementary schools makes it unlikely that early elementary school children will be treated as members or evidence positive moral commitment to the school system. Their commitments are more likely to be personal (e.g., to the teacher). The middle school years seem to present the optimum conditions for the emergence of the type 2 school.

In the structurally loose situations—particularly in bureau-cratic arrangements—the maintenance of classroom boundaries would be a special problem. Therefore, teachers will be likely to develop strategies for excluding others from having knowl-edge of their performance, and will resist administrative moves to "invade" the classroom.

SCHOOL TYPE 3

Professional—Tight—Member—Moral

Probable Location:
Indeterminate, but likely campus setting in rural or subur-ban area.

Probable Size:
Relatively small, often private and residential.

Probable Grade Level:
Students likely to be of junior and senior high school age.

Teacher-Student Relationships:
Typified by reliance on normative strategies of inducement, including ideas of reciprocity and duty. Considerable attention

to tutorial arrangements, little coercion, and practically no use of remunerative strategies. Although student conformity is the expected and common mode of student adaptation, considerable variance may be tolerated.

Intra-Faculty Relationships:

Emphasis on mutualism, respect for perceived competence and excellence. Factionalism, if it develops, is likely to be related to departmental affiliations, subject matter specialties, and similar task-related organizational features.

Administrator-Faculty Relationships:

Administrators are likely to be divided into two categories: those with instructional obligations and those with system maintenance functions. Few middle-level system maintenance administrators (e.g., recruitment officers) will have direct impact on the instructional program. Centralized direction of programs and imposition of professional standards will be the mode, although this is likely to cause considerable tension. Some movement toward structural looseness is likely to be exhibited by the faculty, but may meet administrative resistance from instructionally oriented administrators.

Rationale:

The type of school suggested by type 3 is not very common. The antagonism between professionalism and structural tightness would be likely to create a tension-laden environment. Eventually the tension will be relieved by movement to a structural configuration that has less potential for conflict.

The fact that survival (faculty survival) in such a system would call for considerable student commitment to common values, while at the same time providing a stimulating environment for professional growth, suggests the possibility of a private school, although some highly selective inner-city schools might accomplish the same end.

The professional character of the organization, combined with structural tightness, suggests considerable supervision of instruction. Should this be the case, the supervisors would need to possess professional characteristics that command the respect of the teaching corps. The suggestion of evaluation based on superior position rather than on superior knowledge would probably be resisted.

SCHOOL TYPE 4

Professional—Loose—Member—Moral

Probable Location:
University community.

Probable Size:
Small to medium.

Probable Grade Level:
K–12.

Teacher-Student Relationships:
Same as type 3.

Intra-Faculty Relationships:
Same as type 3.

Administrator-Faculty Relationships:
Administrative authority would be proscribed and limited by faculty policy. Little authority over instructional matters or matters relating to students would be granted to administrators. Efforts on the part of administrators to direct or evaluate the instructional process would be resisted by most—if not all—teachers.

Rationale:

This school type was discussed in detail in an earlier section of this book. The reader is referred to pages 177–179 for a detailed rationale.

SCHOOL TYPE 5

Bureaucratic—Tight—Member—Calculative

Probable Location:

Small towns and villages—especially bedroom communities for middle-level management and commuting white collar workers; the "exurbs."

Probable Size:

Usually sufficiently large to meet Conant's definition of the comprehensive high school, that is, more than one hundred in a graduating class.

Probable Grade Level:

Secondary schools, grades 9–12.

Teacher-Student Relationships:

The relationship between faculty and students may reflect considerable strain as the membership orientation encourages the use of normative strategies of inducement, but calculative involvement makes student conformity with such inducements problematic. It is likely that teachers, particularly those with experience in the system, will make unfavorable comparisons of the present generation of students and those of by-gone years, that is, unfavorable to the present generation of students.

Intra-Faculty Relationships:

There is strong likelihood of considerable factionalism. Teachers who accept the calculative definitions of the students and adjust their teaching strategies accordingly will be seen as less sensitive to demands for "respect" than are the teachers who hold to an insistence that students "ought" to be morally involved. Conversely, teachers who accept student calculative involvement are likely to perceive other teachers as provincial, old-fashioned, and "school marmish."

Administrator-Faculty Relationships:
Administrative insistence on structural tightness may cause some antagonism, especially with those teachers who are willing to use remunerative and social exchange strategies in order to deal effectively with calculative students.

Rationale:
This type of school evidences a basic cleavage between the way the school structure defines the position of the student (member) and the way the student relates to that structure (calculative involvement). To the extent that the calculative involvement results from mildly negative orientations—as opposed to mildly positive orientations—the cleavage and structural tensions will be intensified. The effect can be devastating to faculty morale and result in a breakdown in the relationship between faculty and students.

A situation like this one seems most likely to occur in situations where a relatively stable community, such as a rural village, comes to be populated with a significant portion of families who manifest values substantially at odds with the local traditions. Thus, it seems likely that some of the rural communities that have had a rapid influx of college-oriented, upwardly mobile executives and white collar workers would be a prime location for such a structural development. In the long run, however, the situation is unstable. If the executive and college-oriented parents gain political power (e.g., dominate the board of education), it is likely that administrators and teachers will come to accept a definition of students as clients as a more appropriate means of coming to grips with a hostile external environment.

SCHOOL TYPE 6

Bureaucratic—Loose—Member—Calculative

Probable Location:
Same as type 5.

Probable Size:
Same as type 5.

Probable Grade Level:
Generally the same as school type 5, with slightly more tendency to be located at elementary level.

Teacher-Student Relationships:
The relationships between teachers and students will be quite similar to the situation in school type 5. The existence of more structural looseness will, however, encourage some teachers to engage in activities that induce students and parents to develop loyalties to the individual teacher. For example, some teachers who are able to maintain the boundaries of their classrooms and effectively use strategies appropriate to calculative students, for example, remunerative and social exchange strategies, may develop independent power bases among parents who view the function of the school to prepare their children for college.

Intra-Faculty Relationships:
Because of the existence of structural looseness, teachers will be less likely to be aware of the classroom performance of colleagues. Most factions, therefore, will develop around issues related to the more public functions of schools, such as the election of cheerleaders and honor students. Factionalism is, however, an almost certain consequence of this type of structure.

Administrator-Faculty Relationships:
Given the fact that the structural antagonisms which exist in this type of school are often a response to antagonisms in the larger community, the situation in the structurally loose school is

likely to be quite explosive in regard to teacher-administrator relationships. Being bureaucratic, the administrative structure is likely to be top-heavy with individuals with long experience in the system and loyalties to those who hold positions in the traditional power structure. In response to competing pressures, recruitment is likely to bring in teachers with more cosmopolitan views and orientations. Structural looseness may make it possible for these teachers to develop cohesive groups that are cosmopolitan in orientation and further intensify conflict between the school and other parts of the community.

Rationale:

The basic difference between the type 6 and type 5 schools is the existence of structural looseness in the type 6 school, but this condition is of no minor consequence. Structural tightness provides teachers loyal to the administration and the bureaucratic administrators with a means of policing potentially dissident individuals; structural looseness limits this potential. Structural looseness does not cause the development of anti-administrative factions or cause teachers to develop individual loyalties among parents and students. It does, however, provide conditions that will support such developments should they arise from other sources like competition for control of school policy by identifiable power groups in the community.

SCHOOL TYPE 7

Professional—Tight—Member—Calculative

Probable Location:
Inner-city.

Probable Size:
Indeterminate but likely small as compared with size of other administrative units in the same school system.

Probable Grade Level:
Upper elementary and junior high.

Student-Teacher Relationships:
From the point of view of students, the relationship is uneasy. Teachers represent repressive adult authority. On the other hand, students are sufficiently committed to the school to desire to gain the benefits they perceive the school as offering. In schools with this type of structure, teachers will rely on social exchange, psychological affective, and remunerative strategies. Teachers will attempt to use normative strategies as well, but they are likely to be less effective with mildly negative students.

Intra-Faculty Relationships:
Considerable esprit de corps may be present. The faculty and administration may view their relationship as one of a team. Structural tightness suggests that individual teachers may exercise little autonomy but professional orientations suggest that decisions are made on the basis of competence rather than formal position.

Administrator-Faculty Relationships:
Professional orientations and structural tightness generally are sources of tension when they occur together. The more the administrator comes to act from the basis of position-related authority rather than as an implementor of teacher-made and teacher-directed policy, the greater the antagonism is likely to become. In brief, the relationship between teachers and administrators in this type of setting is always in delicate balance, and is unlikely to hold up under hostile reactions from students or the community.

Rationale:
Although this type of school is probably quite rare, it seems likely that it would be most likely to be found in modestly experimental undertakings in "problem" schools. Given the volatile nature of the situation (the structure is quite incongruent), such

an arrangement is unlikely to survive for long. On the other hand, such a structure could be created by intentionally placing professionally oriented teachers and faculty into a setting where students were somewhat motivated to gain the benefits of schooling, although not totally committed to school per se. Quasi-experimental inner-city schools seem a likely place for development. Similarly, some of the alternative schools that developed during the late 1960's probably manifest the characteristics suggested by this type school.

SCHOOL TYPE 8

Professional—Loose—Member—Calculative

Probable Location:
Inner-city.

Probable Size:
Same as type 7.

Probable Grade Level:
K–6.

Teacher-Student Relationships:
Typically, faculty-student relationships would be more personalistic than in most school arrangements, with teachers relying on psychological affective strategies to induce students to accept the norms of the school.

Intra-Faculty Relationships:
Similar to type 7.

Administrator-Faculty Relationships:
Colleagual and democratic, with considerable attention to the facilitating and expediting functions of management.

Rationale:

This type of school is likely to be found in some of the community oriented neighborhood schools in urban America. Structural looseness suggests that individual teachers would be encouraged to rely on personal qualities as well as professional skills. In a sense, such a school is dependent on the personal qualities of the teachers recruited, and the maintenance of the system depends on recruiting teachers who are professionally competent and personally willing to deal with mildly alienated students.

SCHOOL TYPE 9

Bureaucratic—Tight—Member—Alienative

Probable Location:

Urban, inner-city fringe.

Probable Size:

Relatively large.

Probable Grade Level:

High school.

Teacher-Student Relationships:

Hostility, distrust, and antagonism will typify faculty-student relationships in this type school. Faculty insistence that students accept membership roles and student alienation are incompatible structural conditions. The situation is nearly impossible to maintain and will shift quickly to some other structural form.

Intra-Faculty Relationships:

Factionalism of faculties in this kind of school is likely to become severe, and extreme fragmentation is likely to occur. Some of the sources of factionalism will be issues relevant to the control of students, maintenance of academic and discipline standards, and curriculum reform. It is likely that nonacademic faculty (e.g., vocational teachers) will form significant power blocks in the school.

Administrator-Faculty Relationships:
Faculty with long experience in the school will be likely to identify with administrators. Newer faculty will tend to view administrators with distrust and alarm. Some new faculty may see the administration as insensitive to the needs of students; others will see the administration as hesitant to use coercive measures like expulsion.

Rationale:
The situation of this school has been fully discussed (see chapter 9). The reader is reminded that this is a school in transition and one that is extremely volatile.

SCHOOL TYPE 10

Bureaucratic—Loose—Member—Alienative

Probable Location:
Same as school type 9.

Probable Size:
Same as school type 9.

Probable Grade Level:
High school.

Teacher-Student Relationships:
Generally the same as school type 9, with slightly more chance that individual teachers will have a significant impact on some students.

Intra-Faculty Relationships:

Similar to type 9, but with even more probability that coalitions of fragmented groups will turn into an anti-administration bloc. This will be the case especially if the administration is new to the school building. The anti-administration bloc will, perhaps, find it convenient to use the new administration as a scapegoat.

Administrator-Faculty Relationships:

Communication between faculty and administrators will probably break down in this type of situation. Administrators will be unable to exercise positive control over classroom activities and any effort to establish some control will be resisted by some teachers. On the other hand, many teachers will view the looseness of the structure as a further sign of administrative weakness and laxity.

Rationale:

This school, like the type 9 school is highly volatile. The volatility stems from much the same sources as in the type 9 setting. The type 10 school is, however, often more tension-ridden than the type 9, partly because the type 10 school is frequently evolved out of the type 9 structure. When this is the case, the type 10 school not only has the problems endemic to the structure it manifests, but also contains the history of the type 9 antagonisms. For example, should the administration in a type 9 school suddenly resign or be replaced, the likely result would be the emergence of a type 10 structure. A new administrator would find it difficult to maintain the structural tightness suggested in the type 9 setting, especially in the face of a fragmented faculty and alienated students.

It should be understood, however, that this situation is so volatile that it will not be likely to last. One probable outcome is that the administrator will engage in mass reassignment of staff, "tighten down," and move the school to a configuration more like the type 33 (bureaucratic, tight, product, alienative).

SCHOOL TYPE 11

Professional—Tight—Member—Alienative

Probable Location:
The incongruence of structure is such that this type school would be a rare occurrence and would probably not develop in other than urban centers and experimental schools. This structure is also conceivable in some residential, mental health–oriented correctional institutions.

Probable Size:
Usually quite small, perhaps a distinct subunit within an existing school program, such as special education classes which are set apart.

Probable Grade Level:
Though grade level is not an important factor here, this type of structure is unlikely to exist prior to grade 4 as student alienation, at least in significant numbers of students, is unlikely to have crystallized prior to that time.

Teacher-Student Relationships:
Likely to be typified by a remedial diagnostic orientation on the part of the teacher, and some forms of hostile response on the part of students. Students might adapt with considerable evidence of retreatism and an unusual amount of rebellion. The teachers' response to these adaptive behaviors would probably exclude coercion and would lean toward the use of psychological affective and normative strategies.

Intra-Faculty Relationships:
Because the size of faculties affected by structures like this one is quite small, there will probably be little factionalism within the group, although there may be a great deal of tension between the faculty and the "outside" world. This will be the case particularly when the type 11 structure represents a distinct

subunit within a school system that is *not* tied to a particular building, such as special programs like a system-wide driver education program or special education. The faculty is likely to be quite cohesive.

Administrator-Faculty Relationships:

The likelihood is that administrator-faculty relationships will be relatively benign in this type of structure. Usually such structures will only develop around programs that are so special or highly technical that they are granted considerable autonomy from the routine of administrative life.

Rationale:

It is difficult to conceive of this type of structure being at all viable at the system level, and it seems a highly unlikely occurrence at the building level. Yet, inspection of schools and an examination of the literature suggest the possibility that some kinds of special programs may take on characteristics similar to the ones implicit in the type 11 structure. For example, some schools establish special programs to deal with students who are alienated, although the school may not label them so. (Schools often lump alienated students in with students who are brain-damaged, mentally ill, and physically handicapped.) When this occurs, the staff recruited, particularly if they have a therapeutic and humanistic bent, may attempt to develop a structure in which students are identified as members, given rights, duties, and obligations, and which reflects considerable tightness of structure. The tightness of structure may result from nothing more than insistence on staff and team decisions concerning the treatment of any child.

SCHOOL TYPE 12

Professional—Loose—Member—Alienative

Probable Location:
Same as school type 11.

Probable Size:
Same as school type 11.

Probable Grade Level:
Same as school type 11.

Teacher-Student Relationships:
Same as school type 11.

Intra-Faculty Relationships:
The faculty would probably be more individualistic and less prone to engage in team planning, consultative arrangements, and so on, but on the whole would be quite similar to the faculty in the type 11 arrangement.

Administrator-Faculty Relationships:
Same as school type 11.

SCHOOL TYPE 13

Bureaucratic—Tight—Client—Moral

Probable Location:
Same as school type 5.

Probable Size:
Same as school type 5.

Probable Grade Level:
Same as school type 5.

Teacher-Student Relationships:

The membership orientation of the student body suggests that the students will identify with the teachers. Because, however, teachers would be likely to employ more social exchange and remunerative strategies than might be appropriate in a member setting, some students may come to perceive the teachers as somehow too distant, too cold, and too aloof—indeed, too academic.

Intra-Faculty Relationships:

There will be some strain in faculty relationships but the nature, intensity, and consequences of that strain are problematic and generally dependent on the orientation of administrators. For example, if the building principal accepts the definition of students as clients, teachers who respond to the membership claims of students are apt to be viewed as too soft, lenient, and without standards. If, however, the administrator accepts the membership claims of students, he may be viewed by some teachers as too lenient.

Administrator-Faculty Relationships:

Much that could be said about administrator-teacher relationships is implicit in the section above. One further observation does seem in order. The students' membership orientation arises from some source, whether prior school experience or some base in the community. There will certainly be forces in the school and in the community that support the membership claims of students. The administrator in this situation is caught in a difficult public relations problem. He is always in danger of being accused of coddling incompetent students, catering to the whims of parents, or, conversely, of supporting callous teachers who have no real interest in the personal well-being of students.

Rationale:

This kind of school is the likely result of a dramatic power shift in a community. For example, college-educated and upwardly mobile parents tend to be politically sophisticated and can exercise influence on school policy that is far out of proportion to the relative number of this group. When this happens, recruitment and policy decisions of the school may come to reflect the perceived needs of the more "calculative" students, to the distress, if not the detriment, of students who are morally involved. Educators often overlook the fact that being a cheerleader or a basketball player may have very different meanings to the boy or girl who plans to marry and settle down right after graduation and the student who goes on to college. In the former case, cheerleading- and basketball-based friendships, as well as the status that derives from these activities, may translate into friendships in the small-town adult world of work and homemaking. In the latter case, the chief benefit may be another activity to report to the college admissions officer.

SCHOOL TYPE 14

Bureaucratic—Loose—Client—Moral

Probable Location:
Established suburbs.

Probable Size:
Relatively large.

Probable Grade Level:
High school.

Teacher-Student Relationships:
The relationships between faculty and students will be quite similar to those described in the types 1 and 2 schools. The client orientation will, however, be a potential source of dissatisfaction, especially for extremely committed students.

Intra-Faculty Relationships:

Communications among faculty are likely to be limited to talk about students and administrators. Classroom boundaries will be carefully maintained.

Administrator-Faculty Relationships:

Relationships between administrators and faculty will be carefully defined. For example, how parent complaints about teachers will be handled will probably be a matter of agreed-on policy.

Rationale:

The type 14 school is the likely outcome of the drift and thrust of events in a type 2 school situation that is undergoing a modest influx of calculative students and that is attempting to accommodate the demands for excellence by hiring "highly qualified" teachers. Some public school teachers—especially some that have advanced degrees—seem to take the university as their model, thus the client orientation. Furthermore, the loose structure fits with their conception of the necessity of academic freedom. Frequently, schools in established suburbs create this type of structure, largely through the unintentional consequences of recruitment.

SCHOOL TYPE 15

Professional—Tight—Client—Moral

Probable Location:

Schools for the mildly retarded—especially residential schools.

Probable Size:

Varies, and is probably not a significant factor.

Probable Grade Level:
Adolescent.

Teacher-Student Relationships:
Considerable role strain on the part of teachers, with students making considerably more demands for personal attention than most teachers are willing to give.

Intra-Faculty Relationships:
The nature of intra-faculty relationships will depend in large part on the specific means by which structural tightness is maintained. If tightness is maintained through a cooperative, team-based endeavor, cohesion is likely to be high, but if tightness is maintained by means of rigid status hierarchy (e.g., M.D.'s who are psychiatrists are more influential in decisions than Ph.D. psychologists), factions are apt to develop.

Administrator-Faculty Relationships:
The existence of tensions at this level will be dependent on factors like those mentioned in regard to intra-faculty relationships.

Rationale:
Client-moral arrangements are always a bit uneasy. When combined with the tensions inherent in professional-tight settings, it seems likely that the nature of the clientele and the goals of the staff would need to be clear and probably narrow in scope. Residential schools for mildly retarded children seem most likely to have these qualities.

SCHOOL TYPE 16

Professional—Loose—Client—Moral

Probable Location:
University community, or community with significant population of highly educated citizens.

Probable Size:
Moderate to small.

Probable Grade Level:
K–12.

Teacher-Student Relationships:
Teacher-student relationships would be typified by reliance on normative inducement strategies, with some use of psychological affective strategies. The moral involvement of students suggests a great deal of conformity with inducements of these types.

Intra-Faculty Relationships:
Relationships between and among faculty members will probably be marked by considerable role differentiation, the differentiation being based on perceived competence and expert knowledge.

Administrator-Faculty Relationships:
Administrators will either be representative of the faculty (e.g., colleagual governance) or will not be involved in professional decision areas.

Rationale:
The client orientation is generally compatible with a professional orientation. Indeed, this type of school is probably quite stable. The structure suggests considerable competence on the part of faculty and administrators, as well as stability in the community served. Though such an arrangement is possible

elsewhere, the similarity between this structure and the structure of some colleges suggests that a community that would demand or tolerate such an arrangement is likely to have had considerable educational experience.

SCHOOL TYPE 17

Bureaucratic—Tight—Client—Calculative

Probable Location:
Upper middle class suburb.

Probable Size:
Relatively large.

Probable Grade Level:
Grades 7–12.

Teacher-Student Relationships:
Teacher-student relationships will be typified by heavy reliance on normative, remunerative, and social exchange strategies. Students will exercise considerable active control over teachers, in that they will make claims as clients and their judgment, as clients, will carry weight in the bureaucratic hierarchy.

Intra-Faculty Relationships:
Relationships among faculty will probably be compartmentalized and be related to administrative units and subunits. For example, departments will probably be significant units for faculty groupings, as will the academic level taught (e.g., seniors or freshmen).

Administrator-Faculty Relationships:
Typically, a superordinate-subordinate relationship, with more of a tone of managerial competence than benevolent pa-

ternalism. Teachers tend to be viewed as skilled technicians. Frequently, administrators will hold advanced degrees and speak in management terms. Something of the air of the business corporation will permeate the school.

Rationale:

See chapter 9 for an elaboration of the nature of this school and how and why it takes on the structure it has.

SCHOOL TYPE 18

Bureaucratic—Loose—Client—Calculative

Probable Location:
Same as type 17.

Probable Size:
Same as type 17.

Probable Grade Level:
Grades 1–6.

Teacher-Student Relationships:
Considerable reliance will be placed on remunerative strategies, with some reliance on normative strategies with older students, and psychological affective strategies with younger ones. Students will constitute a serious boundary threat at the classroom level.

Intra-Faculty Relationships:
There will probably be little chance or desire for cross-faculty communication about teaching concerns. Almost all communications will be vertical; few will be horizontal. Teacher isolation will be typical.

Administrator-Faculty Relationships:

There will be considerable tension concerning supervision of instruction, but also an overt acceptance of the legitimacy of bureaucratic authority. The moral leader type of teacher would find this arrangement an acceptable one.

Rationale:

The fundamental difference between the type 17 and type 18 schools can best be pointed up as the difference between the stereotype of the well-run elementary school and the well-run secondary school. The coordination of secondary school activities is thought to require considerably more structural tightness, than the coordination of the elementary school. Therefore, structural tightness, when leavened with "scientific management and experimental programs," is more likely to be manifest at the secondary level than at the elementary level.

SCHOOL TYPE 19

Professional—Tight—Client—Calculative

Probable Location:

Generally a rural or small-town location but likely to serve urban students. May be a private school.

Probable Size:

Varies but is usually a matter of intentional policy.

Probable Grade Level:

Grades 6–12.

Teacher-Student Relationships:

Teacher and student positions, rights, and obligations are apt to be carefully defined and supported by tradition as well as policy. Perhaps relationships best defined as cordial but proper, with faculty assuming a tutorial role rather than a mentor role. Few students will adopt faculty members as role models, although there may be considerable mutual respect.

Intra-Faculty Relationships:

The faculty will be likely to be quite sophisticated and cosmopolitan in their orientations. Factionalism, if it develops, will be around issues related to standards and programs more than around issues related to individual students. There will be some strain involved related to the existence of professional modes of organization and structural tightness. If these issues crystallize, they are likely to be couched in terms of creativity, imagination, academic freedom, and individualism.

Administrator-Faculty Relationships:

Administrators are likely to have been selected with some attention to faculty recommendation. Strains between administrators and teachers will be largely over issues relating to standards and academic freedom.

Rationale:

This type of school is unlikely to exist other than to serve a very select clientele. The faculty would need to be particularly talented in order to cope with some of the inherent tensions implicit in the professional-tight situation. Furthermore, the leadership structure would need to be staffed with exceptionally high-caliber individuals. All of these factors suggest a private school for affluent young men and women.

SCHOOL TYPE 20

Professional—Loose—Client—Calculative

Probable Location:
Suburban.

Probable Size:
Moderate to large.

Probable Grade Level:
Grades 7–12.

Teacher-Student Relationships:
Typically based on a tutorial model. Significant personal attachments and affiliations between some teachers and students may develop, but more frequently, the relationships would be typified by reliance on social exchange, normative, and remunerative patterns of inducement.

Intra-Faculty Relationships:
Relationships between and among faculty members would be based on a colleagual model. Considerable support would be given to the idea of teacher autonomy. At the same time, however, considerable concern would be evidenced regarding the quality of teaching performance, and student comment on teacher performance would be carefully considered.

Administrator-Faculty Relationships:
Administrator-faculty relationships would also be based on a colleagual model. Administrator and faculty roles would be carefully defined and tension would be likely to develop concerning the managerial demands for efficiency and the teachers' claims of autonomy of action and decision making.

Rationale:
The existence of structural looseness makes this school one that can take on a relatively permanent character, assuming it

can be staffed with individuals who can meet the role requirements. Some suburban high schools seem to have the resources
to attract the necessary staff. Furthermore, there is reason to
believe that suburban students—particularly children of upwardly mobile parents—may be more calculative than are other
students. All of these factors suggest that the type 20 school
is likely to be found in upper middle class suburbs, although the
requirements of staffing make the occurrence of this type
school—even in the suburbs—less frequent than the type 17
school.

SCHOOL TYPE 21

Bureaucratic—Tight—Client—Alienative

Probable Location:
   Rural and urban, most likely a correctional institution.

Probable Size:
   Varies.

Probable Grade Level:
   Grades 6–12.

Teacher-Student Relationships:
   In this structure, the relationships between teachers and
students are likely to be quite strained. Many teachers will
operate as technicians and managers. Students will be likely
to rebel from time to time. Teachers may come to place considerable reliance on remunerative strategies and behavior modification techniques.

Intra-Faculty Relationships:
   The frustration some teachers will feel in attempting to
apply prescribed solutions may lead to some intra-faculty tensions. A considerable amount of bureaucratic scapegoating is

likely to occur; pro- and anti-administration groups are likely to develop and become quite cohesive.

Administrator-Faculty Relationships:

In the face of a hostile or alienated clientele the administration is likely to place considerable emphasis on loyalty to authority and overt signs of conformity. Staff-line modes of operation are probably typical in this type of setting, with larger institutions having rather subtle gradations of authority and responsibility.

Rationale:

Organizations that are forced to deal with alienative participants, particularly when the participants are viewed as clients, are in a difficult position. The idea of client connotes voluntarism, yet the alienation suggests forced participation. The client orientation encourages the use of strategies that seem likely to encourage positive commitment, such as psychological affective strategies, but the realities of alienation and bureaucratic authority mitigate against the effective use of such approaches. Consequently, there is a tendency to move to approaches that are—at times—borderline coercive. The strain implicit in this relationship, that is, the client-alienative one, tends to encourage the development of bureaucratic authorities' tendency toward punishment-centered administration.

SCHOOL TYPE 22

Bureaucratic—Loose—Client—Alienative

Probable Location:

Impoverished rural areas and inner-city.

Probable Size:

Moderate to large.

301

Probable Grade Level:
   K–12.

Teacher-Student Relationships:
   There will be considerable variance in the nature of student-teacher relationships, depending largely on the personal qualities of the individual teachers.   However, bureaucratization tends to force teachers to relate to students in prescribed ways.   This will mitigate against the more personalistic qualities of teacher-student interactions.   As representatives of the system, teachers will be likely to receive considerable hostile reaction from students.

Intra-Faculty Relationships:
   The relationships between and among faculty will tend toward factionalism.   The factions will be likely to cluster around orientations toward the exercise of control in classrooms, that is, issues of discipline and decorum.

Administrator-Faculty Relationships:
   There is a strong possibility of strained and antagonistic relationships in this type of setting.   The looseness of structure suggests that the administrators' interference in the operation of classrooms would be met with hostile reaction from teachers, yet student alienation suggests that many teachers would find need to bring organizational power—particularly coercion—to bear on students.   If the administrator is perceived as unable or unwilling to exercise coercion, there is likely to be considerable resentment from some faculty groups.

Rationale:
   This school type seems to typify the kind of situation frequently observed in a school with severe "discipline" trouble. Many teachers look at structural looseness as evidence that the administration is weak; administrators look at classroom chaos as a sign of teacher incompetence.   The basic difference between this situation and the alienative-member setting is that fewer

of the faculty will be committed to the notion that students should—somehow—be encouraged to be positively involved. Containment and cynicism seem more likely to be the attitudes toward students here. To say the least, the environment is unhealthy and will likely take on a configuration like the type 21 or type 33 schools.

SCHOOL TYPE 23

Professional—Tight—Client—Alienative

Probable Location:
Similar to type 11.

Probable Size:
See type 11.

Probable Grade Level:
See type 11.

Teacher-Student Relationships:
Similar to type 11, with the possibility of greater receptivity to and reliance on remunerative strategies of inducement.

Intra-Faculty Relationships:
Similar to type 11.

Administrator-Faculty Relationships:
Similar to type 11.

Rationale:
The type 11 and type 23 schools are the same, except in the definition of the position of students in the organization, that is, client vs. member. Alienated students are more likely to be

treated as clients than as members, since the polar incongruence between alienation and membership makes that relationship difficult to maintain. Furthermore, a view of the student as client opens up alternative paths of action, such as the use of remunerative strategies, which are not so *clearly* available in the member setting.

SCHOOL TYPE 24

Professional—Loose—Client—Alienative

See types 11 and 12 for description. With the exceptions that the client definition makes this type more likely to occur in the "real world" and that there may be more tendency toward more impersonalization, the type 24 school is precisely the same as the type 12.

SCHOOL TYPE 25

Bureaucratic—Tight—Product—Moral

Probable Location:
Rural consolidated, perhaps newly integrated.

Probable Size:
Middle size.

Probable Grade Level:
Grades 7–12.

Teacher-Student Relationships:
The product orientation of the school, combined with student moral involvement, suggests the possibility of serious communications and human relations problems between teachers and

students. The impersonal nature of product orientations and mechanistic treatments that flow from this orientation may result in morally involved students who will react negatively to being treated as things.

Intra-Faculty Relationships:

Relationships within the faculty will probably be strained, at least to the extent that some individual faculty members identify with the student claims as morally involved participants. In such schools it would not be surprising to see the development of a split between so-called behaviorists and so-called humanists.

Administrator-Faculty Relationships:

The relationship between faculty and administrators will depend in great part on the degree to which the administration is responsible for and supportive of the *product* definition of students. If this definition is the result of administrative initiative, it is likely that some faculty will be alienated from the administration and attempt to form alliances with community groups that share their views.

Rationale:

The situation represented in school type 25 is unstable and cannot survive over time. Eventually students will become less morally committed to the system, or the system will begin to be modified to accommodate more student membership claims. Short of events like forced integration, the establishment of a new school, or consolidation, it is unlikely that such a structure could be found. In newly integrated schools, particularly in the South, there does seem to be a tendency to move toward scientific management procedures, behavior modification techniques, and similar product-oriented designs. It seems likely that rural students, both black and white, are more inclined toward moral involvement with community institutions than might be the case in more urban areas. Therefore, it seems likely that a school like type 25 would be more frequently located in newly consolidated or desegregated schools in rural areas.

SCHOOL TYPE 26

Bureaucratic—Loose—Product—Moral

Probable Location:
Same as type 25.

Probable Size:
Same as type 25.

Probable Grade Level:
Same as school type 25, with slightly more tendency to elementary school.

Teacher-Student Relationships:
Generally, student-teacher relationships will be similar to the type 25 school, although the existence of bureaucratic expectations and a loose structure increases the likelihood that teachers will engage in some form of bureaucratic scapegoating as a device to gain student acceptance of teacher direction. Teachers who use techniques like bureaucratic scapegoating and psychological affective strategies will be likely to be quite successful with students, but they may be at odds with colleagues and administrators.

Intra-Faculty Relationships:
Relationships among faculties of this type of school will be quite similar to the type 25 situation, with the possible exception that faculty are apt to unite in an anti-administration bloc if classroom boundaries are invaded (e.g., if supervision becomes more frequent than past practices indicate should be expected).

Administrator-Faculty Relationships:
A product orientation, combined with bureaucratic expectations, suggests that administrators will place considerable reliance on indirect measures of teacher effectiveness, such as student test scores. Direct classroom observation would cause some difficulties, but bureaucratic coordination—particularly in a product setting—suggests systematic efforts at quality control.

Rationale:

The shift of the type 25 school from tight to loose structure (thus becoming type 26) increases the possibility of teachers' exercising more idiosyncratic influence with students. Students who are morally involved are predisposed to respond positively to what they perceive to be the moral authority of the system. Thus, the type 26 school creates nearly optimum conditions for the development of social exchange and psychological affective strategies. It is equally true, however, that this type of structure encourages impersonal relationships between teachers and students. In the long run, therefore, who the teacher is and what the teacher believes may be the most important variable in determining how student-teacher relationships will develop.

SCHOOL TYPE 27

Professional—Tight—Product—Moral

Probable Location:

Inner-city or rural, especially in impoverished rural areas.

Probable Size:

Small, and likely to be experimental.

Probable Grade Level:

K–8, with tendency toward upper elementary.

Teacher-Student Relationships:

Teachers will give considerable emphasis to immediate gratification of student needs, use remunerative rewards, and engage in considerable diagnostic activity. Students, on the other hand, will attempt to impose a more personalistic definition on the relationship, leading perhaps to some role strain for the teacher.

Intra-Faculty Relationships:

This type of school is likely to be very small. Indeed, it is likely that the entire faculty will number fewer than eight members. There would be little factionalism, and if factionalism did develop, it would probably lead to a structural shift, that is, the emergence of a more stable school type.

Administrator-Faculty Relationships:

It is unlikely that administrator and teacher roles would be sufficiently differentiated to make this relationship relevant, but when differentiation does occur, it is likely to cause strain.

Rationale:

This situation is very unstable, and can exist only when there is minimum internal strain, particularly tensions between and among faculty and/or administrators. Such a structure is likely to occur only in "intentional" programs or schools, that is, schools established to follow specific procedures or orientations. Some of the experimental schools for gifted poor children that have been established in inner cities and in Appalachia seem to possess many of the qualities of the type 27 school. It is interesting, furthermore, that most of these schools seem to fail, or are significantly modified, after the initial founders move from the scene. Perhaps the structural incongruence is so great that the strain can be tolerated only by very committed and insightful teachers.

SCHOOL TYPE 28

Professional—Loose—Product—Moral

Probable Location:

Same as school type 27.

Probable Size:

Small to medium size, but will tend to be larger than the type 27 school.

Probable Grade Level:
Same as school type 27.

Teacher-Student Relationships:
Same as school type 27.

Intra-Faculty Relationships:
Same as type 27, with, perhaps, slightly less communication and interdependence.

Administrator-Faculty Relationships:
There is likely to be more role differentiation because of larger size, but the existence of structural looseness decreases the strain this might cause in a professional setting.

Rationale:
Structural looseness decreases the amount of incongruence represented in the type 27 school and thus decreases the need to maintain a small school size. Furthermore, increase in size increases the likelihood of specialization and competency-based role differentiation.

SCHOOL TYPE 29

Bureaucratic—Tight—Product—Calculative

Probable Location:
Private school, perhaps a military academy.

Probable Size:
Medium to small.

Probable Grade Level:
Grades 7–12.

Teacher-Student Relationships:
Teacher-student relationships will be typified by impersonality and clear superordinate-subordinate orientations. Stu-

dents will influence teachers, but the nature of that influence will be difficult to observe because it will be largely *sub rosa*. The concept of classroom democracy, for example, would be unlikely to find favor in this type of institution.

Intra-Faculty Relationships:

These relationships, too, will be based on clear notions of superordination-subordination. Each instructor is a representative of the system. Teachers will evaluate one another on the basis of bureaucratic competence and organizational effectiveness, at least as much as on professional competence and effectiveness in instruction. Innovation and deviation from established routine will be frowned on.

Administrator-Faculty Relationships:

The superordinate-subordinate principle, with emphasis on regularity, punctuality, and orderliness, will typify the relationship between teachers and administrators. Administrative command and lack of teacher autonomy will probably lead administrators to give special attention to the task of faculty orientation.

Rationale:

This structure suggests predictability, regularity, rigidity, and impersonalization. Though it is probably true that public schools are often as rigid as some of the more unimaginative military schools, open admissions policies in public schools make it likely that students will be, or become, alienated. In the private school (e.g., military academy) selective admission and retention are mandatory. Therefore, it seems more probable that a military academy would have a sizable proportion of calculative students.

SCHOOL TYPE 30

Bureaucratic—Loose—Product—Calculative

Probable Location:
Rural consolidated.

Probable Size:
Medium.

Probable Grade Level:
Grades 4–7, perhaps a middle school.

Teacher-Student Relationships:
Similar to the type 25, with somewhat less probability of negative reaction to impersonality.

Intra-Faculty Relationships:
Discussions between and among faculty members are likely to concern individual students or individual faculty members. Structural looseness will be maintained at the cost of communication concerning classroom tasks. Task-related teams may develop considerable cohesion, but for the most part, communication between and among faculty will be limited.

Administrator-Faculty Relationships:
Almost all of the contacts between teachers and administrators will be colored by the threat of evaluation. A product orientation suggests considerable attention to quality control; structural looseness suggests careful attention to the maintenance of classroom boundaries.

Rationale:
The presence of calculative students makes the impersonal nature of a product orientation seemingly less costly in human terms. There is a fine line between product and client, and, given careful attention to skill, technique, and specialization, it is easy for teachers and administrators to rationalize impersonal behavior as technical competence and necessary professional

311

distance. These conditions seem most likely to prevail in middle school years, if for no other reason than that these students are less likely to rebel than are older students.

SCHOOL TYPE 31

Professional—Tight—Product—Calculative

This school type is similar to the type 27 school in every respect, except that students are calculative rather than morally involved. Since calculative involvement includes mildly negative orientations toward school, it does, however, seem likely that the type 31 school will occur more frequently than does the type 27.

SCHOOL TYPE 32

Professional—Loose—Product—Calculative

This school is similar to school type 28 in all respects, but like school type 31, it probably appears more frequently in the "real world."

SCHOOL TYPE 33

Bureaucratic—Tight—Product—Alienative

Probable Location:
Inner-city.

Probable Size:
Large.

Probable Grade Level:
K–12, most likely 7–12.

Teacher-Student Relationships:
Teacher-student relationships best described as manipulative, hostile, distrustful. Teachers will place considerable reliance on remunerative and coercive strategies, often under the guise of behavior modification.

Intra-Faculty Relationships:
Typically, there will be considerable factionalism in schools like this one. Often factions will center around pro- and anti-union sentiments, pro- and anti-administration sentiments, and racially or ethnically based controversies. Most of these conflicts will, however, be *sub rosa*. When they do come into the open, however, they are likely to be quite severe.

Administrator-Faculty Relationships:
A great deal of centralization and bureaucratic routine will typify the relationships between faculty and administrators. Most communication will be one way—from administrators to faculty—with little person-oriented discussion; that is, most communication will be task-centered. Potential for strain and cleavage is always present, but without some outside support, lower-level participants (teachers and students) are unlikely to be able to resist the pressures for conformity to bureaucratic expectations.

Rationale:
See chapter 9.

SCHOOL TYPE 34

Bureaucratic—Loose—Product—Alienative

This school is precisely like school type 33, with the exception of structural looseness. The existence of structural looseness could be a source of considerable tension, particularly between teachers and administrators. Given alienated students, some teachers will feel the need for considerable administrative support at the classroom level. On the other hand, teachers who are able to function without such support may see administrative support as administrative interference and a threat to autonomy. Thus, it seems likely that the school type 34 is even more tension-prone than is school type 33. Indeed, school type 33 without outside interference is quite stable.

SCHOOL TYPE 35

Professional—Tight—Product—Alienative

Probable Location:
Residential school for children with severe behavior disorders.

Probable Size:
Small to medium-sized facility as compared with "correctional" institutions for adolescents.

Probable Grade Level:
Children of any age might be found in this type of setting, but these structures seem most likely with relatively young children ages 6–11.

Teacher-Student Relationships:
Therapeutic is the best term to describe the relationship between teachers and students in this type of setting. The hostility of the alienated student will be accepted as a fact of life, a condition to be faced.

Intra-Faculty Relationships:
Given the likelihood of an intermixing of medical staff, psychiatric staff, and professional educators, there is likely to

be some tension on the faculty, much of which is the result of differences in status between medical personnel and others. It is likely, however, that the administration will be so arranged as to encourage team approaches to specific client problems, and thus offset some of these tensions.

Administrator-Staff Relationships:

It seems likely that colleagual governance would be supported in this type of structure, although it may be that the medically trained staff will have more administrative authority than do other professionals.

Rationale:

This type of setting is not likely to arise in the typical public school setting. Dealing with alienated students in a professional manner requires considerable separation between the school and the larger society. Vilification of community norms is expected in this type of setting. When confronted with alienated students, the typical public school is likely to respond to the situation as a problem of control rather than a problem of treatment.

SCHOOL TYPE 36

Professional—Loose—Product—Alienative

School types 11, 12, and 24 are all quite similar to the type 36 structure. The existence of alienated students in a *product* setting does, however, suggest that the type 36 school would be even more likely than types 11, 12, and 24 to be a special program or special school within the larger system. Furthermore, it seems likely that the teachers in the type 36 school would be disposed to the systematic use of remunerative strategies and behavior modification techniques. Diagnostic testing would play a large role in this setting.

Bibliography

Adams, J. Stacy. "The Structure and Dynamics of Behavior in Organizational Boundary Roles." Unpublished manuscript, University of North Carolina at Chapel Hill.

Adams, Raymond S., and Biddle, Bruce J. *Realities of Teaching: Explorations with Video Tape.* New York: Holt, Rinehart and Winston, Inc., 1970.

American Educational Research Journal, "Message from the Editors." 42 (Summer, 1973), 173.

Amidon, Edmund, and Flanders, Ned A. *The Role of the Teacher in the Classroom: A Manual for Understanding and Improving Teachers' Classroom Behavior.* Minneapolis: Paul S. Amidon and Associates, 1963.

Amidon, Edmund, and Hunter, Elizabeth. *Improving Teaching: The Analysis of Classroom Verbal Interaction.* New York: Holt, Rinehart and Winston, Inc., 1966.

Astin, A. W. "A Re-Examination of College Productivity," *Journal of Educational Psychology,* 52 (1961), 173–178.

Bales, R. F. "Task Roles and Social Roles in Problem Solving Groups," in *Readings in Social Psychology,* 3rd ed. Edited by E. E. Maccoby, T. M. Newcomb, and E. L. Hartley. New York: Holt, Rinehart and Winston, Inc., 1958.

Barker, Roger, et al. *Big School—Small School: Studies of Effects of High School Size upon the Behavior and Experiences of Students.* University of Kansas: Midwest Psychological Field Station, 1962.

Barr, A. S. "The Measurement and Prediction of Teaching Efficiency: a Summary of Investigations," *Journal of Experimental Education,* 16 (June, 1948), 203–283.

Becker, Howard S. "The Teacher in the Authority System of the Public School," *Journal of Educational Sociology,* 27 (Nov., 1953), 128–141.

Biddle, Bruce J., and Thomas, Edwin J., eds. *Role Theory: Concepts and Research.* New York: John Wiley & Sons, Inc., 1966.

Bidwell, Charles E. "The Sociology of Education," in *Encyclopedia of Educational Research,* 4th ed. Edited by R. Ebel. New York: Macmillan Publishing Co., Inc., 1969, pp. 1241–1254.

Bidwell, Charles E. "The School as a Formal Organization," in *Handbook of Organizations.* Edited by James G. March. Chicago: Rand McNally & Company, 1965, pp. 972–1022.

Blau, Peter M. *Bureaucracy in Modern Society.* New York: Random House, 1956.

Boocock, Sarane S. *An Introduction to the Sociology of Learning.* Boston: Houghton Mifflin Company, 1972.

Bowles, Samuel. "Towards Equality of Educational Opportunity," *Harvard Educational Review,* 38 (1968), 89–99.

Bredemeier, H. C. "Schools and Student Growth," *The Urban Review,* 2 (1968), 21–27.

Brookover, Wilbur B. "Sociology of Education: A Definition," *American Sociological Review,* 14 (June, 1949), 407–415.

Butts, R. Freeman, and Cremin, Lawrence A. *A History of Education in American Culture.* New York: Holt, Rinehart and Winston, Inc., 1953.

Campbell, Ernest Q., and Alexander, C. Norman. "Structural Effects and Interpersonal Relations," *American Journal of Sociology,* 71 (Sept., 1965), 284–289.

Cohen, Elizabeth G. "Open Space Schools: The Opportunity to Become Ambitious," *Sociology of Education,* 46 (Spring, 1973), 143–161.

Cohen, Elizabeth G. "Sociology and the Classroom: Setting the

Conditions for Teacher-Student Interaction," *Review of Educational Research,* 42 (1972), 441–451.

Coleman, James S. *The Adolescent Society: The Social Life of the Teenager and Its Impact on Education.* New York: Free Press, 1961.

Coleman, James S., et al. *Equality of Educational Opportunity.* U.S. Department of Health, Education and Welfare, Office of Education. Washington, D.C.: U.S. Government Printing Office, 1966.

Coleman, James S. "Reward Structure and Allocation of Effort," in *Mathematical Methods in Small Group Processes.* Edited by Jean H. Criswell et al. Stanford: Stanford University Press, 1962.

Conant, James B. *The American High School Today: A Final Report to Interested Citizens.* New York: McGraw-Hill Book Company, Inc., 1959.

Corwin, Ronald G. *A Sociology of Education: Emerging Patterns of Class, Status and Power in the Public Schools.* New York: Appleton-Century-Crofts, 1965.

Corwin, Ronald G. "Education and the Sociology of Complex Organizations," in *On Education: Sociological Perspectives.* Edited by Donald Hansen and Joel Gerstl. New York: John Wiley & Sons, Inc., 1967.

Cosby, Bill. *Why Is There Air?* Warner Brothers Recording.

DeCecco, John P. *The Psychology of Learning and Instruction: Educational Psychology.* Englewood Cliffs, N.J.: Prentice-Hall, Inc., 1968.

Domas, S. J., and Tiedman, D. V. "Teacher Competence: An Annotated Bibliography," *Journal of Experimental Education,* 19 (Dec., 1950), 101–218.

Dreeben, Robert S. *The Nature of Teaching: Schools and the Work of Teachers.* Glenview, Ill.: Scott, Foresman and Company, 1970.

Dreeben, Robert S. *On What Is Learned in School.* Reading, Mass.: Addison-Wesley Publishing Company, 1968.

Dunkin, Michael, and Biddle, Bruce J. *The Study of Teaching.* New York: Holt, Rinehart and Winston, Inc., 1974.

Durkheim, Emile. *Education and Sociology.* Translated by

Sherwood D. Fox. Glencoe, Ill.: Free Press of Glencoe, 1956.

Durkheim, Emile. *The Rules of Sociological Method.* New York: Free Press, 1966.

Etzioni, Amitai. *A Comparative Analysis of Complex Organizations: On Power, Involvement, and Their Correlates.* New York: The Free Press of Glencoe, Inc., 1961.

Feldmesser, Robert A. Review of *An Introduction to the Sociology of Learning* by Sarane S. Boocock. *Contemporary Sociology: A Journal of Reviews,* 2 (1973), 649.

Flanders, Ned A. *Teacher Influence, Pupil Attitudes, and Achievements.* U.S. Department of Health, Education and Welfare, Office of Education, Cooperative Research, Monograph No. 12, 1960.

Flanders, Ned A., and Havumaki, Sulo. "Group Compliance to Dominative Teacher Influence," *Human Relations,* 13 (1960), 67–82.

Francis, Roy G., and Stone, Robert C. *Service and Procedure in Bureaucracy: A Case Study.* Minneapolis: University of Minnesota Press, 1956.

Gage, N. L. "Paradigms for Research on Teaching," in *Handbook of Research on Teaching.* Edited by N. L. Gage. Chicago: Rand McNally & Company, 1963, pp. 94–141.

Getzels, Jacob W., and Jackson, P. W., "The Teacher's Personality and Characteristics," in *Handbook of Research on Teaching.* Edited by N. L. Gage. Chicago: Rand McNally & Company, 1963.

Getzels, Jacob W., and Thelen, Herbert A. "The Classroom As a Unique Social System," in *The Dynamics of Instructional Groups: Socio-Psychological Aspects of Teaching and Learning.* Chicago: University of Chicago Press, 1960, pp. 53–82.

Getzels, Jacob W., et al. *Educational Administration as a Social Process: Theory, Research, Practice.* New York: Harper & Row, Publishers, Inc., 1968.

Getzels, Jacob W., et al. "Socialization and Social Structure in the Classroom," in *Review of Child Development Research,* Vol. 2. Edited by L. W. Hoffman and M. L. Hoffman. New York: Russell Sage Foundation, 1966.

Goffman, Erving. *The Presentation of Self in Everyday Life.* Garden City, N.Y.: Doubleday & Co., Inc., 1959.

Good, Thomas L., Biddle, Bruce J., and Brophy, Jere E. *Teachers Make a Difference.* New York: Holt, Rinehart and Winston, Inc., 1975.

Good, Thomas L., and Brophy, Jere E. *Looking in Classrooms.* New York: Harper & Row, Publishers, Inc., 1973.

Goode, William J. *The Family.* Englewood Cliffs, N.J.: Prentice-Hall, Inc., 1964.

Goodlad, John I. *School, Curriculum, and the Individual.* Waltham, Mass.: Blaisdell Publishing Co., 1966.

Gordon, C. Wayne. *The Social System of the High School: A Study in the Sociology of Adolescence.* Glencoe, Ill.: Free Press of Glencoe, 1957.

Gray, Farnum, et al. "Little Brother Is Changing You," *Psychology Today,* 7 (1974), 42–46.

Gross, Neal, et al. *Implementing Organizational Innovations: A Sociological Analysis of Planned Educational Change.* New York: Basic Books, 1971.

Hansen, Donald. "The Uncomfortable Relation of Sociology and Education," in *On Education: Sociological Perspectives.* Edited by Donald Hansen and Joel Gerstl. New York: John Wiley & Sons, Inc., 1967.

Hargreaves, David H. *Social Relations in a Secondary School.* New York: Humanities Publishing Company, 1967.

Harvey, Edward. "Technology and the Structure of Organizations, "*American Sociological Review,* 33 (April, 1968), 247–249.

Havighurst, Robert J., and Neugarten, Bernice L. *Society and Education,* 4th ed. Boston: Allyn and Bacon, Inc., 1975.

Herriot, Robert E., and Muse, Donald N. "Methodological Issues in the Study of School Effects," in *Review of Research in Education.* Edited by Fred N. Kerlinger. Itasca, Ill.: F. E. Peacock Publishers, Inc., 1973.

Homans, George C. *The Human Group.* New York: Harcourt, Brace & World, Inc., 1950.

Homans, George C. *Social Behavior: Its Elementary Forms.* Harcourt, Brace & World, Inc., 1961.

Houston, Robert W., and Howsam, Robert B., eds. *Competency-Based Teacher Education: Progress, Problems and Prospects.* Chicago: Science Research Associates, 1972.

Jackson, Philip W. *Life in Classrooms.* New York: Holt, Rinehart and Winston, Inc., 1968.

James, William. *Talks to Teachers on Psychology: And to Students on Some of Life's Ideas.* New York: Henry Holt and Company, 1939.

Jencks, Christopher, et al. *Inequality: A Reassessment of the Effect of Family and Schooling in America.* New York: Basic Books, Inc., 1972.

Jewett, Robert E. "An Educational Theory Model: Theory of Local and Cosmopolitan Influentials," in *Contruction of Educational Theory Models.* Edited by Elizabeth Steiner Maccia, George S. Maccia, and Robert E. Jewett. Cooperative Research Project No. 1632. Columbus, Ohio: Ohio State University Research Foundation, 1963, pp. 282–297.

Johnson, David W. *The Social Psychology of Education.* New York: Holt, Rinehart and Winston, Inc., 1970.

Kahn, Robert L., et al. *Organizational Stress: Studies in Role Conflict and Ambiguity.* New York: John Wiley & Sons, Inc., 1964.

Katz, Daniel, and Kahn, Robert L. *The Social Psychology of Organizations.* New York: John Wiley & Sons, Inc., 1966.

Kaufman, Bel. *Up the Down Staircase.* Englewood Cliffs, N.J.: Prentice-Hall, Inc., 1964.

Koerner, James D. *The Mis-education of American Teachers.* Baltimore: Penguin Books, 1963.

Larkin, Ralph W. "Contextual Influences on Teacher Leadership Styles," *Sociology of Education,* 46 (1973), 471–479.

Lenke, Hal. "Surviving, More or Less," *Peabody Journal of Education.* 49 (1972), 126–137.

Lewin, K. R., Lippitt, Ronald, and White, R. K. "Patterns of Aggressive Behavior in Experimentally Created 'Social Climates,'" *Journal of Social Psychology,* 10 (May, 1939), 271–299.

Maccoby, E. E., Swanson, Guy E., Newcomb, T. M., and Hartley, E. L., eds., *Readings in Social Psychology.* New York: Holt, Rinehart and Winston, Inc., 1958.

Martindale, Don. *The Nature and Types of Sociological Theory.* Boston: Houghton Mifflin Company, 1960.

McDill, Edward L., and Rigsby, Leo C. *Structure and Process in Secondary Schools: The Academic Impact of Educational Climates.* Baltimore: Johns Hopkins University Press, 1973.

Merton, Robert K. *Social Theory and Social Structure.* New York: Free Press, 1968.

Mills, C. Wright. *The Sociological Imagination.* New York: Oxford University Press, Evergreen edition, 1961.

Moeller, Gerald H. "Bureaucracy and Teachers' Sense of Power," *Administrators Notebook,* 11 (Nov., 1962).

Moreno, J. L. *Who Shall Survive? A New Approach to the Problem of Human Interrelations.* Washington, D.C.: Nervous and Mental Disease Publishing Co., 1934.

Morris, Richard T. "A Typology of Norms," *American Sociological Review,* 21 (1956).

New York Times. "U.S. Modifies Its Own Behavior, Ends Jail Study," Feb. 10, 1974, Sec. 4, p. 7.

Parsons, Talcott. "The School Class As a Social System: Some of Its Functions in American Society," *Harvard Educational Review,* 29 (1959), 297–318.

Riley, M. W. "Sources and Types of Sociological Data," in *Handbook of Modern Sociology.* Edited by R. Faris. Chicago: Rand McNally & Company, 1964.

Robinson, W. S. "Ecological Correlations and the Behavior of Individuals," *American Sociological Review,* 15 (1950), 351–357.

Rosenthal, Robert, and Jacobson, Lenore. *Pygmalion in the Classroom.* New York: Holt, Rinehart and Winston, Inc., 1968.

Rouscoulp, Charles G. *Chalkdust on My Shoulder.* Columbus, Ohio: Charles Merrill, 1969.

Ryans, David G. *Characteristics of Teachers: Their Description, Comparison, and Appraisal: A Research Study.* Washington, D.C.: American Council on Education, 1960.

Sarason, Seymour B. *The Culture of the School and the Problem of Change.* Boston: Allyn and Bacon, Inc., 1971.

Sexton, Patricia C. *Education and Income: Inequalities of Educational Opportunity in Our Public Schools.* New York: Viking Press, 1961.

Sherif, Muzafer, et al. *Intergroup Conflict and Cooperation: The Robbers Cave Experiment.* Norman, Okla.: University Book Exchange, University of Oklahoma, 1961.

Silberman, Charles E. *Crisis in the Classroom: The Remaking of American Education.* New York: Random House, 1970.

Simmel, Georg. *The Sociology of Georg Simmel.* Translated and edited by Kurt H. Wolff. Glencoe, Ill.: Free Press of Glencoe, 1950.

Simon, A., and Boyer, E., eds. *Mirrors For Behavior: An Anthology of Observation Instruments.* Philadelphia: Research For Better Schools, Inc., 1970.

Smith, Louis M., and Geoffrey, William. *The Complexities of an Urban Classroom: An Analysis Toward a General Theory of Teaching.* New York: Holt, Rinehart and Winston, Inc., 1968.

Sociological Resources for the Social Studies. *Leadership in American Society: A Case Study of Black Leadership.* Boston: Allyn and Bacon, Inc., 1969.

Spady, William G. "The Impact of School Resources on Students," in *Review of Research in Education I.* Edited by Fred N. Kerlinger. Itasca, Ill.: F. E. Peacock Publishers, Inc., 1973.

Timasheff, Nicholas S. *Sociological Theory: Its Nature and Growth.* New York: Random House, 1967.

Trump, J. Lloyd, and Baynham, Dorsey. *Focus on Change: Guide to Better Schools.* Chicago: Rand McNally & Company, 1961.

Waller, Willard. *The Sociology of Teaching.* New York: John Wiley & Sons, Inc., 1932, reprinted, 1967.

Walton, John. "Anti-Scholastic Bias in the Study of Equality of Educational Opportunity," *Intellect*, 102 (Oct., 1973), 36–37.

Weber, Max. *The Theory of Social and Economic Organization.* Translated by A. M. Henderson and Talcott Parsons. New York: Oxford University Press, 1947.

Whyte, William H., Jr. *The Organization Man.* New York: Doubleday-Anchor, 1956.

Williams, Robin M., Jr. *American Society: A Sociological Interpretation,* ed. 2. New York: Alfred A. Knopf, Inc., 1960.

Wilson, Everett K. *Sociology: Rules, Roles and Relationships.* Homewood, Ill.: Dorsey Press, 1966.

Wilson, L. Craig. *The Open Access Curriculum.* Boston: Allyn and Bacon, Inc., 1971.

Woodward, Joan. *Industrial Organization.* London: Oxford University Press, 1965.

Wrong, Dennis. "The Over-Socialized Conception of Man in Modern Sociology," *American Sociological Review,* 26 (1961), 183–193.

Index